Hibernia

Literature and Nation in
Victorian Ireland

A series of facsimile reprints chosen and introduced by
JOHN KELLY

Charles Gavan Duffy and others

The Spirit
of the
Nation
1845

Woodstock Books
Poole · Washington D.C.
1998

This edition first published 1998 by
Woodstock Books
c/o Cassell plc, 3 Fleets Lane
Poole, England BH15 3AJ
and
Books International
P.O. Box 605, Herndon
VA. 20172
U.S.A.

ISBN 1 85477 223 6
New matter copyright © John Kelly 1998

British Library Cataloguing-in-Publication Data
A catalogue record for this book is
available from the British Library

Printed and bound in Great Britain by
Smith Settle
Otley, West Yorkshire LS21 3JP

Introduction

It was certain that under the editorship of Charles Gavan
Duffy the *Nation* newspaper would publish patriotic songs
and ballads; what was totally unexpected was the popularity
that those ballads were destined to achieve. The surprise at
their success had literary consequences; reading through the
early files of the *Nation* it is apparent that the editors are
trying to hammer out a rough and ready aesthetic as they go
along, an aesthetic shaped in part by their altering percept-
ions of their readership and the constantly changing
political situation in Ireland as O'Connell's Repeal Movement
made persistent but unsuccessful constitutional assaults on
an obdurate Tory government. Even *The Spirit of the Nation*, a
selection made from the poems published during the first
two years of the paper's existence, is evidence of shifting
aims and ambitions; as we shall see, it went through three
significantly different editions in the space of eighteen months.
   Duffy, the youngest of six children of a Catholic shop-
keeper in Monaghan, had begun his journalist career on the
Northern Herald, edited by the United Irishman Charles
Hamilton Teeling, and after a period working with the
O'Connellite *Morning Register* in Dublin had returned to
Belfast to take charge of the bi-weekly *Belfast Vindicator*. This
he quickly turned into a vigorous and effective nationalist
organ, and he found that its impact was palpably enhanced
by poems he took to publishing in its pages. During a visit
to Dublin in 1842, he was introduced by John Blake Dillon, a
Connaught Catholic whose father had been dispossessed for
supporting the 1798 Rebellion, to Thomas Davis, and after
an animated discussion as they strolled through Phoenix
Park the three resolved to found a new kind of nationalist
weekly paper in Dublin. Davis, the posthumous son of a
Protestant officer in the British Army, had been born in Co.
Cork, but moved to Dublin as a boy. After graduating from
Trinity College he was called to the Irish Bar in 1838, but his
interest lay in journalism rather than the law; he contributed
articles to the *Dublin Citizen*, and in 1841 he and Dillon had
become joint editors of the *Morning Register*. This venture
was a disappointment, but their collaboration with Duffy
seemed to promise better success. They all agreed that
O'Connell's political and practical movement would be
immeasurably strengthened by a campaign that educated
and raised national consciousness. The institution of a
National Board of Education in the 1830s had effected a

growing if often rudimentary literacy among a younger generation which now constituted a popular potential readership for the new weekly. Each of the founders put education at the top of their journalistic priorities; as Duffy recalled, 'our purpose was the same – to raise up Ireland morally, socially, and politically, and put the sceptre of self-government into her hands'. Their goal was national independence for Ireland through repeal if possible or force if necessary, but they realised that education was opening up new possibilities for Irish nationalism. Later, when charged by a correspondent with retarding the progress of repeal by devoting too much time to education, they retorted that the allegation was 'doubly mistaken. A trained and instructed people is not alone necessary to do the work – for you cannot . . . "light a fire with damp faggots" – but to render it useful when it is done. Repeal does not mean a ready-made cure for all our evils, but simply the power and opportunity of prescribing for them ourselves. Is it not our main duty, then, to take care that the people and their representatives shall have knowledge, that they may be able to do so wisely and successfully?'

Their hopes of reaching a new popular audience were turned into a triumphant reality when the first issue of the *Nation* appeared on 15 October 1842. Under its motto 'To create and foster public opinion in Ireland, and make it racy of the soil', and offering incisive articles on Irish political, social and cultural affairs, the first issue was sold out within a day, with copies soon changing hands for two or three times the published price. The paper quickly achieved a circulation of over 10,000 copies, an unheard-of figure in the Ireland of its day, and boasted with justice that it was the largest paper ever published in Ireland; it also calculated that, since many of its subscribers were public reading rooms, its actual readership approached 300,000. Apart from its coverage of national and international news, its uncompromising assertion of Irish rights and unwavering promotion of Irish self-respect found an immediate response among a people who felt that they had been for too long the butt of English disesteem and bad governance. An editorial in the first number insisted that for 'all the nicknames that serve to delude and divide us . . . there are, in truth, but two parties in Ireland: those who suffer from her National degradation, and those who profit by it'. There was never a better moment to come to the aid of Ireland, it urged, since old parties were breaking up and 'Whiggery, which never had a soul, has now no body . . .'.

One of the most effective ways of coming to the aid of Ireland was, it decided, through poetry. Besides James Clarence Mangan's poem celebrating 'Our First Number', the opening issue also printed a 'Poets' Corner', which contained two poems by John Cornelius O'Callaghan, 'Lord Stanley in Ireland' (over his initials) and 'The Exterminators' Song' (over the pseudonym 'Gracchus'), and an anonymous piece, 'We Want No Swords'. Nationalist poems and ballads now became a regular feature in each number. The second week saw the publication of 'Awake and Lie Dreaming No More' by 'The Author of the Deserted College' (i.e. John Coen), and 'Stanzas Written at the Grave of — ' by 'Carolan' (Dr John Thomas Campion). But the second number also found the paper beginning to articulate its policy towards nationalism and the place of poetry in that agenda. The editor, reporting that a correspondent had complained of 'the fierce democracy' of the first number, warned that there would be a great deal more in the same spirit: 'We come to our work . . . unshackled by any connexion with Whig or Tory, and determine to take nothing for granted in the science of politics.' This fierce independence was to extend to poetry, and when another writer suggested 'that the present rage for singing should be taken advantage of to train up choirs for the church' the editor retorted that 'for our part, we will endeavour to teach the people to sing the songs of their country, that may keep alive in their minds the love of fatherland'. The third number explained in more detail the place that poetry was to take in the national fight:

Ireland, a rising, vigorous, and virtuous nation (unlike England), is now, in fact, as of old, essentially a poetic or bardic land, with a fresh, imaginative population, exquisitely alive to those generous and lofty, or keen and brilliant flashes of man's nobler nature, to which poetry supplies at once the most musical and effective utterance. Our POET'S CORNER, therefore, shall be regularly supplied with numerous varied effusions, in this fascinating department of literature, from our ablest pens; so that the ramparts of the fortress of corruption, which we propose to level, may be cleared by the lighter but unceasing crackle of such sparkling musketry, while the lower portions of the wall may be broken through by the more solid fire of prose, with which they shall be vigorously battered.

As an indication of just how seriously the editors took poetry, the regular 'Poets' Corner' feature was now supplemented with a new and entirely separate series, 'Songs of the Nation', which ran in the body of an editorial page. The first poem to appear in this new column was Duffy's 'Faugh a Ballagh' (printed as 'Fag an Baleac' in *The Spirit of the Nation*), a defiant poem, written, as Duffy later confessed, to boost national morale at a time of despondency. A note under the title announced that this was 'A National Hymn, chaunted in full chorus at the last Symposium of the Editors and Contributors of THE NATION'. Thomas Davis would certainly have been present at this cheery gathering, and it may have inspired his first foray into verse, for the same issue printed his poem 'My Grave' under the pseudonym, 'A True Celt' (hereafter he usually abbreviated this to 'The Celt'). Duffy relates that when he had first proposed the publication of ballads Davis assured him that 'he had never published a verse', but within a fortnight 'brought me the "Death of Owen Roe", his second published poem, which for dramatic power and vigour has scarcely been excelled since the era of the old Scottish ballads and week after week, for three years, he poured out songs as spontaneously as a bird'. Not only did Davis keep up a steady flow of verse in various kinds, but his poems inspired other writers, and the editors reported immediately after his 'The Men of Tipperary' appeared in the fourth number that they had 'been overwhelmed with imitations'.

At first Duffy was delighted with the unsolicited manu-scripts brought by every post, and he recalled that people were so amazed by the sudden burgeoning of this new literary talent that they suspected recognised writers such as William Carleton and Thomas Moore of contributing to the paper under pseudonyms. In fact, as he goes on to reveal,

effectual help came from known and unknown recruits. Of the known writers Clarence Mangan was the best. The unknown ones were as great a surprise to the founders of the *Nation* as to the public. I can still recall the mixture of delight and alarm with which I read contributions from new correspondents so striking and effective, so far above the range of Poet's Corner verses, that I was tormented by a suspicion that they must be plagiarisms or adaptations of poems which had escaped my reading. A scratchy school-boy manuscript written on ruled paper, which might easily have repelled an impatient man from further inquiry, proved when deciphered to be William's resonant Munster War Song, and John Keegan's fine peasant verses came in a handwriting on which scythe and spade had left their broad marks and De Jean Fraser's town lyrics in a feminine scrawl which gave little promise at first sight of the vigour and feeling they disclosed.

But the contributors turned out to be a mixed bag; inspiration all too frequently exceeded accomplishment, and the editors soon found themselves obliged to use a regular feature, 'Answers to Our Correspondents', for dispensing literary guidance. The week-to-week advice proffered in this column constitutes the aesthetic which informs *The Spirit of the Nation* and is, finally, inspired by the editors' mission to instruct their readers. In the case of poetry this educational policy had two main goals. The first, both in importance and chronologically, was to teach the history of Ireland so as to increase political awareness and national self-confidence. Only later was the paper concerned to comment on the form rather than content of the poems they were sent.

In dealing with historical and political verse, the editors soon found that they had to steer a course between the Scylla of over-strident militancy and the Charybdis of despondent defeatism. *The Nation* wanted poems that lifted Irish spirits and reminded the people of their martial and historic triumphs. It did not want lachrymose verse in what it considered the defeatist Jacobite style of the eighteenth century, nor that strain of melancholy that had found voice in some of Thomas Moore's *Irish Melodies*. As early as its fourth number the paper announced that it would not publish the poem, 'Sighs for Erin', submitted under the initial 'F', because it 'don't suit us':

We are not of the whining school of politicians; and we don't know what Ireland has to sigh for. God has given her all the gifts of nature in abundance . . . there is nothing to be effected by snivelling such doleful ditties as Mr. F's 'Sighs for Erin.'

In the same number, and at the other extreme, it had to warn the fire-eating 'Turlough' that the editors were 'literary agitators, not military enthusiasts' and could not 'sympathize with his exterminating doctrine'. Advising him to take a cold bath, it quoted from his 'Curse of the Irish Renegadoes':

> Arise blessed Patrick! complete thy good work;
> Unkennel these reptiles wherever they lurk;
> These black, bloated vipers, and renegades vile –
> Oh, pitiless, slay, and unvenom our isle.

This duality was to continue throughout the coming years, although censure fell more often and more heavily on over-despondent rather than over-militant poems. Thus, six months after its first number, the paper again found it necessary to reprimand some of its contributors and to spell out its aesthetic policy:

It is really too provoking that people will continue to 'bother' us with elegiac and sentimental nonsense, which they call poetry. . . . Be it known, then, that we write and publish national ballads to revive historical recollections, which is material to the honour of our people to keep fresh in their memory; that we furnish political songs to stimulate flagging zeal, or create it where it does not exist. . . . But are we, therefore, to fill our pages with whining monodies over the blighted hopes of a man-milliner, or pious didactics versified from the pages of an evangelical magazine? Certainly not . . .

O'Connell's Repeal campaign came to a climax in 1843 – announced as 'Repeal Year' – with a series of 'Monster Meetings' which attracted audiences numbered in hundreds of thousands at carefully selected historic sites, and it was easy to be convinced that this show of massed solidarity would shortly bring about legislative independence and Irish freedom. In this situation the contributor 'M.A.W.' was admonished on 20 May that, while his lines were 'simple and pretty' and reminiscent of Goldsmith,

we fear the utter absence of passion and energy render them unsuited to the present state of the public mind. When the struggle is over we will listen to dulcet lines on the beauty of our country; now we want stirring ones to teach us the duty we owe her, and the price her redemption is worth.

But the struggle never was over. The British government banned O'Connell's culminating Monster Meeting at Clontarf in October 1843 and immediately indicted him, and Gavan Duffy, on charges of seditious conspiracy. This produced a corresponding change in the *Nation*'s policy towards poetry. Warlike historical ballads continued to appear, but now somewhat less frequently and often bearing unwonted disclaimers. And side by side with these more typical *Nation* ballads were poems which struck a new note of caution. Thus the hitherto uncompromising 'Sliabh Cuilinn' (John O'Hagan) penned the more subdued 'Our Hopes' (see p. 234):

> Let them mock at our hopes as idle dreams,
> We'll cling to them closer still.

A week later the paper prefaced verses from 'A Peasant', extolling the wholesome and peaceable sentiments of attachment to the soil, a gentle desire for freedom, and religious toleration, with a note asserting that the 'land that has peasant-boys capable of writing, or even enjoying such verses as the subjoined, need never despair. She has a more irresistible power than standing armies, or monster navies.' A little later M.J. Barry contributed 'Bide Your Time' (p.102), the admonitory refrain set in capitals that its message might not be lost:

> BIDE YOUR TIME – your worst transgression
> Were to strike, and strike in vain . . .

This change in emphasis was not lost on the *Nation's* political enemies. The Conservative and Unionist periodical *Blackwood's Magazine* published a parody of the new manner, a sneering ballad entitled 'Bide Our Time':

> Bide your time, bide your time,
> Patience is the true sublime;
> Heroes? bottle up your tears –
> Wait for ten, or ten-score years;
> Shrink from blows, but rage in rhyme –
> Bide your time, bide your time.

To which a no doubt smarting *Nation* responded gamely that 'neither scolding or jibing, bayonets or proclamations, shall push us a hair's-breadth from the track whereon prudence beckons us. We will bide our time, and to some purpose.'

In fact a change in the *Nation's* poetic direction can be detected before Clontarf, although political events accelerated it. As early as March 1843 an article on 'Native Literature' wondered whether 'a strong stimulant like political poetry must vitiate the taste in almost the same proportions as it excites the passions', and made an analogy between the fiery poteen of political verse and the subtle Château Margaux of non-political poetry. Part of the problem was that imitation had become formulaic, and on 18 September 1843, shortly before Clontarf, the paper, deploring the stock-diction and unthinking blood-thirstiness of the ballads now being submitted, proclaimed itself 'altogether sick of war-songs in which the old images and phrases are repeated to weariness'. Indeed, the sheer amount of bad verse cascading into the *Nation's* office demanded self-protective measures. 'Every poet is not a patriot – why should every patriot be a poet?' complained the editor, and a little later, alleging that he had 'been compelled to burn a cart-load of verses, in all moods and measures, during the present week', begged for a twelve-month truce 'with our poetic friends'.

As hope of imminent political redress faded after October 1843, the *Nation* turned more consistently to its educational mission. An index of this change is the editorial attitude to those contributors who tried to imitate the verse of Thomas Moore. In the early days Moore's poetry was deplored on political grounds, and a correspondent who suggested that the paper should occasionally republish some of his *Irish Melodies* was ticked off in no uncertain manner:

The Heavens forbid – Moore's melodies are full of whining lamentations over our eternal fall, and miserable appeals to our masters to regard us with pity 'while they rivet our chains'. We have learned to speak a different language now – and we fancy the throbbings of the popular heart find a better interpretation in the less polished, but more vigorous verses, of the poets of our own gallant band. *They* neither fear nor doubt for their country.

But, a little later, those imitating Moore and Thomas Campbell are told to desist not on political grounds, but because they have not the skill to model themselves on such 'polished writers . . . whom no amount of natural talent would enable them to compete with till after long and laborious training', and are directed to 'measure their strength' by the work of Burns. The other models most frequently recommended were 'the great masters of ballad poetry' – Scott, Coleridge, Southey, Macaulay, Tennyson, Schiller – and 'above all, *Percy's Collection of Ancient Ballads'*. For those who could read French, Béranger was prescribed, and a number of his ballads were translated for the *Nation* by several hands, including John O'Hagan and John Barry.

Meanwhile, the tired predictability of much of the submitted verse grew ever more wearisome. 'Young gentlemen aspiring to poetry must really say something new', the paper scolded,

or, if there be nothing new under the sun, say old things in a new fashion. We have no fancy for being told three-score-and-ten times a-week that the Repeal flag is 'flung on the gale' – that the harp 'is taken from the willow', that this is the 'Emerald Island', and that the ships of Ireland will sail 'into the harbour of freedom at last'.

The editors also protested against 'the wholesale imitation of the *Nation's* national and historical ballads':

There is a medium in everything, and we find we lose our appetite apace after reading a score of sanguinary songs of a morning, reeking with the blood of the Saxon, or the better blood that he has shed. A bundle of rejected communications, which lately fell by accident into a tea-and-tract party of old ladies, drove them, we understand, into hysterics, like an explosion of gunpowder.

In this vein, the editors, recalling Leigh Hunt's proposal 'to confine poetry for the future to the final words of lines' since 'a person of the least ingenuity could not fail to read the entire story of most modern poems in these catch-words', made merry over the rhyme scheme of M.S.D.'s 'The Captive Patriots'. 'Who is so dull', they enquired, 'as to need that the lines should be supplied to these rhymes? – band, land!, brave, slave. blest, ocean's breast. pause, cause, hand, native land':

Here we have, as plainly as if it were written down, a question implying the patriotism of the 'band' suffering for their native 'land'; a declaration that they are too 'brave' to bear the name of 'slave'; with an apostrophe to the isle by nature 'blest', which, of course, suggests loveliest gem in 'ocean's breast'; then 'pause' and 'cause' is an obvious incentive to action, and 'hand' and 'land' indicate exactly what it is to effect. After this we need scarcely say that the verses are:

> How honoured is the patriot band
> Now suffering for their native land!
> Those gallant spirits, true and brave,
> Who spurn the hated name of slave.
> That land by Heav'n and nature blest,
> 'The loveliest gem in ocean's breast'.
> 'Tis cowards only basely pause,
> To struggle in her sacred cause,
> And calmly see oppression's hand
> Spread ruin o'er their native land.

The editors increasingly saw their function as encouraging work with any sign of promise and tersely rejecting the stale and incompetent. In the second category the put-downs could be devastating: 'M', who 'offers his lines for whatever they are worth, and has written twice on the subject, is informed they are worth nothing', while 'James', 'who "has not much time for study" ought to leave alone writing till he has.' Another versifier is informed that he 'writes in a strain like an irritated turkey-cock', and yet another 'is respectfully informed that repeal does not rhyme to gale in either English or Irish'. Defending themselves against letters 'accusing us of harshness to our poetic correspondents, and admonishing us that we ought to foster young genius till it grows into maturity' the editors replied that this was

all quite true; but are we to foster nonsense or idiocy? . . . We foster genius or even talent when we can find it . . . but are we, therefore, to be guilty of the cruelty of encouraging a taste for scribbling among those whom nature never intended to touch pen and ink?

For, as they also pointed out, it was not only the writers who were betrayed by false encouragement, but also the readers. Thus, the editors were 'sorry to reject the "Song of the Wexfordman," for the writer has got sound notions in his head; but it really is not poetry; and as we have charge of the education of the people, we dare not pass spurious songs upon them'.

Two criteria were insisted upon above others: detailed historical accuracy and linguistic and social authenticity. Noting that 'The Song of the Ejected Tenant' was 'not without considerable merit', the editors went on to complain that 'it has the great fault of not being Irish. Neither the character of the thoughts, nor the structure of the language, is that of an Irish peasant.' And the paper refused to publish J.T.C.'s 'Battle of Tyrrell's Pass' despite some 'decidedly good bits', because the author did not know enough about the period:

He should read the history of that Battle . . . surely he has not done justice to his subject. . . . Be it also said to him that we'll publish no more battle generalities unless of great excellence. The man too ignorant or too lazy to learn the particular events, costume, character, and localities of a battle, cannot succeed in making it into a ballad.

By October 1844, only two years after its founding, the *Nation* felt able to declare that it had created a new standard in Irish poetry by which all future contributions would have to be judged:

'T.L's' verses would have been tolerable last year, and valuable two years ago; but such a generation of poets has since arisen, that they are now inadmissible, unless by doing injustice to something better. There is only one way of securing admission to our pages, but it is an unfailing one – It is by exceeding those who have possession of them. Let the worst man go to the wall.

Indeed, by the end of 1844, Duffy and Davis could anticipate that the first stage of the revival of Irish poetry which the *Nation* had inaugurated was about to close, and, if pushed, would probably have agreed that *The Spirit of the Nation*, then going though what in effect was its third and final incarnation (the advertisement stated unequivocally that the work 'will not be resumed'), was the fitting monument to that phase. They had already inaugurated two new projects, a 'Ballad History of Ireland' and a series to be called 'Songs for the Street and the Field', which were to divert the impetus of the *Spirit* into more specific channels. The Ballad History was to give a chronological account of Irish history, and was 'designed *chiefly* to present the actual facts of history to the people in a popular and picturesque form', since it was 'by fiction, infinitely more than by the serious records of history, that Wallace and Bruce have become familiar to their countrymen. To produce the same effect, we must make fact our foundation . . '. 'Songs for the Times' was deliberately targeted on the bourgeoisie, and the poems intended for it were to be 'simple in expression, and written to a popular air, that they may find their way at once to the drawing-rooms of the middle classes and the workshops of intelligent mechanics'. Another series was contemplated for the peasantry, and 'intended to supersede the miserable street ballads' against which the paper had frequently railed. But above and beyond these, as an article of 21 December 1844 explained, the editors were anticipating an entirely new phase in Irish poetry:

We observe in our verse-writers too exclusive a devotion to songs of war and triumph. The magical influence they have had upon the national mind accounts for and excuses this partiality; but they have done their work, and there is other work to do. The native poetry of every people begins by being bold and picturesque, and by degrees grows condensed and suggestive. The second state is before us.

And it commended 'The Right Road' (p. 120) by Davis and 'Munster' (p. 241) by 'Sliabh Cuilinn' in *The Spirit of the Nation* as 'specimens of the class we mean'.

Notwithstanding its immense and continuing influence on later generations, *The Spirit of the Nation* was, then, precisely situated both historically and culturally, and an account of its genesis bears witness to the shifting political influences which shaped its form and contents. The first suggestion for such an anthology, made by a correspondent 'Patricius' (probably John Coen) on 18 February 1843, was that the Repeal Association should translate poems from the *Nation* into Irish and circulate them 'by thousands in the provinces, as music and poetry are the best possible popular agitators'. This proposed Gaelic version (which was to be mooted at frequent intervals over the coming years) came to nothing, but on 25 March 1843 the *Nation* announced that at 'the suggestion of many correspondents' it was about to provide 'singing for the millions' by 'reprinting the best political songs, national ballads, epigrams, and squibs, that have appeared in our journal, in a little book, with the title of the *Spirit of the Nation*, which we will sell, or rather give away, for sixpence'. It was hoped 'to circulate it by tens of thousands among the people', and the announcement, recalling 'that those who make the laws and those who make the songs for a nation divide its government between them', resolved to modify, as far possible, 'the bad measures' of the Irish Adminstration by 'the good measures' of the *Nation's* poets.

The little book of 76 pages was duly published in paper covers on 15 May, with the title page sporting the inevitable harp enwrought with shamrocks. In his preface Davis proclaimed that the sole object of the anthology was to benefit the people of Ireland: 'A book that contemplates neither praise nor profit is a genuine novelty, and will, we expect, receive a "Cead Mile Failte" [A hundred thousand welcomes] which the stranger never asks for from our countrymen in vain.' He also pointed out that special care had been taken to get the correct spelling of the Gaelic words and phrases, and that the editors had 'consulted the best Irish scholars, and adopted their orthography, which we expect will become general'. This was at Davis's own initiative, and part of his – at this time unpopular – campaign to revive the use of and respect for the Irish language. Insisting that 'to understand History, Topography, or Romance, it was indispensable to study native nomenclature', he persuaded the noted Gaelic scholars John O'Donovan and Eugene O'Curry to check the Irish spellings, and, according to Duffy, 'the first appearance of the genuine Gaelic patronymics created consternation'.

This first issue of *The Spirit of the Nation* contained 55 poems and 6 epigrams, nearly all pseudonymous, most of which were retained in the present 1845 edition. The book opened with John O'Hagan's 'Ourselves Alone', and he also contributed 'The Voice of the Nation', but, as in the final compilation, the lion's share was provided by Davis ('My Grave', 'The Men of Tipperary', 'The Death of Sarsfield', 'My Land', 'Death of Owen Ruadh O'Neill', and 'O'Sullivan's Return'), and by Duffy ('Fag an Bealach', 'Song of Ulster', 'The Spirit of the Times', 'Song of Sorrow', and 'Literary Leisure'). Other contributions included Edward Walsh's 'The Irish War Song, 1843', and 'The Munster War Song' and 'The Leinster War Song' by Richard D'Alton Williams, while John Kells Ingram's poem, 'The Memory of the Dead', was prudently signed 'S — T.C.D.'.

By 20 May the *Nation* was already noting errors: despite the 'special care' mentioned in Davis's preface, some Irish phrases and words had been wrongly spelled 'in imitation of the sound, and not according to Irish orthography', and the editors were not 'at all contented with the airs suggested in the contents. Some of these airs are Scotch, and some are not characteristic. We shall be obliged for suggestions on this head.' It was promised that various typographical errors would be corrected in the second edition ('which we find will be necessary immediately'), and the article ended with a modest disclaimer: 'We are far from estimating the bulk of these songs highly; but any national are better than the best alien verses. A beginning has been made, and the carrying out must be left to abler hands.'

The immediate and extraordinary success of the book clearly astounded the editors, not least because a good deal of the praise came from unexpected social and political quarters. The *Morning Post*, the Tory government's paper, confessing that the lyrics 'surprise us very much', found that they 'exhibit more poetic force of this ballad kind than we supposed to exist at present. . . . We should like to know who the anonymous rebel is that writes these Repeal ballads. Formerly the ballads for the Irish common people were distinguished for nothing but humorous slang of the coarsest kind, but here are verses fit to stir the heart of men.' Not less astonishing, Isaac Butt – at this time a Conservative alderman and leading Unionist spokesman – held up a copy of *The Spirit of the Nation* at an Anti-Repeal Meeting on 14 June 1843, and proclaimed that 'these ballads were written with a poetic pen worthy of a better cause, and the writer, whoever he was, unquestionably deserved the name of poet, and had the inspiration of a poet'. Other reviews appeared in *The Quarterly Review* (by John Gibson Lockhart), the *Leeds Times* and *The Tablet*.

This attention no doubt accelerated the already brisk sales and by the end of July the entire first edition was, as the *Nation* announced, almost exhausted: half the last thousand was gone 'and it sells at the rate of above a hundred a day'. 'It will gratify our readers to learn', the *Nation* added, 'that a great number of copies has gone among the very highest class in England'. A second edition was in preparation by early September, and in November 1843 a completely new collection, Part II of *The Spirit of the Nation*, was published in the same format and at the same price. In his preface to this Part, Davis admitted the Young Irelanders' astonishment at the success of the first Part:

We hardly hoped that their popularity could extend beyond our own class and country. But the Tory had praised them more than the Liberal; the Anti-Repealer as much as the Nationalist, while their success in foreign countries has at least equalled their success here. . . . The Irish Press thought them excellent for Ireland, the *Morning Post* said that they were superior to anything they had supposed to exist at present; the *Leeds Times* thought them a great achievement; and the *Tablet* called them the music of the battlefield.

Like Part I, this book also had 76 pages but it contained slightly fewer contributions (50 poems and 5 epigrams). Once again Davis was well represented with 'The West's Asleep', 'Song of the Volunteers of 1782', and 'A Rally for Ireland', but two other poets who were to feature largely in the 1845 edition were also much in evidence: Richard D'Alton Williams with 'The Rath of Mullaghmast', 'Winter', 'The Lion and the Serpent', 'The Vision', 'Adieu to Innisfail', and 'The Gathering of Leinster, 1648', and Michael Joseph Barry with 'Hymn of Freedom', 'The Arms of '82', 'Stand Together', 'The Wexford Massacre', and 'Erin Aboo'. All the poets retained their anonymity, but the book was placed in the hands of the small-time Dublin printer and publisher James Duffy, so laying the foundation, Gavan Duffy (who was no relation) later claimed, of his 'great prosperity'.

Both Parts of *The Spirit of the Nation* were now on sale, priced 6d. and the publisher also offered the two together, bound up 'in fancy cloth' for 1s. 6d. By late January 1844 he was already talking of two new editions: 'one for the drawing-room, in the most beautiful style of typographic art; the other for the millions, in a little pocket volume that the farmer can take to the fair, and the labourer to the field with him, and which either can purchase for a trifle.' These plans proceeded slowly; but in late April the *Nation* announced the 'Library Edition' of *The Spirit of the Nation*, which would 'appear in six numbers in quarto size, on beautiful paper'. The first part of this edition was published on 1 July, and a new part followed on the first of each month during the summer and autumn. (In the event, there were finally eight parts, the last one published on Christmas Eve 1844). Advertisements promised that each part would 'contain two new airs composed for this work, and two scarce and old Irish airs with pianoforte accompaniments. The names of the writers of the poems will, in most cases, be prefixed to them.' This is the origin of the present volume, for early in 1845 the separate parts were published with music in one volume priced at half a guinea.

This final version contained 348 pages and 147 poems, and was significantly different from the previous two editions. Not only were there many new poems, but a number of the original items had been discarded, and all the Epigrams were omitted. As James Duffy had promised, nearly all the names of the contributors were published. This may have been partly because the poets wanted to bask in their unexpected celebrity, but it was also designed to put an end to much wild speculation: both the *Morning Post* and Isaac Butt had supposed all the poems to be the work of the same hand, the *Leeds Times* had identified 'The Celt' (Thomas Davis) as Kate O'Connell, the Liberator's daughter, and there were 'sundry speculations in the American papers as to the authorship of particular songs in THE NATION, every one of which was erroneous'. Nevertheless a few of the poets retained their pseudonyms for personal, social, or political reasons. These included 'Sliabh Cuilinn' (John O'Hagan, an up-and-coming lawyer, who was to marry the daughter of the Lord Chancellor of Ireland), 'Theta' (Terence MacMahon Hughes, Gavan Duffy's cousin and editor of *The London Magazine and Charivari*), 'Spartacus' (the radical and accomplished London wood-engraver, William J. Linton), and 'Fermoy' (John Pigot, the socialite son of the first Catholic Lord Chief Baron of the Exchequer for nearly two centuries). John Coen, still a Trinity College student, signed himself 'Author of the Deserted College'; Mrs Ellen Fitzsimons, another of O'Connell's three daughters, disguised her identity under the initials 'L.N.F.'; and John Kells Ingram, soon to be elected a Fellow of loyalist Trinity College, even dropped the initials 'S—T.C.D.' in favour of complete anonymity – a wise precaution since 'The Memory of the Dead' had by now been denounced by the Attorney-General at the State Trials, and by Sir Robert Peel in Parliament. Other contributors either could not be traced (for instance the author of 'The Peasant Girls' [p. 149]), or, like the author of 'Father Mathew' (p. 87), preferred to remain unidentified ('We know the latter', the *Nation* revealed, 'and the delicacy of his position, but his scent is safe with us').

The final version of the anthology indicates the growing 'professionalization' of the poetry in the *Nation*. Although there were thirty contributors, two-thirds of the poems were the work of only six writers (all members of the paper's 'inner circle'), and Davis, with 43 pieces, made up well over a quarter of the book. This was partly owing to the manner in which the final edition was published, for a notice in the *Nation* on 7 September 1844 announced that 'future numbers of the new edition of the "Songs and Ballads of the Nation" will consist chiefly of pieces not hitherto collected in *The Spirit of the Nation*, but published in THE NATION since the issue of the second part of that book ten months ago.' In this time it had become increasingly difficult for newcomers to gain access to the *Nation's* pages, since, as the paper explained on 7 December 1844, 'by increasing the difficulty of admission to our pages, we will give a new stimulus to self-culture and honourable ambition', and in inaugurating the series 'Songs for the Times', the editors announced that they 'neither invite nor refuse assistance beyond that of our immediate habitual contributors'. In his memoirs, Duffy divulges the names of these 'habitual contributors'. The select group which first 'composed the weekly meeting' comprised, besides Duffy himself, Davis, Dillon, Pigot, and John O'Hagan, all of whom had been educated at Trinity College and all of whom had been called to the Bar. This clique was later joined by a handful of others, nearly all of whom had also been educated at Trinity College and then gone on to the Bar. Denis Florence MacCarthy, an affable Catholic barrister, who wrote under the name 'Desmond', contributed nine poems to *The Spirit of the Nation*, and was later to achieve fame for his translations of Calderon's plays. The Cork-born Michael Joseph Barry, who wrote as 'M.J.B.', 'Beta', and 'Brutus', was imprisoned with O'Connell and Duffy in 1844, and contributed fourteen poems to the anthology; he later went back on his nationalist views, became a leader-writer for *The Times*, and ended life as a police magistrate in Dublin. Denny Lane, who used the pseudonym 'Donall Na Glanna', was one of the most popular of the Young Ireland leaders, and published 'Cate of Araglen' in the anthology. A man of prolific ideas, he found difficulty in applying himself to any one task, and Davis, a good friend, described him as a fine fellow 'but hardly selfish enough for a great success'. Thomas MacNevin, a gifted scholar and orator, and Michael Doheny, a self-educated lawyer from a humble background, made up the rest of this charmed circle, and it also admitted one poet recruited as a result of his contributions to the paper. This was Richard D'Alton Williams, the illegitimate son of a Tipperary landowner, who as 'Shamrock' wrote patriotic, religious, lyrical and humorous poetry, and who printed six poems in *The Spirit of the Nation*. Duffy recalled that early in the first year of the paper,

a poem reached us from Carlow College which may take its place in literary history with the boyish pastorals of Pope, and the boyish ballads of Chatterton. It was scrawled in the angular, uncertain hand of a student, and scarcely invited examination. But it proved to be a ballad of surpassing vigour, full of new and daring imagery, which broke out like a tide of lava among the faded flowers and tarnished tinsel of modern poetry.

This was Williams's 'Munster War Song', published on 7 January 1843 (see p. 194), and he went on to submit numerous poems to the *Nation* (including parodies of well-known poems by Davis and O'Hagan). When he came to Dublin as a medical student in 1844, he was invited to the weekly suppers, where Gavan Duffy recalled him as a 'sensitive student reared in the country, intoxicated with the new pleasure of brilliant talk, but too modest to open his mouth'.

As we have seen, the treatment of the major themes in *The Spirit of the Nation* modified after the suppression of the Clontarf meeting in October 1843, and, since the final form of the anthology was structured roughly in the chronological order in which the poems had appeared in the *Nation*, many of the poems in the last part are less optimistic about the immediate success of Irish agitation, and urge the necessity for patience and education. Yet certain stances remain constant. Whereas Jacobite poetry of the eighteenth century had gestured with less and less visionary conviction to salvation from without – the return of the Old or Young Pretender from the Continent in the guise of Erin's lover – the poets of the *Nation* insist upon self-help. The watch-word of John Keegan's 'Devil May Care' is '*Sin fein*', a phrase Arthur Griffith was to borrow for a new political party preaching Irish self-sufficiency at the turn of the twentieth century. John O'Hagan's 'Ourselves Alone' carries the same message of self-reliance. Nor do the *Nation* poets permit themselves to luxuriate in Messianism, preferring popular action. O'Connell is celebrated in some early poems, but as a leader and organizer of the people, and Davis honours his 'True Irish King' not because he has succeeded by hereditary right, but because he is elected by popular will:

> The poorest, and highest, choose freely to-day
> The chief, that to-night, they'll as truly obey;
> For loyalty springs from a people's consent,
> And the knee that is forced had been better unbent –
> The Sasanach serfs no such homage can bring
> As the Irishmen's choice of A TRUE IRISH KING!

The various poems celebrating Irish battle prowess against Dane and Saxon, whether at Beal-an-atha-Buidhe or Glendalough, Ramilles or Fontenoy, enforce the idea that, given equal terms, the Irish are more than a match for their oppressors, and even those poems acknowledging defeat do not linger, as Thomas Moore often dwelt, on the plangencies of failure, but conclude with rousing prophecies of imminent revival. An important incitement to action and defiance, especially in the poems written before Clontarf, is a desire for vengeance kept burning by the recollection of past and present wrongs. Thus Frazer's 'The Gathering of the Nation', written in September 1843, towards the culmination of the Monster Meetings, looks forward to the Saxons' long-deserved come-uppance, while M.J. Barry's 'Hymn of Freedom', published in the same month, ends with a prayer to the God of Vengeance. In many other poems, too (for example, Michael Doheny's 'O'Neil's Vow' and George Phillips's 'Brothers Arise!'), the fight for freedom is associated with God's will, and Irish resistance seen as a holy and righteous war against the forces of evil. This love of freedom extends beyond Ireland: tyranny everywhere is deplored, even when exercised by Ireland's potential allies France and the United States, and Davis's 'A Ballad of Freedom' is a powerful protest against European Imperialism in all its manifestations.

Another recurrent theme is the need for Irish unity, and for Orangemen to throw in their lot with nationalists. This point is made in direct appeals such as John O'Hagan's 'The Irish Catholic to his Protestant Brother', 'Beta's' 'Stand Together', J. D. Frazer's 'Song for July 12th', and Davis's optimistic conviction that 'Orange and Green will carry the Day'. More subtle and compelling is his simile in 'Celts and Saxons' illustrating how the various settlers in Ireland have been assimilated by the river of time to produce the fruitful soil of the Nile delta:

> As Nubian rocks, and Ethiop sand
>   Long drifting down the Nile,
> Built up old Egypt's fertile land
>   For many a hundred mile;
> So Pagan clans to Ireland came,
>   And clans of Christendom,
> Yet joined their wisdom and their fame
>   To build a nation from.

Apart from these recurrent themes, there are groups of poems which grow out of specific contemporary events. The 'Irish Arms' Bill' and 'The Slaves' Bill' by William Drennan, together with R.D. Williams's allegorical 'The Lion and the Serpent', are three of the numerous poems published by the

Nation in protest against a Government bill in the summer of 1843 strictly licensing and controlling fire-arms in Ireland. O'Hagan's 'The Thirtieth of May' and Davis's 'Sweet and Sad' are inspired by the imprisonment of O'Connell, Duffy and others in Richmond gaol after their conviction for seditious conspiracy in 1844. Gavan Duffy's 'Saint Laurence's Address to the Irish Princes at Peace with the Invader' ostensibly recalls events that occurred in 1171, but is, in fact, a warning to O'Connell in late October 1844 not to flirt with the Whigs or proceed with his plans to water down Repeal demands (Madden's article and poem on the Bishop of Ross two weeks later may have had the same purpose). For, notwithstanding poetic contributions to the *Nation* by O'Connell's sons John and Maurice, and his daughter Mrs Ellen Fitzsimons ('L.N.F.'), tensions between the Young Irelanders and the O'Connellites became increasingly apparent. The Young Irelanders were finally to secede from the Repeal Association in July 1846 because they refused to rule out the use of armed resistance under all circumstances, but the last stanza of O'Hagan's 'Aid Yourself and God will aid You' anticipates the grounds of disagreement as early as 23 December 1843. The poem advises the Irish people, in the apparently cautious post-Clontarf manner, to 'Watch and wait, your hour abiding . . . Trusting in your Leader's guiding'. But what, asks the final stanza, if nothing comes of all this patience, and every peaceful effort is thwarted? The one remedy then is physical force:

> On, true heart that never alters,
> On, stout arm, no terrors weaken,
> Bruce's star and Tell's your beacon;
> Strike – that stroke, is many a day due,
> AID YOURSELVES AND GOD WILL AID YOU.

The political implications of the poems published in *The Spirit of the Nation* had long troubled Unionist readers, and even those English reviewers sympathetic to Irish national aspirations found them disquieting. The pro-Irish radical paper, the *Leeds Review,* described the publication of the anthology as

a very serious matter both to friends and foes. . . . Earnestness, like the grip of death, breathes throughout every line, and in every word there is a soul armed with swords. . . . Neither can we mistake the spirit of these songs. They mean simply this, and no more – FREEDOM – by peaceable means if we can get it – but if not – FREEDOM.

The Tablet thought that the songs had 'the smell of powder and battle-field about them', and a friendly article in *Ainsworth's Magazine* noted nervously that they inculcated 'in words that burn, lessons of redress, of freedom – too often, we fear, of vengeance – that might, perhaps, tingle in colder ears than those to which they are addressed'. Tory commentators were more outspoken. William Thackeray, stung to anger by the *Nation's* swingeing attack on his friend, the Irish novelist Charles Lever, alleged in *Fraser's Magazine* that 'there is bad blood, bitter, brutal, un-Christian hatred in every single ballad in *The Nation*'. The ultra-Orange *Banner of Ulster*, ignoring the *Nation's* ecumenical overtures, observed tersely that there was 'a spice of originality about some of those rogues – not original genius, but original stupidity'. But the most sustained political critique of the poems appeared in *The Times*, which found the poems 'instinct with the same feeling of burning hostility to Norman and Saxon, of fierce aspirations for liberty, battle, vengeance, and triumph, which form the staple of the great Agitator's speeches. Like those speeches, they are written with considerable vigour and talent of that rough and ready kind which will tell on the minds of an excited people.' And it went on to uncover the hidden agenda in the *Nation's* method:

Poetry is one of the most convenient instruments in the world for saying what you please. Nobody has a right to know exactly how much you may or may not mean. Let a man but make his thoughts rhyme, and there is hardly any account of treason and iniquity that he may not utter without giving anybody a right to say positively that he intends it. But when to the license of poetry are joined the facilities of history – when writers do but pay criminal justice the compliment of casting their exciting appeals to modern national feeling into the ever transparent form of historical allusion, and of winging them with the privileged and ambiguous vehemence of verse, no sedition appears too daring to be spoken, no atrocity too great to be recommended with impartiality.

O'Connell, it went on to allege, had been preaching disguised treason, but 'even his mischievous exhortations are as nothing when compared with the fervour of rebellion which breathes in every page of these verses, disguised, or but hardly disguised, under the very penetrable mask of allusion to other times.'

The Times picked out for particular condemnation Duffy's 'The Muster of the North', a ballad treatment of a particularly sensitive incident in the Rebellion of 1641, in which the dispossessed native Irish rose up against the Ulster settlers and killed several thousand of them. But greatly exaggerated accounts of the 'Bloody Massacre' quickly spread to England, where they were accepted as true, and the persistent memory bedevilled Anglo-Irish relations for many years (scenes depicting the killings still feature in Orange Lodge banners to this day). Duffy, who was born in Ulster, and had suffered from Orange bigotry in his youth, did nothing in his poem to understate the rebels' desire for vengeance:

Pity! no, no, you dare not Priest – not you, our Father, dare
Preach to us now that Godless creed – the murderer's blood to spare;
To spare his blood, while tombless still our slaughtered kin implore
'Graves and revenge' from Gobbin-Cliffs and Carrick's bloody shore!

'These burning words are not inserted in the popular newspaper of the day as a mere specimen of poetical diction', *The Times* admonished, 'they are written to commend and direct the public mind, and they are very well calculated, indeed, for their purpose. . . . If anyone doubts that the Irish movement has a character, and that character is one of revenge, and that revenge is too likely to be a bloody one, we advise him to keep clear of the *Spirit of the Nation*.' These criticisms hit home to the extent that Duffy felt obliged to publish an explanatory and exculpating note with the poem when it was republished in the final edition of the book (see pp. 26-30). He had perhaps felt a little uneasy from the beginning, for a prose preface to the poem on its first appearance in the *Nation* warned those 'who look for any allusions, open or covert, to the present time, will look in vain', although it also extolled such ballads as 'the best nutriment for the nationality and public spirit of a country – the recollection of the men and achievements they celebrate act on its youth like a second conscience – they become ashamed to disgrace a land that was the mother of such men.'

But it was not 'The Muster of the North' which attracted the severest official censure. That distinction went to John Kells Ingram's celebration of the United Irishmen, 'The Memory of the Dead', first recited at the *Nation's* St. Patrick Day's party in 1843. This poem was cited by the Attorney General during the state trial of O'Connell and Duffy in January 1844 as an example of the way the Repeal Association 'sought to circulate among the people, to poison their minds and to unsettle their allegiance', and it was later denounced by the Prime Minister in a crowded House of Commons. Ingram was an improbable dissident: the son of a Protestant clergyman, he was at this time a student at Trinity College, Dublin, where he was destined to become Professor of Oratory and English, Regius Professor of Greek, and Vice-Provost – and also a confirmed Unionist. It was not only enemies in the government who took offence at the poem; O'Connell was not pleased to have the *Nation* cited by the prosecution in evidence against him and shortly after his release from Richmond complained that 'passages I disapproved of and condemned were read against me'. But the experience of prison made even Gavan Duffy more cautious. Presented in September 1844, shortly after his release, with a seditious ballad by 'Spartacus' (William J. Linton), he protested that unless

Spartacus wants us to resume Richmond, or rather to face something worse, he will not just at present expect us to print his Insurgent Songs. He is not made to be a ruler of his time who cannot use its forms. Up-hill is what tries the wind. Spartacus should spare his *contemporary* war-songs, and use his fine talents on historical subjects or spiritual ones.

If there was disagreement among the reviewers about the political validity of *The Spirit of the Nation*, there was remarkable uniformity about the superior quality of the poetry itself. *The Tablet* detected 'decidedly more of the real lyrical spirit about them than any of our modern songs', and *Ainsworth's Magazine* found that 'as poems, they alike charm and surprise. They are wonderfully earnest, biting, passionate – all pathos now, now all fury – always musical and full of thought – seldom wanting either in sweetness or in strength. This, admiration is obliged to say. Who the writers may be, and what else they may have written, we know not; but never, in our recollections, were political songs poured forth with such profusion and power.' Even Conservative contemporaries praised the book's technical accomplishment, and the anthology became a model of what 'true' Irish poetry should be until Yeats gradually eased Davis from his pedestal in the 1890s. It is easy to see why Yeats was alarmed by the artistic cul-de-sac Young Ireland poetry presented, although Yeats, being notoriously tone deaf, was incapable of appreciating the greater power of the words when accompanied by the appropriate air. What he objected to was the palpable design of the poetry, the constant sacrifice of content to form. As we have seen, the editors were not unaware of these faults, and castigated contributors who fell too facilely into stock diction and responses. Nevertheless, they themselves were also too committed to their didactic purposes, and too precipitate in their procedures, to escape many of the faults they censured. Davis always prized literature for its propaganda value; writing to Smith O'Brien about a volume of Irish ballad poetry, he praised it as 'every way good. Not an Irish Conservative of education but will read it, and be brought nearer to Ireland by it. That is a propagandism worth a thousand harangues such as you ask me to make.' He advised would-be contributors to the *Nation* that feeling should always come before style, for 'in all cases we think simplicity and heartiness needful to the perfect success of a song', and he disparaged the lyrics of Marlowe, Jonson and Waller for their excess of technique over emotion. There was little danger that either he or the other *Nation* poets would fall into this error. In March 1844 'Oscar' was informed that he wrote 'well', but that 'he seems to have no object in view, no truth to enforce, no falsehood to expose, no principles to develope [*sic*], and fine writing without an object is an abomination. If he will try some practical question, which he has considered, he will do well, and we will be glad to see the result.' An Oscar of a later generation would have deplored such advice, but the *Nation* poets had no doubts that verse must have a definite ulterior aim. Duffy recalled that Irish history 'was *ransacked* . . . for examples of public spirit and public services, and for warning against national sins and errors' (my italics), and he describes Davis as striking off a ballad 'at a heat' with 'unfinished lines, perhaps, and blanks for epithets which did not come at once' – for an example of this see his 'Tone's Grave' [p. 130]. Davis was a young man in a hurry, and his friend the artist Sir Frederick Burton warned him that neither mere determination nor financial prizes could ever

produce either art or nationality . . . You should give Ireland first a decided national school of poetry – that is song – and the other phases will soon show themselves. This I must allow is being done – but the effect is not complete. You know that this mode is the only possible one, as well as I do, but you have lurking hopes that things can be forced. Ah, my dear friend – free spiritual high-aiming art cannot be forced.

Burton stresses here the relationship between poetry and song, and this was a connection that both Duffy and Davis insisted upon. An important influence on Davis's thinking about Irish music and poetry, as upon his historiography, was the French historian, Augustin Thierry. An unsigned article in the *Nation* of 26 November 1842, almost certainly by Davis, quoted Thierry's essays on Irish character from the *Censeur* of 1829 to the effect that the Irish national identity was kept alive by poetry and especially music. This is an idea that Davis endorsed in his article 'Ethnology', where he wrote that 'musical characteristics are, perhaps, the most spiritual and safe from confusion of any that can be imagined, and the surest to last in a country, if it be independent, or if it be rude'. These views were informed by his personal experience, for one of his relations reported to Duffy that she had seen him while a boy 'more than once in tears, listening to a common country fellow playing old airs on a fiddle'. Duffy, too, had been introduced to the emotive power of ballads at an early age, when songs were 'common at every dinner table, and some rude local ballad was ordinarily the favourite. I have seen tears fall like rain as a man familiar with "the time of the troubles" sang in slow tender tones of genuine feeling . . . or faces flush with pride over Rory O'Moore'. Since, unlike Davis, Duffy had grown up in a vehemently Orange district, he also knew the value of ballads in reinforcing communal solidarity. From the beginning, many of the poems were printed in the *Nation* with a recommended air, but, as we have seen, the airs suggested in the first edition of *The Spirit of the Nation* disappointed the editors, since some 'are Scotch, and some are not characteristic'. They asked 'for suggestions on this head', and were to continue to encourage their readers to collect and submit country tunes. In the event, most of the music published in the final edition was collected and arranged by two of their own number. John Edward Pigot ('Fermoy'), was a gifted musician and composed the airs for many of the lyrics, including 'Dear Land', 'The Memory of the Dead', 'Our Own Again', and 'The Hymn of Freedom', as well as adapting 'Our Own Green Isle' to the 'Caravat Jig', and arranging the tune of 'O'Connell's March' to Barry's 'The Green Flag'. He was aided in this work by William Elliott Hudson, a barrister and generous patron of many Irish cultural initiatives, who provided the music for 'Men of Tipperary', 'War Song A.D. 1597', 'Oh, for a Steed', 'Repealer's Trumpet Calls', 'The Sword', and 'Bide Your Time'. Most of the music had been arranged by May 1844, when the *Nation* announced that if 'the music offered for the songs of THE NATION be spirited and characteristic, we will print it in the paper – but the principal songs have already been set by competent persons for the forthcoming edition of *The Spirit of the Nation*.'

The Irish musicologist Grattan Flood has pointed out that of the seventeen 'original' airs published in 1845, only a dozen are genuinely original, the others being variants of existing tunes. Nevertheless, many of the most celebrated poems in *The Spirit of the Nation* – including 'The West's Asleep', 'A Nation Once Again', 'The Memory of the Dead', 'Cate of Araglen', 'Annie Dear', 'The Penal Days', 'Oh! the Marriage', 'The Welcome', 'O'Donnell Abu', 'Why, Gentles, Why', and 'Watch and Wait' – owe much of their lasting fame to their musical setting, and no account of the popularity and effect of the book can ignore the crucial part played by the music in its reception.

Davis was very proud of this edition. Writing to Pigot he described the music as 'very well done, and the paper and letterpress are superb. Nothing like them has ever been attempted here before.' He was also delighted with the Irish typography and the care taken with the transliteration of Irish phrases and names. But perhaps what gave him greatest joy was the title page, by Frederic Burton. The drawing was unsigned since Burton was not a Young Irelander, nor, indeed, a nationalist; he later confessed to Lady Gregory that it 'was Davis who asked me to do it and there was nothing I could refuse Davis'. Davis reciprocated by devoting an essay to decoding 'this most beautiful design, the most original and thoughtful that we have yet seen in this country'. He explained that over the central pillar stone 'an Irish eagle is soaring from a serpent, vast, wounded and hissing – the bird is safe – need we translate the allegory?' The young, harp-bearing bard he interpreted as having 'one great mission, the dream of his childhood before him', and, having travelled the land to awaken 'the slumbers of ages', he 'treads on a broken chain, yet he has no eye nor hand for these tokens of fame, he is full of his great thought, abstracted from all else, even from his own echoes.' His singing has released the old harper from a spell in which he 'sat tranced and clutching his harp of broken chords', so that now 'his hand is rising, and there is life coming into his huge rocky face'. 'Two young brothers in arms (friends and patriots) are looking wildly at the passing bard, and as his song swells louder, there is fierce daring in their eyes and limbs. They are in old Irish costume . . . one wears the gold torque of an Irish knight, the other grasps a yet sheathed sword – it will be drawn':

Disconnected from this immediate group (and sunk in the corners of the structure, beneath whose antique arch the minstrel has passed) are figures of the four provinces. Leinster sits gazing in historic grief at the shield bearing England's leopards. Under that shield is a skull, the emblem of Dermod's fatal treason. But Leinster, that holds Dublin and Tara, and Clontarf, and Wexford (the last adventurers for liberty) may forgive her friend for telling the treason of her king, and the more so, as a fairer being never made sorrow sweet. To Munster – exuberant Munster – a child is leading lambs, and he totters under this rich sheaf. Ulster is seated among the basalt rocks of the Causeway. She has hope and anxiety in her face and action; and she proudly shows the red hand of O'Neill on her shield. And Connaught sits on the shore, the wave comes as a wild subject to her fair feet, and dreaming she looks where the sun sinks behind the western waters. Nothing can surpass the grace of form, the simple force of thought, the noble disposition of limb and drapery, and the masterly lightness of touch in all these figures.

In *Young Ireland*, published in 1880, Duffy remarked that an edition of *The Spirit of the Nation* had been required every year since its first publication, and that it had 'influenced the mind of Ireland as deeply and permanently as the poems of Robert Burns influenced the mind of Scotland'. This was no idle boast, and in 1885 the *Nation* felt able to assert that in the 1840s its columns 'teemed with poetry, rich, impetuous, glowing, and so abundant that we believe no country has ever produced such an amount of poetry of equal quality in the same space of time'. An enthusiastic young relative of Arthur Griffith informed the Leinster Literary and Debating Society in 1889 that Davis, Duffy and Dillon had attracted to the *Nation* 'a galaxy of Geniuses unparalleled in the History of any country', and Padraic Colum points out that Thomas Davis was 'the evangelist' for such young men: 'they read and re-read him until some of them knew certain of his pages by heart'.

But gradually things changed. Yeats set his face against the Young Irelanders, believing that their propagandist themes and rough and ready style were cramping the development of Irish poetry, and his counter arguments, and the example of his own and others' work gradually eroded the pre-eminence of *The Spirit of the Nation*, although it continued in print well into the twentieth century. Gavan Duffy, the last of the Young Irelanders, now grown old, watched these developments with impatience. Writing to the Irish clergyman and man of letters Stopford Brooke in July 1899, he hoped for 'an analysis and vindication of national poetry. Some critics have made the marvellous discovery that it is altogether deficient in the qualities we applaud in Keats. Of course it is. Its business is to stir the heart of a nation, and the rude strains of "Scots w'ae hae" or "Rule Britannia" or the "Shan Van Vocht" do that in a way no sentimental poet ever could rival.' He was true to *The Spirit of the Nation* to the last, and on 9 February 1903 expended his last dying breath on whispering a stanza of John O'Hagan's 'Dear Land' (see p. 22):

> When comes the day, all hearts to weigh,
>   If staunch they be, or vile,
> Shall we forget the sacred debt
>   We owe our mother isle?
> My native heath is brown beneath,
>   My native waters blue;
> But crimson red o'er both shall spread,
>   Ere I am false to you,
>   Dear land –
>   Ere I am false to you.

J.K.

The Spirit of the Nation

DUBLIN: PUBLISHED BY JAMES DUFFY, 23, ANGLESEA-STREET.

The Spirit of the Nation.

BALLADS AND SONGS

BY

THE WRITERS OF "THE NATION,"

WITH

ORIGINAL AND ANCIENT MUSIC,

ARRANGED FOR THE VOICE AND PIANO-FORTE.

DUBLIN:

PUBLISHED BY JAMES DUFFY,

23, ANGLESEA-STREET.

1845.

DUBLIN:

PRINTED BY T. COLDWELL.

50, CAPEL-STREET.

PREFACE.

————

It is hardly necessary to tell our Irish readers that the Ballads and Songs, collected here, were originally published, from week to week, in THE NATION newspaper, since its establishment in October, 1842.

Two-thirds of the verses in this volume have never been reprinted from the newspaper till now; but a portion of them are re-edited from the original SPIRIT OF THE NATION.

In March, 1843, we printed a little sixpenny book, containing the poems which had appeared in our paper up to *that date*. Last autumn a second part appeared.

The success of the work was marvellous.

It was seized on by Ireland's friends as the first bud of a new season, when manhood, union, and nationality, would replace submission, hatred, and provincialism. It was paraded by our foes as the most alarming sign of the decision and confidence of the national party, and, accordingly, they arraigned it in the press, in the meeting, in parliament, and, finally, put it on its trial with "the conspirators of Ireland."

Its circulation was proportionate.

It went through several editions here, was extracted into all the periodicals in Britain, and, passing to America, was reprinted by a dozen publishers. It is to be found everywhere, from the English Admiral's cabin to the Irish peasant's—from Dublin to Boston, to Sydney, and to Calcutta.

Yet that little book was coarsely printed, was full of typographical errors, contained some unmistakeable rubbish, and had no music. The work which is here offered to Ireland contains thrice as many poems, is almost free from errors of the press, is beautifully printed, not unfavoured by art, and companioned with more music than many a costly collection.

There are in this volume no less than seventeen original airs composed for it, and twenty-two old Irish airs, arranged for the voice with piano accompaniments.

Among the old airs are many of the finest and scarcest. Most of the original airs are of a proud and fierce character, and peculiarly fitted for bands and chorus singing.

The greatest achievement of the Irish people is their music. It tells their history, climate, and character; but it too much loves to weep. Let us, when so many of our chains have broken, when our strength is great and our hopes high, cultivate its bolder strains—its raging and rejoicing; or, if we weep, let it be like men whose eyes are lifted, though their tears fall.

Music is the first faculty of the Irish, and scarcely any thing has such power for good over them. The use of this faculty and this power, publicly and constantly, to keep up their spirits, refine their tastes, warm their courage, increase their union, and renew their zeal, is the duty of every patriot. We are now putting in their reach a number of new and noble airs, and others so scarce as to be little known, and so beautiful, as to deserve to be known by every one. Will not the temperance bands learn to play these airs, and the young men, ay, and the young women, of the temperance societies learn to sing our songs, and chorus them till village and valley ring? If they do, we care not into how many or how few of the drawing-rooms of England or America this book of ours will reach. It will have done its work, and entered into the heart of Ireland, for good and for ever.

Nation Office, 1st January, 1845.

THE
SPIRIT OF THE NATION.

FÁG AN BEALAĊ.*

"Hope no more for Fa-ther-land; All its ranks are thinn'd or broken,"—Long a base and cow-ard band Recreant words like these have spoken;

---

* Fág an bealach, *clear the way.* "The ᵫ is scarcely heard in speaking, and is omitted in some printed works (incorrectly)."—*Owen Connellan's Practical Grammar of the Irish Language, p. 98.* Thus: ᴀ' ᴛᴇᵫᴊᴇ, *the fire;* ᴀ' ᴃᴇᴀʟᴀᴄ, *the way.*

B

But WE preach a land a-wok-en; Fa-ther-land is true and tried,

As your fears are false and hol-low; Slaves and Dastards, stand a-side—

Knaves and Trai-tors, ꝼáꝫ ꜵꞃ beꜵ-ꝇꜵċ! Knaves and Trai-tors, ꝼáꝫ ꜵꞃ beꜵꝇꜵċ!

FÁG AN BEALAĊ.*

A National Hymn.

BY CHARLES GAVAN DUFFY.

I.

" Hope no more for Fatherland,
  All its ranks are thinned or broken;"
Long a base and coward band
  Recreant words like these have spoken.
  But WE preach a land awoken;
Fatherland is true and tried
  As your fears are false and hollow:
Slaves and Dastards stand aside—
  Knaves and Traitors, *FÁG AN BEALAĊ!*

II.

Know, ye suffering brethren ours,
  Might is strong, but Right is stronger;
Saxon wiles or Saxon powers
  Can enslave our land no longer
  Than your own dissensions wrong her:

---

* *FÁG AN BEALAĊ,* " Clear the road;" or, as it is vulgarly spelt, *Faugh a Ballagh,* was the cry with which the clans of Connaught and Munster used in faction fights to come through a fair with high hearts and smashing shillelahs. The regiments raised in the South and West took their old shout with them to the Continent. The 87th, or Royal Irish Fusileers, from their use of it, went generally by the name of "The Faugh a Bollagh Boys." "Nothing," says Napier, in his *History of the Peninsular War*—"nothing so startled the French soldiery as the wild yell with which the Irish Regiments sprung to the charge;" and never was that haughty and intolerant shout raised in battle, but a charge, swift as thought and fatal as flame, came with it, like a rushing incarnation of *FÁG AN BEALAĊ!*

B 2

Be ye one in might and mind—
 Quit the mire where Cravens wallow—
And your foes shall flee like wind
 From your fearless *FÁG AN BEALAĊ!*

III.

Thus the mighty Multitude
 Speak in accents hoarse with sorrow—
" We are fallen, but unsubdued;
 " Show us whence we Hope may borrow,
 " And we'll fight your fight to-morrow.
" Be but cautious, true, and brave,
 " Where ye lead us we will follow;
" Hill and valley, rock and wave,
 " Shall echo back our *FÁG AN BEALAĊ!*"

IV.

Fling our Sun-burst to the wind,
 Studded o'er with names of glory;
Worth, and wit, and might, and mind,
 Poet young, and Patriot hoary,
 Long shall make it shine in story.
Close your ranks—the moment's come—
 NOW, ye men of Ireland follow;
Friends of Freedom, charge them home—
 Foes of Freedom, *FÁG AN BEALAĊ!* *

---

* To make the general tone, and some of the allusions in this song intelligible, we should, perhaps, mention that it was written in October, 1841, when the hope and spirits of the people were low; and published in the third number of the *Nation*, as the Charter-Song of the contributors.

LAMENT FOR THE DEATH OF EOĠAN RUAḊ O'NEILL,

(COMMONLY CALLED OWEN ROE O'NEILL.)

BY THOMAS DAVIS.

Time—10th Nov., 1649. Scene—Ormond's Camp, County Waterford. Speakers—A Veteran of Owen O'Neill's clan, and one of the horsemen, just arrived with an account of his death.

I.

"Did they dare, did they dare, to slay Owen Roe O'Neill?"
'Yes, they slew with poison him, they feared to meet with steel.'
"May God wither up their hearts! May their blood cease to flow!
May they walk in living death, who poisoned Owen Roe!"

II.

'Yes! from Derry we were marching, false Cromwell to o'erthrow,
And who can doubt the tyrant's fate, had he met Owen Roe?
But the weapon of the Saxon met him on his way,
And he died at Cloċ Uaċtair, upon Saint Leonard's Day.'

III.

"Wail, wail ye for The Mighty One! Wail, wail ye for the Dead;
Quench the hearth, and hold the breath—with ashes strew the
    head.
How tenderly we loved him! How deeply we deplore!
Oh! it breaks my heart to think we shall never see him more.

IV.

Sagest in the council was he, kindest in the hall,
Sure we never won a battle—'twas Owen won them all.
Had he lived—had he lived—our dear country had been free;
But he's dead, but he's dead, and 'tis slaves we'll ever be.

v.

O'Farrell and Clanrickarde, Preston and Red Hugh,
Audley and MacMahon—ye are valiant, wise, and true;
But—what, what are ye all to our darling who is gone?
The Rudder of our Ship was he, our Castle's corner stone!

vi.

Wail, wail him through the Island! Weep, weep for our pride!
Would that on the battle-field our gallant chief had died!
Weep the Victor of Beinn Burb—weep him, young man and old;
Weep for him, ye women—your Beautiful lies cold!

vii.

We thought you would not die—we were sure you would not go,
And leave us in our utmost need to Cromwell's cruel blow—
Sheep without a shepherd, when the snow shuts out the sky—
Oh! why did you leave us, Owen? Why did you die?

viii.

Soft as woman's was your voice, O'Neill! bright was your eye,
Oh! why did you leave us, Owen? why did you die?
Your troubles are all over, you're at rest with God on high;
But we're slaves, and we're orphans, Owen!—why did you die?"

THE ARMS OF EIGHTY-TWO.

BY M. J. BARRY.

i.

They rose to guard their fatherland—
   In stern resolve they rose—
In bearing firm—in purpose grand—
   To meet the world as foes.
They rose as brave men ever do;
    And, flashing bright,
    They bore to light
The Arms of "Eighty-two!"

II.

Oh! 'twas a proud and solemn sight
  To mark that broad array,
Come forth to claim a nation's right
  'Gainst all who dared gainsay;
And despots shrunk, appall'd to view
    The men who bore
    From shore to shore,
  The Arms of "Eighty-two!"

III.

They won her right—they passed away—
  Within the tomb they rest—
And coldly lies the mournful clay
  Above each manly breast;
But Ireland still may proudly view
    What that great host
    Had cherished most—
  The Arms of "Eighty-two!"

IV.

Time-honoured comrades of the brave—
  Fond relics of their fame,
Does Ireland hold one coward slave
  Would yield you up to shame?
One dastard who would tamely view
    The alien's hand
    Insulting brand
  The Arms of "Eighty-two?"

THE IRISH CATHOLIC TO HIS PROTESTANT BROTHER.

" Oh, Paddy, my boy,
What makes you so shy
To join with your Protestant brother,
Your brother ?
Sure, you 'll never thrive,
Unless you contrive
To be on good terms with each other,
Each other.''

Old Song.

I.

WHAT curse is on our land and us,
That bigot strife so long has lasted—
That every cheering prospect thus
Is by its fatal influence blasted!
That still, when round our banner green
The dawning hope of freedom rallies,
Religious discord comes between,
To mix her poison in the chalice!

II.

Religious discord! Oh! shall man,
The worm by doubt and darkness bounded,
His fellow-creature dare to ban,
For faith, in God, sincerely founded!
A holier gospel let us preach,
In spite of angry bigots' railing—
His own eternal hope to each;
But love and peace through all prevailing.

III.

And are not all our ties the same—
One sod beneath—one blue sky o'er us;
True Irish both, in heart and name—
One lot, or dark, or bright before us?

A thousand links about us wound
   To peace and mutual kindness urge us ;
The very seas that gird us round
   Speak UNION in their sleepless surges.

IV.

Remember glorious eighty-two,
   And wakening Freedom's voice of thunder ;
That spirit first was roused by YOU,
   Which burst at length *my* bonds asunder.
How bright, though brief, the halo then
   That o'er our common country lighted !
Alas ! the spoiler came again—
   He came, and found us disunited !

V.

Our annals stained with blood and tears
   Still preach this warning, this example,
The wicked feuds of byegone years
   At once beneath our feet to trample.
To have but one distinction known,
   One line from henceforth drawn among us,
The line of false and true alone,
   Of those who love and those who wrong us.

VI.

Unite with me, then, brother mine,
   Oppressor and oppressed no longer,
A bond of peace we 'll round us twine
   Than all the Saxon's fetters stronger.
Be Ireland's good our common creed,
   Her sacred cause alone enlist us ;
With gallant hearts and God to speed,
   What power on earth will dare resist us ?

                      SLIAḂ CUILINN.

c

O'CONNELL.

I.

I saw him at the hour of pray'r, when morning's earliest dawn
Was breaking o'er the mountain tops—o'er grassy dell and lawn;
When the parting shades of night had fled—when moon and stars
  were gone,
Before a high and gorgeous shrine the chieftain kneel'd alone.
His hands were clasp'd upon his breast, his eye was raised above—
I heard those full and solemn tones in words of faith and love:
He pray'd that those who wrong'd him might for ever be forgiven;
Oh! who would say such prayers as *these* are not received in heaven?

II.

I saw him next amid the best and noblest of our isle—
There was the same majestic form, the same heart-kindling smile!
But grief was on that princely brow—for others still he mourn'd,
He gazed upon poor fetter'd slaves, and his heart within him
  burned:
And he vowed before the captive's God to break the captive's
  chain—
To bind the broken heart, and set the bondsman free again;
And fit he was our chief to be in triumph or in need,
Who never wrong'd his deadliest foe in thought, or word, or deed!

III.

I saw him when the light of eve had faded from the West—
Beside the hearth that old man sat, by infant forms caress'd;
One hand was gently laid upon his grandchild's clustering hair,
The other, raised to heaven, invoked a blessing and a pray'r!
And woman's lips were heard to breathe a high and glorious strain—
Those songs of old that haunt us still, and ever will remain
Within the heart like treasured gems, that bring from mem'ry's cell
Thoughts of our youthful days, and friends that we have loved so
  well!

IV.

I saw that eagle glance again—the brow was marked with care,
Though rich and regal are the robes the Nation's chief doth wear;*
And many an eye now quailed with shame, and many a cheek now
    glow'd,
As he paid them back with words of love for every curse bestow'd.
I thought of his unceasing care, his never-ending zeal;
I heard the watchword burst from all—the gathering cry—*Repeal:*
And as his eyes were raised to heaven—from whence his mission
    came—
He stood amid the thousands there a monarch save in name !

Astrea.

SONNET.

BY E. N. SHANNON, TRANSLATOR OF DANTE, AUTHOR OF "TALES OLD AND NEW."

In fair, delightful Cyprus, by the Main,
    A lofty, royal seat, Love's dwelling stands:
    Thither I went, and gave into his hands
An humble scroll, his clemency to gain.
Sire, said the writing, Thyrsis, who in pain
    Has served thee hitherto, this boon demands—
His freedom—neither should his suit be vain,
    After six lustres' service in thy bands.
He took the scroll, and seemed to pore thereon:
    But he was blind, and could not read the case.
    Seeming to feel his grievous want full sore—
Wherefore, with stern and frowning air, anon,
    He said, and flung my writing in my face—
    Give it to DEATH—we two will talk it o'er.

---

* Written during his Mayoralty.

c 2

OUR OWN LITTLE ISLE.

AIR.—*The Lapabat Jig.*

ERIN—*OUR OWN* LITTLE ISLE.

I.

Oh! Irishmen! never forget—
'Tis a *foreigner's farm*—your own little isle;
Oh! Irishmen! when will you get
　Some *life* in your hearts for your poor little isle?
　　Yes! yes!—we've a dear little spot of it!
　　　Oh! yes!—a sweet little isle!
　　Yes! yes!—if Irishmen thought of it,
　　　'Twould be a dear little, sweet little isle!

II.

Then, come on and rise, ev'ry man of you—
Now is the time for a stir to be made;
Ho! Pat! who made such a lamb of you?
　Life to your soul, boy, and strength to your blade!
　　Yes! yes!—a dear little spot of it!
　　　Oh! yes!—a sweet little isle!
　　Yes! yes!—if Irishmen thought of it,
　　　Erin once more is *our own* little isle!

III.

Rise! heartily! shoulder to shoulder—
We'll show 'em strength with good humour *go leór!*
Rise! rise! show each foreign beholder
　We've *not* lost our love to thee, Erin *a stór!*
　　For oh! yes!—'tis a dear little spot of it!
　　　Yes! yes!—a sweet little isle!
　　Yes! yes!—the Irish *have* thought of it;
　　　Erin for ever—*our own* little isle!

IV.

Never forget what your forefathers fought for, O!
　When, with "O'Neill" or "O'Donnell aboo!"
Sassenaghs ev'rywhere sunk in the slaughter, O!
　Vengeance for insult, dear Erin, to you!

For oh! yes!—a dear little spot!
   Yes! yes!—a sweet little isle;
   Yes! yes!—if Irishmen thought of it,
    Erin once more is *our own* little isle!

v.

Yes, we *have* strength to make Irishmen free again;
   Only UNITE—and we'll conquer our foe;
And never on earth shall a foreigner see again
   Erin a province—though lately so low.
     For oh! yes!—we've a dear little spot of it!
     Yes! yes!—a sweet little isle!
     Yes! yes!—the Irish *have* thought of it;
      Erin *for ever*—OUR OWN little isle!

FERMOY.

EIBLIN A RUIN.

BY THOMAS DAVIS.

Air—" Eiblin A Ruin."

I.

WHEN I am far away,
       Eiblin a Ruin,
Be gayest of the gay,
       Eiblin a Ruin.
Too dear your happiness,
For me to wish it less—
Love has no selfishness,
       Eiblin a Ruin.

II.

And it must be our pride,
       Eiblin a Ruin,
Our trusting hearts to hide,
       Eiblin a Ruin.

They wish our love to blight,
We'll wait for Fortune's light—
The flowers close up at night,
   Eiblin a Ruin.

III.

And when we meet alone,
   Eiblin a Ruin,
Upon my bosom thrown,
   Eiblin a Ruin,
That hour, with light bedeck'd,
Shall cheer us and direct,
A beacon to the wreck'd,
   Eiblin a Ruin.

IV.

Fortune, thus sought, will come,
   Eiblin a Ruin,
We'll win a happy home,
   Eiblin a Ruin;
And, as it slowly rose,
'Twill tranquilly repose,
A rock 'mid melting snows,
   Eiblin a Ruin.

TYROL AND IRELAND.

" Ye gather three ears of corn, and they take two out of the three. Are ye contented?
are ye happy? But there is a Providence above, and there are angels, and when we
seek to right ourselves, they will assist us."—*Speech of Hofer to the Tyrolese*: 1809.

I.

AND Hofer roused Tyrol for this,
 Made Winschgan red with blood,
Thal Botzen's peasants ranged in arms,
 And Inspruck's fire withstood.

For this! for this! that but a third
   The hind his own could call,
When Passyer gathered in her sheaves;
   Why, *ye* are robbed of all.

II.

Up rose the hardy mountaineers,
   And crushed Bavaria's horse,
I' th' name of Father and of Son,*
   For *this* without remorse.
Great Heaven, for this! that Passyer's swains
   Of half their store were reft;
Why, clods of senseless clay, to you
   Not ev'n an ear is left!

III.

'Midst plenty gushing round, ye starve—
   'Midst blessings, crawl accurst,
And hoard for your land cormorants all,
   Deep gorging till they burst!
Still—still they spurn you with contempt,
   Deride your pangs with scorn;
Still bid you bite the dust for churls,
   And villains basely born!

IV.

Oh, idiots! feel ye not the lash—
   The fangs that clutch at gold?
From rogues so insolent what hope
   Of mercy do ye hold?
The pallid millions kneel for food;
   The lordling locks his store.
Hath earth, alas! but one Tyrol,
   And not a Hofer more.
                     THETA.

---

* The Bavarian vanguard, composed of 4,000 men, advanced into the defile; and when they had reached midway, the mountaineers hurled down upon their heads huge rocks, which they had rolled to the verge of the precipice in the name of the Father, the Son, and the Holy Ghost."—*Histoire des Tyroliens.*

D

STAND TOGETHER.

I.

STAND together, brothers all!
Stand together, stand together!
To live or die, to rise or fall,
Stand together, stand together!
Old Erin proudly lifts her head—
Of many tears the last is shed;
Oh! *for* the living—*by* the dead!
Stand together, true together!

II.

Stand together, brothers all!
Close together, close together!
Be Ireland's might a brazen wall—
Close up together, tight together!
Peace!—no noise!—but hand in hand
Let calm resolve pervade your band,
And wait—till nature's God command—
Then help each other, help each other!

III.

Stand together, brothers all!
Proud together—bold together!
From Kerry's cliffs to Donegal,
Bound in heart and soul together!
Unrol the sunburst! who'll defend
Old Erin's banner is a friend—
One foe is ours—oh! blend, boys, blend
Hands together—hearts together!

IV.

Stand together, brothers all!
Wait together, watch together!
See, America and Gall
Look on together, both together!

Keen impatience in each eye—
Yet on "ourselves" do we rely—
"Ourselves alone" our rallying cry!
   And " stand together, strike together !"

BETA.

AWAKE, AND LIE DREAMING NO MORE.

BY THE AUTHOR OF "THE DESERTED COLLEGE."

I.

Ye great of my country, how long will ye slumber?
  Spell-bound, and remote from her once happy shore,
Unmoved by her wrongs and her woes without number:
  Oh! wake thee, awake, and lie dreaming no more!
Awaken to fame, and poor Erin's condition;
To heal all her wounds be your noblest ambition
Oh! break off the spell of the foreign magician.
  Awake, then, awake, and lie dreaming no more!

II.

Not the want of green fields nor of countless resources
  The sons of sweet Erin have cause to deplore,
Nor the want of brave hearts for the muster of forces:
  Awake, then, awake, and lie dreaming no more!
A patriot flame and endearing emotion
Are wanting to bless the sweet isle of the ocean;
Yet Erin is worthy of love and devotion.
  Awake, then, awake, and lie dreaming no more!

III.

Let Fashion no more, in pursuit of vain pleasure,
  To far-distant lands in her train draw you o'er;
In your own native isle is the goodliest treasure:
  Awake, then awake, and lie dreaming no more!
When once love and pride of your country ye cherish,
The seeds of disunion and discord shall perish,
And Erin, dear Erin, in loveliness flourish.
  Awake, then, awake, and lie dreaming no more!

D 2

DEAR LAND.

When comes the day, all hearts to weigh, If staunch they be or

vile, Shall we for-get the sa-cred debt, We owe our mo-ther isle?

My na-tive heath is brown be-neath, My na-tive wa-ters

blue; But crim-son red o'er both shall spread,—E'er I am false to

you, dear land, Ere I am false to you. Ere I am false to

you, dear land, Ere I am false to you.

DEAR LAND.

I.

When comes the day, all hearts to weigh,
    If stanch they be, or vile,
Shall we forget the sacred debt
    We owe our mother isle?
My native heath is brown beneath,
    My native waters blue;
But crimson red o'er both shall spread,
    Ere I am false to you,
                    Dear land—
    Ere I am false to you.

II.

When I behold your mountains bold—
    Your noble lakes and streams—
A mingled tide of grief and pride
    Within my bosom teems.
I think of all your long, dark thrall—
    Your martyrs brave and true;
And dash apart the tears that start—
    We must not *weep* for you,
                    Dear land—
    We must not weep for you.

III.

My grandsire died, his home beside;
    They seized and hanged him there;
His only crime, in evil time,
    Your hallowed green to wear.
Across the main his brothers twain
    Were sent to pine and rue;
And still they turn'd, with hearts that burn'd,
    In hopeless love to you,
                    Dear land—
    In hopeless love to you.

IV.

My boyish ear still clung to hear
　Of Erin's pride of yore,
Ere Norman foot had dared pollute
　Her independent shore:
Of chiefs, long dead, who rose to head
　Some gallant patriot few,
Till all my aim on earth became
　To strike one blow for you,
　　　　　　　　Dear land—
　To strike one blow for you.

V.

What path is best your rights to wrest
　Let other heads divine;
By work or word, with voice or sword,
　To follow them be mine.
The breast that zeal and hatred steel,
　No terrors can subdue;
If death should come, that martyrdom
　Were sweet, endured for you,
　　　　　　　　Dear land—
　Were sweet, endured for you.

　　　　　　　　　SLIAḂ CUILINN.

THE WEXFORD MASSACRE.
1649.

BY M. J. BARRY.

I.

THEY knelt around the Cross divine,
　The matron and the maid—
They bow'd before redemption's sign,
　And fervently they prayed—
Three hundred fair and helpless ones,
　Whose crime was this alone—
Their valiant husbands, sires, and sons,
　Had battled for their own.

II.

Had battled bravely, but in vain—
  The Saxon won the fight,
And Irish corses strewed the plain
  Where Valour slept with Right.
And now, that Man of demon guilt,
  To fated Wexford flew—
The red blood reeking on his hilt,
  Of hearts to Erin true!

III.

He found them there—the young, the old—
  The maiden and the wife;
Their guardian Brave in death were cold,
  Who dared for *them* the strife.
They prayed for mercy—God on high!
  Before *thy* cross they prayed,
And ruthless Cromwell bade them die
  To glut the Saxon blade!

IV.

Three hundred fell—the stifled prayer
  Was quenched in woman's blood;
Nor youth nor age could move to spare
  From slaughter's crimson flood.
But nations keep a stern account
  Of deeds that tyrants do;
And guiltless blood to Heaven will mount,
  And Heaven avenge it, too!

THE IRISH ARMS' BILL.

BY WILLIAM DRENNAN.

I.

My country, alas! we may blush for thee now,
The brand of the slave broadly stamp'd on thy brow!
Unarm'd must thy sons and thy daughters await
The Sassenagh's lust or the Sassenagh's hate.

II.

Through the length and the breadth of thy regions they roam;
Many huts and some halls may be there—but no home;
Rape and Murder cry out "let each door be unbarr'd!
Deliver your arms, and then—stand on your guard!"

III.

For England hath waken'd at length from her trance—
She might knuckle to Russia, and truckle to France—
And, licking the dust from America's feet,
Might vow she had ne'er tasted sugar so sweet.

IV.

She could leave her slain thousands, her captives, in pawn,
And Akhbar to lord it o'er Affghanistán,
And firing the village or rifling the ground
Of the poor murder'd peasant—slink off like a hound.

V.

What then? She can massacre wretched Chinese—
Can rob the Ameers of their lands, if she please—
And when Hanover wrings from her duties not due,
She can still vent her wrath, enslav'd Erin, on you!

VI.

Thus—but why, belov'd land, longer sport with thy shame?
If my life could wipe out the foul blot from thy fame,
How gladly for thee were this spirit outpour'd
On the scaffold, as free as by shot or by sword!

VII.

Yet, oh! in fair field, for one soldier-like blow,
To fall in thy cause, or look far for thy foe—
To sleep on thy bosom, down-trodden, with thee,
Or to wave in thy breeze the green flag of the free!

VIII.

Heaven! to think of the thousands far better than I,
Who for thee, sweetest mother, would joyfully die!
Then to reckon the insult—the rapine—the wrong—
How long, God of love!—God of battles!—how long?

E

THE MUSTER OF THE NORTH.

A.D. 1641.

BY CHARLES GAVAN DUFFY.

I.

Joy! joy! the day is come at last, the day of hope and pride—
And see! our crackling bonfires light old Bann's rejoicing tide,
And gladsome bell, and bugle-horn from Newry's captured
    Towers,
Hark! how they tell the Saxon swine, this land is ours, is OURS!

II.

Glory to God! my eyes have seen the ransomed fields of Down,
My ears have drunk the joyful news, "Stout Phelim hath his
    own."
Oh! may they see and hear no more, oh! may they rot to clay,
When they forget to triumph in the conquest of to-day.

III.

Now, now we'll teach the shameless Scot to purge his thievish
    maw,
Now, now the Court may fall to pray, for Justice is the Law,
Now shall the Undertaker* square for once his loose accounts,
We'll strike, brave boys, a fair result, from all his false amounts.

IV.

Come, trample down their robber rule, and smite its venal spawn,
Their foreign laws, their foreign church, their ermine and their
    lawn,
With all the specious fry of fraud that robbed us of our own;
And plant our ancient laws again, beneath our lineal throne.

---

* The Scotch and English adventurers planted in Ulster by James I. were
called Undertakers.

v.

Our standard flies o'er fifty towers, and twice ten thousand men;
Down have we pluck'd the pirate Red never to rise agen;
The Green alone shall stream above our native field and flood—
The spotless Green, save where its folds are gemmed with Saxon
    blood!

vi.

Pity!* no, no, you dare not Priest—not you, our Father, dare
Preach to us now that Godless creed—the murderer's blood to
    spare;
To spare his blood, while tombless still our slaughtered kin implore
"Graves and revenge" from Gobbin-Cliffs and Carrick's bloody
    shore! †

vii.

Pity! well, if you needs must whine, let pity have its way,
Pity for all our comrades true, far from our side to-day;
The prison-bound who rot in chains, the faithful dead who poured
Their blood 'neath Temple's lawless axe or Parsons' ruffian sword.

viii.

Pity!—could we "forget—forgive," if we were clods of clay,
Our martyred priests, our banished chiefs, our race in dark decay,
And worse than all—you know it, Priest—the daughters of our
    land,
With wrongs we blushed to name until the sword was in our hand!

ix.

They smote us with the swearer's oath, and with the murderer's
    knife,
We in the open field will fight, fairly for land and life;
But, by the Dead and all their wrongs, and by our hopes to-day,
One of us twain shall fight their last, or be it we or they—

---

* Leland, the Protestant Historian, states that the Catholic Priests "*laboured
zealously to moderate the excesses of war;*" and frequently protected the English by
concealing them in their places of worship, and even under their altars.

† The scene of the dreadful massacre of the unoffending inhabitants of Island Magee
by the garrison of Carrickfergus.

E 2

X,

They banned our faith, they banned our lives, they trod us into
    earth,
Until our very patience stirred their bitter hearts to mirth;
Even this great flame that wraps them now, not *we* but *they* have
    bred,
Yes, this is their own work, and now, THEIR WORK BE ON THEIR
    HEAD.

XL

Nay, Father, tell us not of help from Leinster's Norman Peers,
If we shall shape our holy cause to match their selfish fears—
Helpless and hopeless be their cause, who brook a vain delay,
Our ship is launched, our flag's afloat, whether they come or stay.

XIL

Let silken Howth, and savage Slane still kiss their tyrant's rod,
And pale Dunsany still prefer his Monarch to his God,
Little we lack their father's sons the Marchmen of the Pale,
While Irish hearts and Irish hands have Spanish blades and mail

XIIL

Then, let them stay to bow and fawn, or fight with cunning words;
I fear me more their courtly acts than England's hireling swords;
Natheless their creed they hate us still, as the Despoiler hates,
Would God they loved their prey no more, our kinsmen's lost
    estates!

XIV.

Our rude array's a jagged rock to smash the spoiler's power,
Or need we aid, His aid we have who doomed this gracious hour;
Of yore He led our Hebrew sires to peace through strife and pain,
And us He leads the self-same path, the self-same goal to gain.

XV.

Down from the sacred hills whereon a SAINT* communed with God,
Up from the vale where Bagnall's blood manured the reeking sod,
Out from the stately woods of Truagh, M'Kenna's plundered home,
Like Malin's waves, as fierce and fast, our faithful clansmen come.

---

* St. Patrick, whose favourite retreat was Lecale, in the County Down.

XVI.

Then, brethren, *on!*—O'NIAL's shade would frown to see you
    pause—
Our banished Hugh, our martyred Hugh, is watching o'er your
    cause—
His generous error lost the land—he deem'd the Norman true,
Oh, forward! friends, it must not lose the land again in you!

NOTE ON THE MUSTER OF THE NORTH.

The *Times*, newspaper, in the absence of any topic of public interest, having
made this ballad the subject of a leading article, in which extravagant praise of its
literary merits was joined with an equally extravagant misrepresentation of its object
and tendency, it had the hard fortune to run the gauntlet of all the Tory journals in
the empire, and to become the best abused ballad in existence.   It was described as the
Rosg-Cata of a new rebellion—as a deliberate attempt to revive the dead-and-gone
jealousies of the bill of settlement; and the organ of the General Assembly of Ulster
coolly proclaimed the writer to be a man with the intellect, but also with the heart, of
Satan!   Under these circumstances I should not have inserted it in the present edition
of the *Spirit of the Nation* had I not feared that omitting it might be interpreted into
an admission of charges, than which nothing can possibly be more false or ludicrous.   In
writing it, I had simply in view to produce—what it will not be denied an historical
ballad ought to be—a picture of the *actual feelings* of the times in which the scene
is laid; and the sentiments are certainly not more violent than the great masters
of ballad poetry—Scott, for example, in his " Glencoe"—have put into the mouths of
injured men.   Possibly the prejudice in the present case arose from overlooking
the fact that these sentiments are attributed to men who had been plundered of two
provinces by a false king, imprisoned for returning conscientious verdicts, robbed by
enormous fines, persecuted for the exercise of their religion, and subject to a long series
of tyrannies which historians, without exception, have described as cruel and infamous.
To make these men talk coolly, and exhibit all the horror of spilling one drop of human
blood, into which O'Connell has trained the present generation, would be very much
on a par in point of sense and propriety with the old stage custom of dressing Richard
III. in the uniform of the Coldstream Guards.   So little intention, however, was there
to make it available to any political purpose, that there is not a single allusion in the
poem that was not suggested by the circumstances of the period ; while some of them
would be quite inapplicable to any other time, especially to the present.

Babington Macaulay, a Privy Councillor, and Secretary at War under the late
Administration, has written two ballads of the English Commonwealth, a period only
a few years removed from the era of this one, which certainly leave the " Muster of

IRISH WAR-SONG.

BY EDWARD WALSH.

Air—" The world 's turn'd upside down. "

I.

BRIGHT sun, before whose glorious ray,
 Our Pagan fathers bent the knee;
Whose pillar-altars yet can say,
 When time was young, our sires were free—

---

the North" almost as far behind in ferocity as in grace and vigour. For example, he puts this sentiment into the mouth of the Cavaliers :—

  " What, ho! the craven slaves retire;
  On! trample them to mud!
  No quarter!—charge.—No quarter!—fire!
  No quarter!—blood!—blood!—blood!"

And afterwards this unequivocal stimulant to robbery and rape :—

  " Where next? In sooth there lacks no witch,
  Brave lads, to tell us where;
  Sure London's sons be passing rich,
  Her daughters wondrous fair;
  And let that dastard be the theme
  Of many a board's derision,
  Who quails for sermon, cuff, or scream
  Of any sweet Precisian."

And the Puritans are not behind them in savage vigour :—

  " Ho! comrades, scour the plain, and ere ye strip the slain,
  First give another stab to make your guest secure;
  Then shake from sleeves and pockets, their broad pieces and lockets,
  The tokens of the wanton—the plunder of the poor."

It would be monstrous to allege that this accomplished poet has committed any offence, or that he shares in the sentiments of either party because he has described both of them with dramatic spirit and historical truth; and unless it is shewn that I have misrepresented the feelings of the men who seized upon Ulster, in 1641, I am surely entitled to the same defence.

In the original edition the following note was prefixed to the poem; and we retain it as an additional evidence of the actual purpose in view :—

" We deny and have always denied the alleged massacre of 1641. But that the people rose under their Chiefs, seized the English towns and expelled the English settlers, and in doing so committed many excesses, is undeniable—as is equally the desperate provocation. The Ballad here printed is not meant as an apology for these excesses, which we condemn and lament, but as a true representation of the feelings of the insurgents in the first madness of success."

Who seest how fallen their offspring be—
  Our matrons' tears—our patriots' gore ;
We swear before high Heaven and thee,
  The Saxon holds us slaves no more !

II.

Our sun-burst on the Roman foe
  Flash'd vengeance once in foreign field—
On Clontarf's plain lay scathed low
  What power the Sea-kings fierce could wield !
Beinn Burb might say whose cloven shield
  'Neath bloody hoofs was trampled o'er ;
And, by these memories high, we yield
  Our limbs to Saxon chains no more !

III.

The *clairseach* wild, whose trembling string
  Had long the " song of sorrow" spoke,
Shall bid the wild *Rosg-Cata** sing
  The curse and crime of Saxon yoke.
And, by each heart his bondage broke—
  Each exile's sigh on distant shore—
Each martyr 'neath the headsman's stroke—
  The Saxon holds us slaves no more !

IV.

Send the loud war-cry o'er the main—
  Your sun-burst to the breezes spread !
That *slogan* rends the heaven in twain—
  The earth reels back beneath your tread !
Ye Saxon despots, hear, and dread—
  Your march o'er patriot hearts is o'er—
That shout hath told—that tramp hath said,
  Our country's sons are slaves no more !

---

* Literally the " Eye of Battle"—the war-song of the bards.

NATIVE SWORDS,

A VOLUNTEER SONG FOR 1st JULY, 1792.

Air—"Boyne Water."

Marcaiġeaċt na Boinne. THE CAVALCADE OF THE BOYNE.

Moderato
We've bent too long to brag-gart wrong, While force our prayers de-
ri - ded; We've fought too long our - selves a - mong, By

knaves and priests di - vi - ded. U - - ni - ted now, no

more we'll bow, Foul fac - tion, we dis - card it; And now, thank God, our

na - tive sod Has Na - tive Swords to guard it.

F

NATIVE SWORDS,

A VOLUNTEER SONG.—1ST JULY, 1792.

BY THOMAS DAVIS.

Air—"Boyne Water."

I.

WE'VE bent too long to braggart wrong,
    While force our prayers derided;
We've fought too long, ourselves among,
    By knaves and priests divided;
United now, no more we'll bow,
    Foul faction, we discard it;
And now, thank God! our native sod
    Has Native Swords to guard it.

II.

Like rivers, which, o'er valleys rich,
    Bring ruin in their water,
On native land, a native hand
    Flung foreign fraud and slaughter.
From Dermod's crime to Tudor's time
    Our clans were our perdition;
Religion's name, since then, became
    Our pretext for division.

III.

But, worse than all, with Lim'rick's fall
    Our valour seem'd to perish;
Or, o'er the main, in France and Spain,
    For bootless vengeance flourish.
The peasant, here, grew pale for fear
    He'd suffer for our glory,
While France sang joy for Fontenoy,
    And Europe hymn'd our story.

IV.

But, now, no clan, nor factious plan,
  The east and west can sunder—
Why Ulster e'er should Munster fear
  Can only wake our wonder.
Religion's crost, when union's lost,
  And "royal gifts" retard it;
And now, thank God! our native sod
  Has Native Swords to guard it.

SONG FOR JULY 12TH, 1843.

BY J. D. FRASER.

Air—"Boyne Water."

I.

COME—pledge again thy heart and hand—
  One grasp that ne'er shall sever;
Our watchword be—" Our native land"—
  Our motto—" Love for ever."
And let the Orange lily be
  Thy badge, my patriot brother—
The everlasting Green for *me;*
  And—we for one another.

II.

Behold how green the gallant stem
  On which the flower is blowing;
How in one heav'nly breeze and beam
  Both flower and stem are glowing.
The same good soil sustaining both,
  Makes both united flourish:
But cannot give the Orange growth,
  And cease the Green to nourish.

III.

Yea, more—the hand that plucks the flower
  Will vainly strive to cherish :
The stem blooms on—but in that hour
  The flower begins to perish.
Regard them, then, of equal worth
  While lasts their genial weather;
The time's at hand when into earth
  The two shall sink together.

IV.

Ev'n thus be, in our country's cause,
  Our party feelings blended ;
Till lasting peace, from equal laws,
  On both shall have descended.
Till then the Orange lily be
  Thy badge, my patriot brother—
The everlasting Green for *me;*
  And—we for one another.

SONG OF THE VOLUNTEERS OF 1782.

BY THOMAS DAVIS.

Air—"Boyne Water."

I.

HURRAH ! 'tis done—our freedom's won—
  Hurrah for the Volunteers !
No laws we own, but those alone
  Of our Commons, King, and Peers.
The chain is broke—the Saxon yoke
  From off our neck is taken ;
Ireland awoke—Dungannon spoke—
  With fear was England shaken.

II.

When Grattan rose, none dar'd oppose
　　The claim he made for freedom;
They knew our swords, to back his words,
　　Were ready, did he need them.
Then let us raise, to Grattan's praise,
　　A proud and joyous anthem;
And wealth, and grace, and length of days,
　　May God, in mercy grant him!

III.

Bless Harry Flood, who nobly stood
　　By us, through gloomy years,
Bless Charlemont, the brave and good,
　　The Chief of the Volunteers!
The North began; the North held on
　　The strife for native land;
Till Ireland rose, and cow'd her foes—
　　God bless the Northern land!

IV.

And bless the men of patriot pen—
　　Swift, Molyneux, and Lucas;
Bless sword and gun, which "Free Trade" won—
　　Bless God! who ne'er forsook us!
And long may last, the friendship fast,
　　Which binds us all together;
While we agree, our foes shall flee
　　Like clouds in stormy weather.

V.

Remember still, through good and ill,
　　How vain were prayers and tears—
How vain were words, till flashed the swords
　　Of the Irish Volunteers.
By arms we've got the rights we sought
　　Through long and wretched years—
Hurrah! 'tis done, our Freedom's won—
　　Hurrah for the Volunteers!

MY GRAVE.

BY THOMAS DAVIS.

SHALL they bury me in the deep,
Where wind-forgetting waters sleep?
Shall they dig a grave for me,
Under the green-wood tree?
Or on the wild heath,
Where the wilder breath
Of the storm doth blow?
Oh, no! oh, no!

Shall they bury me in the Palace Tombs,
Or under the shade of Cathedral domes?
Sweet 'twere to lie on Italy's shore;
Yet not there—nor in Greece, though I love it more.
In the wolf or the vulture my grave shall I find?
Shall my ashes career on the world-seeing wind?
Shall they fling my corpse in the battle mound,
Where coffinless thousands lie under the ground?
Just as they fall they are buried so—
Oh, no! oh, no!

No! on an Irish green hill-side,
On an opening lawn—but not too wide;
For I love the drip of the wetted trees—
On me blow no gales, but a gentle breeze,
To freshen the turf: put no tombstone there,
But green sods deck'd with daisies fair.
Nor sods too deep: but so that the dew,
The matted grass-roots may trickle through—
Be my epitaph writ on my country's mind,
"He serv'd his country, and lov'd his kind"—
Oh! 'twere merry unto the grave to go,
If one were sure to be buried so.

THE NATION'S FIRST NUMBER.

BY CLARENCE MANGAN.

Air—" Rory O'More."

I.

'TIS a great day, and glorious, O Public! for you—
This October Fifteenth, Eighteen Forty and Two!
For on this day of days, lo! THE NATION comes forth,
To commence its career of Wit, Wisdom, and Worth—
To give Genius its due—to do battle with wrong—
And achieve things undreamed of as yet, save in song.
Then arise! fling aside your dark mantle of slumber,
And welcome in chorus THE NATION'S FIRST NUMBER.

II.

Here we are, thanks to Heaven, in an epoch when Mind
Is unfettering our captives, and couching our blind;
And the Press, with its thunders keeps marring the mirth
Of those tyrants and bigots that curse our fair earth.
Be it ours to stand forth and contend in the van
Of truth's legions for freedom, that birthright of man,
Shaking off the dull cobwebs that else might encumber
Our weapon—the pen—in THE NATION'S FIRST NUMBER.

III.

We announce a New Era—be this our first news—
When the serf-grinding Landlords shall shake in their shoes;
While the ark of a bloodless yet mighty Reform
Shall emerge from the flood of the Popular Storm!
Well we know how the lickspittle panders to Power
Feel and fear the approach of that death-dealing hour;
But we toss these aside—such vile vagabond lumber
Are but just worth a groan from THE NATION'S FIRST NUMBER.

IV.

Though we take not for motto, *Nul n'a de l'esprit,*
(As they once did in Paris) *hors nos bons amis,*
We may boast that for first-rate endowments, our band
Form a phalanx unmatched *in*—or *out* of—the land.
Poets, Patriots, Linguists, with reading like Parr's—
Critics keener than sabres—Wits brighter than stars;
And Reasoners as cool as the coolest cu-cumber
Form the host that shine out in THE NATION'S FIRST NUMBER.

V.

We shall sketch living manners—and men—in a style
That will scarcely be sneezed at, we guess for a while;
Build up stories as fast as of yore Mother Bunch,
And for Fun of all twists take the shine out of " PUNCH ;"
Thus our Wisdom and Quizdom will finely agree,
Very much, Public dear, we conceive, as you see
Do the lights and the shades that illume and adumber
Each beautiful page in THE NATION'S FIRST NUMBER.

VI.

A word more :—To OLD IRELAND our first love is given ;
Still, our friendship hath arms for all lands under Heaven.
WE ARE IRISH—we vaunt it—all o'er and all out ;
But we wish not that England shall "sneak up the spout !"
Then, O Public ! here, there, and elsewhere through the world,
Wheresoe'er TRUTH'S and LIBERTY'S flags are unfurl'd,
From the Suir to the Rhine, from the Boyne to the Humber,
Raise one Shout of Applause for THE NATION'S FIRST NUMBER.

WHAT'S MY THOUGHT LIKE?

BY JOHN O'CONNELL, M.P.

" What's my thought like?
" How is it like? &c.
" What would you do with it ?"
Nursery-Game.

I.

WHAT's my thought like?—What's my thought like?
—Like a column tumbled down—
Its noble shaft and capital with moss and weeds o'ergrown!
How is my thought so like unto a column thus laid low?
Because your thought is Ireland now—laid prostrate;—even so!
What with it would you do?—oh, say—what with it would you do?
Upraise it from the earth again, aloft to mankind's view!
A sign unto all those that mourn, throughout earth's vast domain,
That Heaven rewards the patient, and will make them joy again.

II.

What's my thought like?—What's my thought like?
—Like a gallant ship on shore?
Dismasted all and helpless now, amid the breakers' roar!
Her crew, so faithful once to her, each seeking plank and spar,
To 'scape from her and safety seek, upon the land afar.
How is my thought like such poor ship in peril and distress?
Because your thought is Ireland now, whose peril is no less!
What with it would you do?—oh, say—what with it would you do?
Like to some few but faithful hearts among such vessel's crew—
Stand by her to the last I would! and die, if so decreed,
Ere man should dare to say to me, *You failed her at her need!*

III.

What's my thought like?—What's my thought like?
—Like a land by Nature bless'd
Beyond most other lands on earth—and yet the most distress'd!
A teeming soil—abounding streams—wide havens—genial air—
And yet a people ever plunged in suffering and care!

G

Eight millions of a noble race—high-minded, pure, and good—
Kept subject to a petty gang—a miserable brood!
Strong but in England's constant hate, and help to keep us down,
And blast the smiles of Nature fair, with man's unholy frown!
How is it like my thought, again?—How is it like my thought?
Because your thought is Ireland's self—and even thus her lot!
What with it would you do, again?—What with it would you do?
Work even to the death I would, to rive her chain in two!
To help her 'gainst unnatural sons, and foreign foemen's rage,
And all her hapless People's woes and bitter griefs assuage;
Bid them be happy now, at length, in this their rescued land—
That land no longer marked and cursed with slav'ry's withering
    brand!
No longer Slave to England!—but her Sister, if she will—
Prompt to give friendly aid at need, and to forget all ill!
But holding high her head, and with serenest brow
Claiming, amid Earth's nations all, her fitting station now!
THIS is my thought—it is your thought.
        —If thus each Irish heart
Will only think, and purpose thus, henceforth, to act its part,
Full soon their honest boast shall be—that she was made by them
Great, Glorious, Free!—the Earth's first Flower!
        —The Ocean's brightest Gem!

COME, FILL EV'RY GLASS TO O'ERFLOWING.

BY M. J. BARRY.

AIR—" *One bumper at parting.*"

I.

COME, fill ev'ry glass to o'erflowing,
   With wine, or potheen if you will,
Or, if any think these are too glowing,
   Let water replace them—but fill!

Oh! trust me 'tis churlish and silly
  To ask how the bumper's fill'd up;
If the tide in the heart be not chilly
  What matters the tide in the cup?
Oh! ne'er may that heart's tide ascending
  In shame on our foreheads be seen,
While it nobly can ebb in defending
  Our own glorious colour—the Green!

II.

In vain did oppression endeavour
  To trample that green under foot;
The fair stem was broken, but never
  Could tyranny reach to its root.
Then come, and around it let's rally,
  And guard it henceforward like men;
Oh! soon shall each mountain and valley
  Grow bright with its verdure again.
Meanwhile, fill each glass to the brim, boys,
  With water, with wine, or *potheen,*
And on each let the honest wish swim, boys—
  Long flourish the Gael and the Green!

III.

Here, under our host's gay dominion,
  While gathered this table around,
What varying shades of opinion
  In one happy circle are found!
What opposite creeds come together—
  How mingle North, South, East, and West;
Yet, who minds the diff'rence a feather?—
  Each strives to love Erin the best.
Oh! soon through our beautiful island
  May union as blessed be seen,
While floats o'er each valley and highland
  Our own glorious colour—the Green!

THE MEMORY OF THE DEAD.

Who fears to speak of Nine - ty -Eight? Who blushes at the name? When cow-ards mock the patriot's fate, Who hangs his head for shame? He's all a knave, or half a slave, Who slights his coun - try thus; But a

true man, like you, man, Will fill your glass with us. He's

all a knave, or half a slave, Who slights his coun - try thus; But a

true man, like you, man, Will fill your glass with us.

THE MEMORY OF THE DEAD.

I.

Who fears to speak of Ninety-Eight?
　　Who blushes at the name?
When cowards mock the patriot's fate,
　　Who hangs his head for shame?
He's all a knave, or half a slave,
　　Who slights his country thus;
But a *true* man, like you, man,
　　Will fill your glass with us.

II.

We drink the memory of the brave,
　　The faithful and the few—
Some lie far off beyond the wave—
　　Some sleep in Ireland, too;
All—all are gone—but still lives on
　　The fame of those who died—
All true men, like you, men,
　　Remember them with pride.

III.

Some on the shores of distant lands
　　Their weary hearts have laid,
And by the stranger's heedless hands
　　Their lonely graves were made;
But, though their clay be far away
　　Beyond the Atlantic foam—
In true men, like you, men,
　　Their spirit's still at home.

IV.

The dust of some is Irish earth;
　　Among their own they rest;
And the same land that gave them birth
　　Has caught them to her breast;

And we will pray that from their clay
    Full many a race may start
Of true men, like you, men,
    To act as brave a part.

V.

They rose in dark and evil days
    To right their native land;
They kindled here a living blaze
    That nothing shall withstand.
Alas! that Might can vanquish Right—
    They fell and pass'd away;
But true men, like you, men,
    Are plenty here to-day.

VI.

Then here's their memory—may it be
    For us a guiding light,
To cheer our strife for liberty,
    And teach us to unite.
Through good and ill, be Ireland's still,
    Though sad as theirs your fate;
And true men be you, men,
    Like those of Ninety-Eight.

THE BATTLE OF BEAL-AN-ATHA-BUIDHE.*
A.D. 1598.

BY WILLIAM DRENNAN.

I.

By O'Neil, close beleagur'd, the spirits might droop
Of the Saxon—three hundred shut up in their coop,
Till Bagenal drew forth his Toledo, and swore
On the sword of a soldier, to succour Port Mór.

---

* Won by the great Hugh O'Neil over Marshal Bagenal and the flower of Elizabeth's army, between Armagh and Blackwater Bridge.

II.

His veteran troops, in the foreign wars tried—
Their features how bronz'd, and how haughty their stride—
Stept steadily on; it was thrilling to see
That thunder-cloud brooding o'er BEAL-AN-ATHA-BUIDHE.

III.

The flash of their armour, inlaid with fine gold—
Gleaming matchlocks and cannon that mutteringly roll'd—
With the tramp and the clank of those stern cuirassiers,
Dyed in blood of the Flemish and French cavaliers.

IV.

And are the mere Irish, with pikes and with darts—
With but glibb-covered heads, and but rib-guarded hearts—
Half-naked, half-fed, with few muskets, no guns—
The battle to dare against England's proud sons?

V.

Poor Bonnochts, and wild Gallowglasses, and Kern*—
Let them war with rude brambles, sharp furze, and dry fern;
Wirrastrue† for their wives—for their babes *ochanie*,
If they wait for the Saxon at BEAL-AN-ATHA-BUIDHE.

VI.

Yet O'Neil standeth firm—few and brief his commands—
" Ye have hearts in your bosoms, and pikes in your hands;
Try how far ye can push them, my children, at once;
Fág an Bealach—and down with horse, foot, and great guns.

VII.

They have gold and gay arms—they have biscuit and bread;
Now, sons of my soul, we'll be found and be fed;"
And he clutch'd his claymore, and—"look yonder," laughed he,
" What a grand commissariat for BEAL-AN-ATHA-BUIDHE."

---

* *Buanadh*, a billetted soldier, from *Buanacht*, quarterage.   *Galloglachaibh,*
heavy soldiers.   *Ceitheirn*, a band of light troops, plural of *Ceithearnaigh.*
† *Wirrastrue—A Mhuire as truagh*, Oh! Mary, what sorrow!

VIII.

Near the chief, a grim tyke, an O'Shanaghan stood,
His nostril dilated seemed snuffing for blood ;
Rough and ready to spring—like the wiry wolf-hound
Of Iernè—who, tossing his pike with a bound,

IX.

Cried, "My hand to the Sassanach ! ne'er may I hurl
Another to earth if I call him a churl !
He finds me in clothing, in booty, in bread—
My Chief, won't O'Shanaghan give him a bed ?"

X.

"Land of Owen, abu !" and the Irish rush'd on—
The foe fir'd but one volley—their gunners are gone,
Before the bare bosoms the steel-coats have fled,
Or, despite casque or corselet, lie dying and dead.

XI.

And brave Harry Bagenal, he fell while he fought,
With many gay gallants—they slept as men ought :
Their faces to heaven—there were others, alack !
By pikes overtaken, and taken aback.

XII.

And my Irish got clothing, coin, colours, great store,
Arms, forage, and provender—plunder *go leór !*
They munch'd the white manchets—they champ'd the brown
    chine,
Fillelue ! for that day, how the natives did dine !

XIII.

The Chieftain looked on, when O'Shanaghan rose,
And cried, hearken O'Neil ! I 've a health to propose—
"To our Sassanach hosts !" and all quaff'd in huge glee,
With *Cead mile failte go,* Beal-an-atha-buidhe !

H

THE VOICE OF LABOUR.

A Chant of the City Meetings.

BY CHARLES GAVAN DUFFY.

I.

YE who despoil the sons of toil, saw ye this sight to-day,
When stalwart trade in long brigade, beyond a king's array,
Marched in the blessed light of heaven, beneath the open sky,
Strong in the might of sacred RIGHT, that none dare ask them why?
These are the slaves, the needy knaves, ye spit upon with scorn—
The spawn of earth, of nameless birth, and basely bred as born;
Yet know, ye weak and silken Lords, were we the thing ye say,
Your broad domains, your coffered gains, your lives were ours
    to-day!

II.

Measure that rank, from flank to flank; 'tis fifty thousand strong;
And mark you here, in front and rear, brigades as deep and long;
And know that never blade of foe, or Arran's deadly breeze,
Tried by assay of storm or fray, more dauntless hearts than these;
The sinewy Smith, little he recks of his own child—the sword;
The men of gear, think you they fear *their* handiwork—a Lord?
And undismayed, yon sons of trade might see the battle's front,
Who bravely bore, nor bowed before, the deadlier face of want.

III.

What lack we here of all the pomps that lure your kerns to death?
Not serried bands, nor sinewy hands, nor music's martial breath;
And if we broke the slavish yoke our suppliant race endure,
No robbers we—but chivalry—the Army of the Poor.
Out on ye now, ye Lordly crew, that do your betters wrong—
We are no base and braggart mob, but merciful and strong.
Your henchmen vain, your vassal train, would fly our first defiance;
In us—in our strong, tranquil breasts—abides your sole reliance.

IV.

Aye! keep them all, castle and hall, coffers and costly jewels—
Keep your vile gain, and in its train the passions that it fuels.
We envy not your lordly lot—its bloom or its decayance;
But ye *have* that we claim as ours—our right in long abeyance:
Leisure to live, leisure to love, leisure to taste our freedom—
Oh! suff'ring poor, oh! patient poor, how bitterly you need them!
"Ever to moil, ever to toil," that is your social charter,
And city slave or rustic serf, the TOILER is its martyr.

V.

Where Frank and Tuscan shed their sweat the goodly crop is
    theirs—
If Norway's toil make rich the soil, she eats the fruit she rears—
O'er Maine's green sward there rules no lord, saving the Lord on
    high;
Why are *we* swindled—sabred—starved?—my masters, tell us
    why.
The German burgher and his men, brother with brothers live,
While toil must wait without *your* gate what gracious crusts you
    give.
Long in your sight, for our own right, we've bent, and still we
    bend—
Why did we bow? why do we now? my masters, this must end.

VI.

Perish the past—a generous land is this fair land of ours,
And enmity may no man see between its Towns and Towers.
Come, join our bands—here take our hands—now shame on him
    that lingers,
Merchant or Peer, you have no fear from labour's blistered fingers.
Come, join at last, perish the past—its traitors, its seceders—
Proud names and old, frank hearts and bold, come join and be our
    Leaders.
But know, ye lords, that be your swords with us or with our Wronger,
Heaven be our guide, we Toilers bide this lot of shame no longer!

H 2

THE ANTI-IRISH IRISHMAN.

AIR.—*Féaðaim má'r ail liom.*

Cheerful and with Expression.

From po - lar seas to tor - rid climes, Where - e'er the trace of man is found, What com - mon feel - ing marks our kind, And sanc - ti - fies each

spot of ground? What vir - tue in the hu - man heart The

proud - est tri - bute can com - mand? The dear - est, pur - est,

ho - li - est, best, *The last - ing love of* FA - THER - LAND.

THE ANTI-IRISH IRISHMAN.

BY HUGH HARKAN.

I.

From polar seas to torrid climes,
    Where'er the trace of man is found,
What common feeling marks our kind,
    And sanctifies each spot of ground?
What virtue in the human heart
    The proudest tribute can command?
The dearest, purest, holiest, best,
    The lasting love of FATHERLAND!

II.

Then who's the wretch that basely spurns
    The ties of country, kindred, friends—
That barters every nobler aim
    For sordid views—for private ends?
One slave alone on earth you'll find
    Through Nature's universal span,
So lost to virtue—dead to shame—
    The anti-Irish Irishman.

III.

Our fields are fertile, rich our floods,
    Our mountains bold, majestic, grand;
Our air is balm, and every breeze
    Wings health around our native land.
But who despises all her charms,
    And mocks her gifts where'er he can?
Why, he, the Norman's sneaking slave,
    The anti-Irish Irishman.

IV.

The Norman—spawn of fraud and guile!
    Ambitious sought our peaceful shore,
And, leagued with native guilt, despoiled,
    And deluged Erin's fields with gore!

Who gave the foeman footing here?
  What wretch unholy led her van?
The prototype of modern slaves,
  An anti-Irish Irishman!

v.

For ages rapine ruled our plains,
  And slaughter raised "his red right hand,"
And virgins shriek'd!—and roof-trees blaz'd!
  And desolation swept the land!
And who would not those ills arrest,
  Or aid the patriotic plan
To burst his country's galling chains?
  The anti-Irish Irishman!

vi.

But now too great for fetters grown,
  Too proud to bend a slavish knee,
Loved Erin mocks the tyrant's thrall,
  And firmly vows she shall be free!
But mark yon treacherous stealthy knave
  That bends beneath his country's ban;
Let infamy eternal brand
  That anti-Irish Irishman!

STEADY.

BY R. D. WILLIAMS.

" Courage—your most necessary virtue—consists not in blind resistance, but in knowing when to forbear."—THE NATION, *June* 17, 1843.

I.

STEADY! Host of Freedom, steady!
  Ponder, gather, watch, mature!
Tranquil be, though ever ready—
  Prompt to act—and to endure.

II.

Aimless, rage you not, insanely,
    Like a maniac with his chain,
Struggling madly, therefore vainly,
    And lapsing back to bonds again.

III.

But, observe, the clouds o'er Keeper
    Long collect their awful ire—
Long they swell more dark and deeper;
    When they burst, all heaven's on fire.

IV.

Freedom's barque to port is running,
    But beware the lurking shelves;
And would you conquer tyrants' cunning,
    Brethren, conquer first yourselves.

V.

Though thy cheek insulted burn—
    Though they call thee coward-slave—
Scoff nor blow shalt thou return:
    Trust me, this is *more* than brave.

VI.

Fortitude hath shackles riven,
    More than spear or flashing gun;
Freedom, like the thrones of heaven,
    Is by suff'ring virtue won.

VII.

Though thy brother still deride thee,
    Yield thou love for foolish hate:
He'll, perhaps, ere long, beside thee,
    Proudly, boldly, share thy fate.

VIII.

Steady! steady! ranks of Freedom,
    Pure and holy are our bands;
Heaven approves, and angels lead them,
    For truth and justice are our brands!

O'NEIL'S VOW.

BY MICHAEL DOHENY.

" Quamdiu vita aderit, ipsos impubnabimus pro nostri juris defensione."—*Letter of Domhnall O'Neil, to Pope John in Fordun's Scotichronicon, p.* 923.

I.

How many a year,
In fleet career,
Have circled o'er its blackened strand,
Since first that vow,
Forgotten now,
Was plighted to our native land?
And still the crimes
Of those dark times
Are perpetrated hour by hour,
And Saxon fraud,
By GOD unaw'd,
Goes hand in hand with Saxon power!

II.

This lesson stern
Thou 'st left to learn,
Oft baffled, but unyielding King,
" In peace or strife,
In death or life,
The Saxon bears a poison'd sting.
Then weal or woe,
Strike home the blow,
And shun at least the coward's fate,
And far on high
Your destiny
Shall rank with stars of loftiest state.

I

III.

Domhnall O'Neil
Swears on his steel,
While throbs one pulse, or heaves one breath,
To meet thy hand
With whetted brand,
Invading brigand to the death.
Nor length of years,
Nor blood nor tears,
Defeat, disaster, nor distress,
Shall mar the word
Pledg'd on the sword
He clutches for the merciless."

THE SAXON SHILLING.

BY THE LATE K. T. BUGGY.

I.

Hark! a martial sound is heard—
The march of soldiers, fifing, drumming;
Eyes are staring, hearts are stirr'd—
For bold recruits the brave are coming.
Ribands flaunting, feathers gay—
The sounds and sights are surely thrilling,
Dazzled village youths to-day
Will crowd to take the *Saxon Shilling*.

II.

Ye, whose spirits will not bow
In peace to parish tyrants longer—
Ye, who wear the villain brow,
And ye who pine in hopeless hunger—
Fools, without the brave man's faith—
All slaves and starvelings who are willing
To sell yourselves to shame and death—
Accept the fatal *Saxon Shilling*.

III.

Ere you from your mountains go
   To feel the scourge of foreign fever,
Swear to serve the faithless foe
   That lures you from your land for ever!
Swear henceforth its tools to be—
   To slaughter trained by ceaseless drilling—
Honour, home, and liberty,
   Abandon'd for a *Saxon Shilling.*

IV.

Go—to find, 'mid crime and toil,
   The doom to which such guilt is hurried;
Go—to leave on Indian soil
   Your bones to bleach, accurs'd, unburied!
Go—to crush the just and brave,
   Whose wrongs with wrath the world are filling;
Go—to slay each brother slave,
   Or spurn the blood-stained *Saxon Shilling!*

V.

Irish hearts! why should you bleed,
   To swell the tide of British glory—
Aiding despots in their need,
   Who've changed our *green* so oft to *gory?*
None, save those who wish to see
   The noblest killed, the meanest killing,
And true hearts severed from the free,
   Will take again the *Saxon Shilling!*

VI.

Irish youths! reserve your strength
   Until an hour of glorious duty,
When Freedom's smile shall cheer at length
   The land of bravery and beauty.
Bribes and threats, oh, heed no more—
   Let nought but JUSTICE make you willing
To leave your own dear Island shore,
   For those who send the *Saxon Shilling.*

I 2

THE GIRL OF DUNBUIDE.

BY THOMAS DAVIS.

I.

'Tis pretty to see the girl of Dunbuide
Stepping the mountain statelily—
Though ragged her gown, and naked her feet,
No lady in Ireland to match her is meet.

II.

Poor is her diet, and hardly she lies—
Yet a monarch might kneel for a glance of her eyes;
The child of a peasant—yet England's proud Queen
Has less rank in her heart, and less grace in her mien.

III.

Her brow 'neath her raven hair gleams, just as if
A breaker spread white 'neath a shadowy cliff—
And love, and devotion, and energy speak
From her beauty-proud eye, and her passion-pale cheek.

IV.

But, pale as her cheek is, there's fruit on her lip,
And her teeth flash as white as the crescent moon's tip,
And her form and her step, like the red-deer's, go past—
As lightsome, as lovely, as haughty, as fast.

V.

I saw her but once, and I looked in her eye,
And she knew that I worshipp'd in passing her by;
The saint of the wayside—she granted my pray'r,
Though we spoke not a word, for her mother was there.

VI.

I never can think upon Bantry's bright hills,
But her image starts up, and my longing eye fills;
And I whisper her softly, "again, love, we'll meet,
And I'll lie in your bosom, and live at your feet."

LOVE SONG.

BY CHARLES GAVAN DUFFY.

I.

I LOVE thine eyes of truth and light,
   I love thy smile of joy;
But not to me their beams were bright,
If, as I did, so others might
    Their light enjoy.

II.

Canst thou be true to one alone,
   True beyond all reproach—
Bound like the palmer to one goal,
Thrilled like the magnet by one pole—
    Canst thou be such?

III.

The head that pillows on my breast,
   And calls that home its own,
Must grant to every thought confess'd
As calm and true a place of rest
    To reign alone.

IV.

Ask I too much? Nay, think not so;
   Canst thou not, dearest, guess
He with scant love content to go
Meaneth, in turn, to bestow
    Even yet less.

V.

But the true heart can claim in sooth
   But what it gave—
Candour for candour, truth for truth,
An ebbless tide from age to youth
    Even to the grave.

OURSELVES ALONE.

Moderato. *p* Sotto voce.

1. The work that should to - day be wrought De - fer not till to -
2. *Re - mem -ber when your lot was worse,—— Sunk, tram-pled to the*

p

mor - row; The help that should with - in be sought — Scorn from with - out to
dust; 'Twas long our weak - ness and our curse In stran-ger aid to

Poco piu forte.

bor - row. — Old max - ims these—yet stout and true—They
trust. *And* *if* *at* *length* *we* *proud - ly* *trod* *On*

cresc.

speak in trum - - pet tone, To do at once what
bi - - got *laws* *o'er - - - thrown,* *Who* *won* *that* *strug - gle?*

cresc. *colla parte.*

f

is to do, And trust OUR - SELVES A - - - LONE.
Un - - der *God,* *Our - -selves,—*

f

OURSELVES ALONE.

I.

The work that should to-day be wrought
    Defer not till to-morrow;
The help that should within be sought,
    Scorn from without to borrow.
Old maxims these—yet stout and true—
    They speak in trumpet tone,
To do at once what is to do,
    And trust OURSELVES ALONE.

II.

Too long our Irish hearts we school'd,
    In patient hope to bide;
By dreams of English justice fool'd,
    And English tongues that lied.
That hour of weak delusion 's past,
    The empty dream has flown:
Our hope and strength, we find at last,
    Is in OURSELVES ALONE.

III.

Aye! bitter hate, or cold neglect,
    Or lukewarm love, at best,
Is all we 've found, or can expect,
    We aliens of the west.
No friend, beyond her own green shore,
    Can Erin truly own;
Yet stronger is her trust, therefore,
    In her brave sons ALONE.

IV.

Remember when our lot was worse—
    Sunk, trampled to the dust;
'Twas long our weakness and our curse,
    In stranger aid to trust.

And if, at length, we proudly trod
  On bigot laws o'erthrown,
Who won that struggle ?   Under God,
  Ourselves—OURSELVES ALONE.
v.
Oh, let its memory be enshrined
  In Ireland's heart for ever !
It proves a banded people's mind
  Must win in just endeavour;
It shows how wicked to despair,
  How weak to idly groan—
If ills at *others'* hands ye bear,
  The cure is in YOUR OWN.
VI.
The "foolish word impossible"
  At once, for aye, disdain;
No power can bar a people's will
  A people's right to gain.
Be bold, united, firmly set,
  Nor flinch in word or tone—
We'll be a glorious nation yet,
  REDEEMED—ERECT—ALONE.

SLIAB CUILINN.

THE RATH OF MULLAGHMAST.

BY R. D. WILLIAMS.
I.
O'ER the Rath of Mullaghmast,
On the solemn midnight blast,
What bleeding spectres past,
  With their gash'd breasts bare ?
Hast thou heard the fitful wail
That o'erloads the sullen gale,
When the waning moon shines pale
  O'er the curs'd ground there ?

K

II.

Hark! hollow moans arise
Thro' the black tempestuous skies,
And curses, strife, and cries,
    From the lone Rath swell;
For bloody Sydney, there,
Nightly fills the lurid air
With th' unholy pomp and glare
    Of the foul, deep hell.

III.

He scorches up the gale,
With his knights, in fiery mail;
And the banners of the Pale
    O'er the red ranks rest.
But a wan and gory band
All apart and silent stand,
And they point th' accusing hand
    At that hell-hound's crest!

IV.

Red streamlets, trickling slow,
O'er their clotted *cuilins* flow,
And still and awful woe,
    On each pale brow weeps—
Rich bowls bestrew the ground,
And broken harps around,
Whose once enchanting sound
    In the bard's blood sleeps.

V.

False Sydney! knighthood's stain,
The trusting brave in vain—
Thy guests—ride o'er the plain
    To thy dark cow'rd snare.
Flow'r of Offaly and Leix,
They have come thy board to grace—
Fools! to meet a faithless race
    Save with true swords bare.

VI.

While cup and song abound,
The triple lines surround
The closed and guarded mound,
   In the night's dark noon.
Alas! too brave O'More,
Ere the revelry was o'er
They have spill'd thy young heart's gore,
   Snatch'd from love too soon!

VII.

At the feast, unarm'd all,
Priest, bard, and chieftain fall
In the treacherous Saxon's hall,
   O'er the bright wine-bowl;
And now nightly round the board,
With unsheath'd and reeking sword,
Strides the cruel felon lord
   Of the blood-stain'd soul.

VIII.

Since that hour the clouds that pass'd
O'er the Rath of Mullaghmast,
One tear have never cast
   On the gore-dyed sod;
For the shower of crimson rain,
That o'erflow'd that fatal plain,
Cries aloud, and not in vain,
   To the most high God.

IX.

Tho' the Saxon snake unfold
At thy feet his scales of gold,
And vow thee love untold,
   Trust him not, Green Land!
Touch not with gloveless clasp
A coil'd and deadly asp,
But with strong and guarded grasp
   In your steel-clad hand!

K 2

THE LION AND THE SERPENT.

An Arms'-Bill Fable.

BY R. D. WILLIAMS.

I.

IN days of old the Serpent came
 To the Lion's rocky hall,
And the forest king spread the sward with game,
 And they drank at the torrent's fall;
And the Serpent saw that the woods were fair,
And she long'd to make her dwelling there.

II.

But she saw that her host had a knack of his own,
At tearing a sinew or cracking a bone,
 And had grinders unpleasantly strong;
So she said to herself, " I'll bamboozle the king
With my plausible speech, and all that sort of thing,
 That, since Eve, to my people belong:

III.

" Those claws and those grinders must certainly be
Inconvenient to you as they're dreadful to me—
 Draw 'em out, like a love, I'm so 'frighted!
And, then, since I've long had an amorous eye on
Yourself and your property, dear Mr. Lion,
 We can be (spare my blushes) *united.*"

IV.

So subtle the pow'r of her poisonous kisses,
So deadly to honour the falsehood she hisses,
 The lion for once is an ass.
Before her, disarmed, the poor simpleton stands,
The Union's proclaimed, but the hymen'al bands
 Are ponderous fetters of brass.

v.

The Lion, self-conquer'd, is chained on the ground,
And the breath of his tyrant sheds poison around
    The fame and the life of her slave.
How long in his torture the stricken king lay
Historians omit, but 'tis known that one day,
    The Serpent began to look grave;

vi.

For when passing, as usual, her thrall with a sneer,
She derisively hiss'd some new taunt in his ear—
    He shook all his chains with a roar;
And, observing more closely, she saw with much pain
That his tusks and his claws were appearing again,
    A fact she neglected before.

vii.

From that hour she grew *dang'rously civil*, indeed,
And declared he should be, ere long, totally freed
    From every dishonouring chain.
" The moment, my *dearest*, our friend, the Fox, draws
Those nasty sharp things from your Majesty's jaws,
    You must bound free as air o'er the plain."

viii.

But the captive sprung from his dungeon floor,
And he bow'd the woods with a scornful roar,
    And his burning eyes flash'd flame;
And as echo swell'd the shout afar,
The stormy joy of Freedom's war
    O'er the blast of the desert came.

ix.

And the Lion laugh'd, and his mirth was loud
As the stunning burst of a thunder cloud,
    And he shook his wrathful mane;
And hollow sounds from his lash'd sides come,
Like the sullen roll of a 'larum drum—
    He snapp'd, like a reed, the chain;
And the Serpent saw that her reign was o'er,
And hissing, she fled from the Lion's roar!

THE WEST 'S ASLEEP.

AIR.—"*The Brink of the White Rocks.*" *

---

* As here set this air slightly differs, in the end of the second line, from the version in Bunting's third volume and agrees with that to which Mr. Horncastle sang "The Herring is King." : There is a totally different and still finer air known in the Co. Tipperary by the name of "The Brink of the White Rocks".

Con - naught lies in slum - ber deep. There lake and plain smile

fair and free,'Mid rocks—their guar - dian chi- val-ry—Sing, oh! let man learn

li - ber - ty, From crash - ing wind and lash - ing sea.

THE WEST'S ASLEEP.

BY THOMAS DAVIS.

I.

WHEN all beside a vigil keep,
The West's asleep, the West's asleep—
Alas! and well may Erin weep,
When Connaught lies in slumber deep.
There lake and plain smile fair and free,
'Mid rocks—their guardian chivalry—
Sing oh! let man learn liberty
From crashing wind and lashing sea.

II.

That chainless wave and lovely land
Freedom and Nationhood demand—
Be sure, the great God never plann'd,
For slumbering slaves, a home so grand.
And, long, a brave and haughty race
Honoured and sentinelled the place—
Sing oh! not even their sons' disgrace
Can quite destroy their glory's trace.

III.

For often, in O'Connor's van,
To triumph dash'd each Connaught clan—
And fleet as deer the Normans ran
Through Coirrsliabh Pass and Ard Rathain.*
And later times saw deeds as brave;
And glory guards Clanricarde's grave—
Sing oh! they died their land to save,
At Aughrim's slopes and Shannon's wave.

---

* Vulgarly written Corlews and Ardrahan.

IV.

And if, when all a vigil keep,
The West's asleep, the West's asleep—
Alas! and well may Erin weep,
That Connaught lies in slumber deep.
But—hark!—some voice like thunder spake:
" *The West's awake, the West's awake*"—
Sing oh! hurra! let England quake,
We'll watch till death for Erin's sake!"

THE FIRESIDE.

BY D. F. M'CARTHY.

I.

I HAVE tasted all life's pleasures—I have snatched at all its joys—
The dance's merry measures, and the revel's festive noise;
Though wit flash'd bright the live-long night, and flowed the ruby
    tide,
I sighed for thee—I sighed for thee, my own fireside!

II.

In boyhood's dreams I wandered far, across the ocean's breast,
In search of some bright earthly star—some happy isle of rest;
I little thought the bliss I sought, in roaming far and wide,
Was sweetly centred all in thee—my own fireside!

III.

How sweet to turn at evening's close from all our cares away,
And end, in calm serene repose, the swiftly passing day!
The pleasant books, the smiling looks of sister or of bride,
All fairy ground doth make around one's own fireside!

L

IV.

" My lord" would never condescend to honour my poor hearth ;
" His grace" would scorn a host or friend of mere plebeian birth ;
And yet the lords of human kind whom man has deified,
For ever meet in converse sweet around my fireside !

V.

The poet sings his' deathless songs, the sage his lore repeats,
The patriot tells his country's wrongs, the chief his warlike feats ;
Though far away may be their clay, and gone their earthly pride,
Each godlike mind in books enshrined still haunts my fireside.

VI.

Oh ! let me glance a moment through the coming crowd of years—
Their triumphs or their failures—their sunshine or their tears—
How poor or great may be my fate, I care not what betide,
So peace and love but hallow thee, my own fireside.

VII.

Still let me hold the vision close, and closer to my sight ;
Still—still in hopes elysian, let my spirit wing its flight ;
Still let me dream, life's shadowy stream may yield from out its tide,
A mind at rest—a tranquil breast—a quiet fireside !

DEVIL MAY CARE.

BY J. KEEGAN.

I.

Musha, " Queen of the Sea," is it true what they say
All about the grand " speeching" you had t'other day
About Ireland, and Dan, and Repeal ?   I declare
I think you were bullied ; but, devil may care,
They shan't bully Paddy—so devil may care.

II.

I heard, when a boy, you were gentle and true—
That you lov'd poor old Ireland and Irishmen too—
That your heart was as just as your form was fair,
And I wished you were here ; but the devil may care,
I 've got my own darling—so devil may care.

III.

And you 've got young Albert, and long may you reign,
And lightsome and brightsome, and strong be the chain
That binds you together in love, now so rare
To be found at " Head Quarters ;" but, devil may care,
That's a case for the lawyers—so devil may care.

IV.

But Paddy a " case" of his own has just now,
So off goes my " caubeen," and here 's my best bow ;
My belly is empty, my back is all bare,
I 'm hungry and naked ; but devil may care,
Good times are approaching—so devil may care.

V.

" *Acushla machree*," we are wounded and sore,
So bad that we cannot endure it much more.
A cure we must have, though the Saxons may stare
And " curse like a trooper ;" but devil may care,
" *Sin fein*"* is our watch-word—so devil may care.

VI.

Through many a century of darkness and gloom
We writhed in our sorrow and wept at our doom ;
We begged and implored, but they laughed at our prayer—
The answer they gave us was—" devil may care,"
You 're " mere Irish" rebels—so devil may care.

VII.

But no longer, like cowards, we 'll kneel to the foe—
" Soft words they will butter no parsnips" we know ;
Our RIGHTS they *must* give " on the nail"—" a child's share"
We claim, and *must* get.   By St. Patrick, we swear,
We won't be put off with a " devil may care."

---

* " *Sin fein*"—Ourselves—or " OURSELVES ALONE."

BROTHERS, ARISE!

BY GEORGE PHILLIPS.

[The subjoined address was written to the Irish Nationalists, during the Monster Meetings of 1843, by one of the English Puseyites, and may be fairly taken to represent the sentiments of many of that great party. They cannot but sympathise with a people not only oppressed for conscience sake, but for opinions differing little from their own ; and it is natural that the sympathy of the young and earnest should exhibit the bold and emphatic spirit which breathes through this poem :—]

I.

BROTHERS, arise ! the hour has come
   To strike the blow for truth and God ;
Why sit ye folded up and dumb—
   Why bending kiss the tyrant's rod ?
Is there no hope upon the earth—
   No charter in the starry sky ?
Has freedom no ennobling worth ?
   And man no immortality ?

II.

Ah, brothers ! think ye what ye are !
   What glorious work ye have to do !
And how they wait ye near and far
   To do the same the wide world through.
The wide world sunk in dreams and death,
   With guilt and wrong upon its breast,
Like night-mares choking up its breath,
   And murdering all its holy rest !

III.

Bethink ye, how with heart and brain
   This God-like work were ablest done ;
For man must ne'er go back again
   And lose the triumphs he has won.
Ye who have spurned the tyrant's power,
   And fought your own great spirits free,
Forget not in this trying hour
   The claims of struggling slavery !

IV.

The wise and good! oh, where are they
 To guide us onward to the Right,
Untruth and specious lies to slay,
 And red oppression in its might?
Come forth, my brothers, on with us—
 Direct the battle we would give;
By thousands we would die—if thus
 The millions yet unborn may live.

V.

For what is death to him who dies
 With God's own blessing on his head?
A charter—not a sacrifice—
 A life immortal to the dead.
And life itself is only great
 When man devotes himself to be
By virtue, thought, and deed, the mate
 Of God's own children and the free.

VI.

And are we free? Oh! blot and shame!
 That men who for a thousand years
Have battled on through fire and flame,
 And nourished with their blood and tears—
Religion—Freedom—Civil Right—
 Should tamely suffer traitor hands
To dash them into gloom and night,
 And bind their very God with bands.

VII.

And will ye bear, my brother men,
 To see your altars trampled down;
Shall Christ's great heart bleed out again
 Beneath the scoffer's spear and frown?
Shall priests proclaim that God is not,
 And from the Devil's gospel teach
Those worldly doctrines, unforgot,
 Which burning tyrants loved to preach?

VIII.

Shall traitors to the human right,
    To God and truth, have boundless sway,
And ye not rush into the fight
    And wrench the SACRED CROSS away,
And tear the scrolls of freedom, bought
    With blood of martyrs and the brave,
From men who with derisive sport
    Defy you on the martyr's grave?

IX.

Ah! no!—uprushing—million-strong,
    The trodden people come at last—
Their fiery souls, pent up so long,
    Burst out in flames all thick and fast;
And thunder-words and lightning-deeds
    Strike terror to the Wrong, who flee,
Till, lo! at last the wronger bleeds,
    And dying, leaves the nation free.

O'SULLIVAN'S RETURN.

BY THOMAS DAVIS.

I.

O'SULLIVAN has come
Within sight of his home,
    He had left it long years ago;
The tears are in his eyes,
And he prays the wind to rise,
As he looks tow'rds his castle, from the prow, from the prow,
As he looks tow'rds his castle, from the prow.

II.

For the day had been calm,
And slow the good ship swam,
    And the evening gun had been fir'd;
He knew the hearts beat wild
Of mother, wife, and child,
And of clans, who to see him long desir'd, long desir'd,
And of clans, who to see him long desir'd.

III.

Of the tender ones the clasp,
Of the gallant ones the grasp,
   He thinks, until his tears fall warm:
And full seems his wide hall,
With friends from wall to wall,
Where their welcome shakes the banners, like a storm, like a storm,
Where their welcome shakes the banners like a storm.

IV.

Then he sees another scene—
Norman churls on the green—
   "Ⓞ'Suileabain abú!" is the cry;
For filled is his ship's hold,
With arms and Spanish gold,
And he sees the snake-twined spear wave on high, wave on high,
And he sees the snake-twined spear wave on high.*

V.

"Finghin's race shall be freed
From the Norman's cruel breed—
   My sires freed Beire once before,
When the Barnwells were strewn
On the fields, like hay in June,
And but one of them escaped from our shore, from our shore,
And but one of them escaped from our shore."†

---

  * The standard bearings of O'Sullivan. See O'Donovan's edition of the Banquet of Dún na n-Gedh, and the Battle of Magh Rath, for the Archæological Society, App., p. 349—"Bearings of O'Sullivan at the Battle of Caisglinn."
      "I see, mightily advancing on the plain,
       The banner of the race of noble Finghin;
       His spear with a venomous adder *(entwined)*,
       His host all fiery champions."
Finghin was one of their most famous progenitors.

  † The Barnwells were Normans, who seized part of Beire in the reign of Henry II; but the O'Sullivans came down on them, and cut off all save one—a young man who settled at Drimnagh Castle, Co. Dublin, and was ancestor to the Barnwells, Lords of Trimlestone and Kingsland.

VI.

And, warming in his dream,
He floats on victory's stream,
   Till Desmond—till all Erin is free,
Then, how calmly he 'll go down,
Full of years and of renown,
To his grave near that castle by the sea, by the sea,
To his grave near that castle by the sea!

VII.

But the wind heard his word,
As though he were its lord,
   And the ship is dash'd up the Bay.
Alas! for that proud barque,
The night has fallen dark,
'Tis too late to Adragool to bear away, bear away,
'Tis too late to Adragool to bear away.

VIII.

Black and rough was the rock,
And terrible the shock,
   As the good ship crashed asunder;
And bitter was the cry,
And the sea ran mountains high,
And the wind was as loud as the thunder, the thunder,
And the wind was as loud as the thunder.

IX.

There 's woe in Beire,
There 's woe in Glean Garbh,
   And from Beantraighe unto Dun Ciaran;*
All Desmond hears their grief,
And wails alone their chief—
" Is it *thus*, is it *thus*, that you return, you return,—
Is it *thus*, is it *thus*, that you return?"

---

* In common English spelling these names are Bearra, or Bear—Glengarriff, or
Glengarra—Bantry—Dunkerron.

ADIEU TO INNISFAIL.

BY R. D. WILLIAMS.

Aɪʀ—" Aɴ Ꮮʜ́ᴘᴜɪᴛ5ɪɴ Ꮮᴀ́ɴ."

I.

Adieu !—the snowy sail
Swells her bosom to the gale,
And our barque from Innisfail
   Bounds away.
While we gaze upon thy shore,
That we never shall see more,
And the blinding tears flow o'er,
   We pray.

II.

No múɪᴘɴɪɴ ! be thou long
In peace, the queen of song—
In battle proud and strong
   As the sea!
Be saints thine offspring still—
True heroes guard each hill—
And harps by ev'ry rill
   Sound free!

III.

Tho', round her Indian bowers,
The hand of nature showers
The brightest-blooming flowers
   Of our sphere;
Yet not the richest rose
In an *alien* clime that blows,
Like the brier at home that grows,
   Is dear.

M

IV

'Tho' glowing breasts may be
In soft vales beyond the sea,
Yet ever Ᵹраδ mo Ċроｌδе
        Shall I wail
For the heart of love I leave,
In the dreary hours of eve,
On thy stormy shore to grieve,
        Innisfail!

V.

But mem'ry o'er the deep
On her dewy wing shall sweep,
When in midnight hours I weep
        O'er thy wrongs:
And bring me, steep'd in tears,
The dead flow'rs of other years,
And waft unto my ears
        Home's songs.

VI.

When I slumber in the gloom
Of a nameless foreign tomb,
By a distant ocean's boom,
        Innisfail!
Around thy em'rald shore
May the clasping sea adore,
And each wave in thunder roar,
        " All hail!"

VII.

And when the final sigh
Shall bear my soul on high,
And on chainless wing I fly
        Thro' the blue,
Earth's latest thought shall be,
As I soar above the sea—
" Green Erin, dear, to thee—
        Adieu!"

BOYHOOD'S YEARS.

BY THE REV. CHARLES J. MEEHAN.

I.

Ah! why should I recal them—the gay, the joyous years,
Ere hope was cross'd or pleasure dimm'd by sorrow and by tears?
Or why should memory love to trace youth's glad and sunlit way,
When those who made its charms so sweet are gathered to decay?
The summer's sun shall come again to brighten hill and bower—
The teeming earth its fragrance bring beneath the balmy shower;
But all in vain will mem'ry strive, in vain we shed our tears—
They're gone away and can't return—the friends of boyhood's
    years!

II.

Ah! why then wake my sorrow, and bid me now count o'er
The vanished friends so dearly prized—the days to come no more—
The happy days of infancy, when no guile our bosoms knew,
Nor reck'd we of the pleasures that with each moment flew?
'Tis all in vain to weep for them—the past a dream appears;
And where are they—the lov'd, the young, the friends of boy-
    hood's years?

III.

Go seek them in the cold church-yard—they long have stolen to
    rest;
But do not weep, for their young cheeks by woe were ne'er op-
    press'd:
Life's sun for them in splendour set—no cloud came o'er the ray
That lit them from this gloomy world upon their joyous way.
No tears about their graves be shed—but sweetest flow'rs be
    flung—
The fittest off'ring thou canst make to hearts that perish young—
To hearts this world has never torn with racking hopes and fears;
For bless'd are they who pass away in boyhood's happy years.

M 2

TIPPERARY.

Let Brit - ain boast her Brit - - ish hosts, A - bout them all

right lit - tle care we; Not Brit - ish seas, nor Brit - ish coasts, Can match THE

MAN—THE MAN OF TIP-PE-RA-RY. Tall is his form, his heart is

warm, His spi - - rit light   as   a - ny   fai - ry, His   wrath   is fear-ful

as the storm That sweeps The HILLS—The HILLS of TIPPE-RARY. His wrath is

fear-ful   as the storm That sweeps The HILLS—The HILLS of TIPPE-RARY.

TIPPERARY.

BY THOMAS DAVIS.

I.

Let Britain boast her British hosts,
    About them all right little care we;
Not British seas nor British coasts
    Can match The Man of Tipperary!

II.

Tall is his form, his heart is warm,
    His spirit light as any fairy—
His wrath is fearful as the storm
    That sweeps The Hills of Tipperary!

III.

Lead him to fight for native land,
    His is no courage cold and wary;
The troops live not on earth would stand
    The headlong Charge of Tipperary!

IV.

Yet meet him in his cabin rude,
    Or dancing with his dark-hair'd Mary,
You'd swear they knew no other mood
    But Mirth and Love in Tipperary!

V.

You're free to share his scanty meal,
    His plighted word he'll never vary—
In vain they tried with gold and steel
    To shake The Faith of Tipperary!

VI.

Kind is his girl's soft sunny eye,
    Her mien is mild, her step is airy,
Her heart is fond, her soul is high—
    Oh! she's The Pride of Tipperary!

VII.

Though Britain boasts her British hosts,
    About them all right little care we—
Give us, to guard our native coasts,
    The Matchless Men of Tipperary!

VIII.

Let Britain, too, her banner brag,
    We'll lift The Green more proud and airy;
Be mine the lot to bear that flag,
    And head The Men of Tipperary!

FATHER MATHEW.

ODE TO A PAINTER, ABOUT TO COMMENCE A PICTURE
ILLUSTRATING THE LABOURS OF FATHER MATHEW.

I.

Seize thy pencil, child of art!
    Fame and fortune brighten o'er thee;
Great thy hand, and great thy heart,
    If well thou do'st the work before thee!

'Tis not thine to round the shield,
　　Or point the sabre, black or gory;
'Tis not thine to spread the field,
　　Where crime is crown'd—where guilt is glory.

II.

Child of art! to thee be given
　　To paint, in colours all unclouded,
Breakings of a radiant heaven
　　O'er an isle in darkness shrouded!
But, to paint them true and well,
　　Every ray we see them shedding
In its very light must tell
　　What a gloom *before* was spreading.

III.

Canst thou picture dried-up tears—
　　Eyes that wept no longer weeping—
Faithful woman's wrongs and fears,
　　Lonely, njghtly, vigils keeping—
Listening ev'ry footfall nigh—
　　Hoping him she loves returning?
Canst thou, then, depict her joy,
　　That we may know *the change* from mourning?

IV.

Paint in colours strong, but mild,
　　Our Isle's Redeemer and Director—
Canst thou paint *the man* a *child*,
　　Yet shadow forth the mighty VICTOR?
Let his path a rainbow span,
　　Every *hue* and *colour* blending—
Beaming "peace and love" to man,
　　And alike o'er ALL extending!

v.

Canst thou paint a land made free—
   From its sleep of bondage woken—
Yet, withal, that we may see
   What 'twas *before* the chain was broken?
Seize the pencil, child of art!
   Fame and fortune brighten o'er thee!
Great thy hand, and great thy heart,
   If well thou do'st the work before thee!

THE SONG OF '44.

BY M. J. BARRY.

Air—"*Alley Croker.*"

I.

Come, boys! a toast,
   While traitors boast
They 'll crush our free opinions—
   While smirk, elate
   With hopeful hate,
The despot's fawning minions—
   With heart and cup,
   Each brimming up
In honest exultation,
   Pledge we to-night,
   In foes' despite,
"Old Erin yet a Nation!"
   Dear, loved Erin!
Our own, our cherished Erin!
   Ne'er shall foe
   With tyrant blow,
Again profane thee, Erin!

N

II.

Oh! why not clasp,
In manly grasp,
Our hands—and, by each other
Resolve to stand
For fatherland,
As brother should by brother?
The truths divine,
Your creed and mine,
Are not as bigots read them;
And in one creed
We're both agreed,
That "God made man for freedom."
Dear, loved Erin!
We both will guard thee, Erin!
Ne'er shall foe
With tyrant blow,
Again profane thee, Erin!

III.

If you and I,
By nature's tie,
Were sons of one dear mother,
Should diff'rent views
Of faith infuse
Cold rancour tow'rds each other?
The same dear earth
Has given us birth—
We're sons of one green island;
Then join with me
To make her free—
She's yours as well as my land!
Dear, loved Erin!
Oh! join with me for Erin:
Ne'er let foe,
With tyrant blow,
Again profane our Erin!

A TRAVELLER'S TESTIMONY.

I.

GREEN-VESTED land, with emeralds strewn,
　Wherever wends the pilgrim weary,
With faltering steps and dusty shoon,
　From Rhine to Loire—from Baste to Erie.
He feels still freshlier o'er his heart
　Rush the remembrance of thy beauty;
And owns, all peerless as thou art,
　To love thee, both his joy and duty.

II.

Romantic land! in other climes
　Far brighter suns the skies illumine;
In the warm south, 'mid vesper chimes,
　More dazzlingly bright-eyed is woman;
But sunlight there, like lightning burns,
　While thine streams soft, as crystal waters—
Too warm the southern maids, and turns
　The yearning breast to Erin's daughters.

III.

Oh, matchless land! so well combine
　Thy elements of cloud and splendour,
That earth can boast no vales like thine,
　Nor show a sod with green so tender!
So well in Erin, too, are mixed
　The elements of wit and honour,
That other nations' eyes are fixed
　In hopeless rivalry upon her!

THETA.

N 2

𝔑𝔒 𝔠𝔥𝔯𝔲𝔬𝔦𝔟𝔞𝔦𝔫 𝔲𝔬𝔦𝔟𝔞𝔦𝔫 𝔞́𝔩𝔲𝔦𝔫 𝔬́𝔤.

AIR—𝔑o Ċṟaoibiṅ aoibiṅ áluiṅ óṡ!

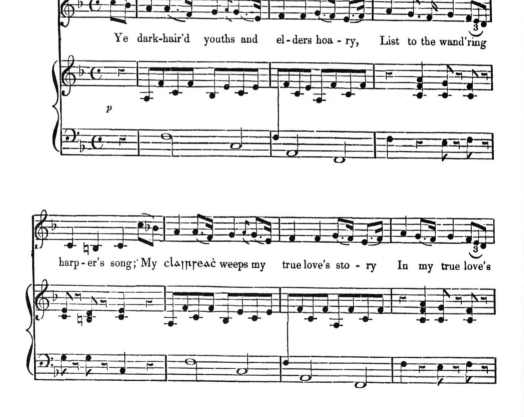

Ye dark-hair'd youths and el-ders hoa-ry, List to the wand'ring harp-er's song; My claiṟṟeaċ weeps my true love's sto-ry In my true love's

na - tive tongue. She's bound and bleed - ing 'neath th' op - press - or;

Few her friends and fierce her foe, And brave hearts cold who

would re - dress her, Ꞁo ċꞃаоı-ƀíꞃ ꞅоı - ƀíꞃ а - Ꞁᵹuꞃ óᵹ!

⁊o Ċᴚᴀoıʙᴀıɴ ᴚoıʙᴀɴɴ ᴀ́ʟᴜıɴ óᵹ.

A.D. 1720.

BY EDWARD WALSH.

AIR—" ⁊o Ċʜᴚᴀóıʙıɴ ᴚoıʙıɴɴ."

I.

YE dark-haired youths and elders hoary
   List to the wand'ring harper's song,
My cláıᴚᴚeᴀċ weeps my true love's story,
   In my true love's native tongue:
She's bound and bleeding 'neath the oppressor,
   Few her friends and fierce her foe,
And brave hearts cold who would redress her—
   ⁊o ċᴚᴀóıʙıɴ ᴀoıʙıɴɴ ᴀ́ʟᴜıɴ óᵹ.

II.

My love had riches once and beauty,
   Till want and sorrow paled her cheek;
And stalwart hearts for honour's duty—
   They're crouching now, like cravens sleek.
Oh Heaven! that e'er this day of rigour
   Saw sons of heroes, abject, low—
And blood and tears thy face disfigure,
   ⁊o ċᴚᴀóıʙıɴ ᴀoıʙıɴɴ ᴀ́ʟᴜıɴ óᵹ.

III.

I see young virgins step the mountain
   As graceful as the bounding fawn,
With cheeks like heath-flow'r by the fountain,
   And breasts like downy ceᴀɴᴀʙᴀɴ.
Shall bondsmen share those beauties ample?
   Shall their pure bosoms' current flow
To nurse new slaves for them that trample
   ⁊o ċᴚᴀóıʙıɴ ᴀoıʙıɴɴ ᴀ́ʟᴜıɴ óᵹ?

IV.

Around my cláirreaċ's speaking measures
  Men, like their fathers tall, arise—
Their heart the same deep hatred treasures,
  I read it in their kindling eyes!
The same proud brow to frown at danger—
  The same long cúil-ḟioñ's graceful flow—
The same dear tongue to curse the stranger—
  Ⴔo ċraóiḃiñ aoiḃiññ áluiñ óʒ!

V.

I 'd sing ye more but age is stealing
  Along my pulse and tuneful fires;
Far bolder woke my chord, appealing,
  For craven Séamur, to your sires.
Arouse to vengeance, men of brav'ry,
  For broken oaths—for altars low—
For bonds that bind in bitter slav'ry—
  Ⴔo ċraóiḃiñ aoiḃiññ áluiñ óʒ!

WAS IT A DREAM?

BY JOHN O'CONNELL, M.P.

I.

It was an empty dream, perchance—yet seemed a vision high,
That in the midnight hour last night arose before mine eye,
Two figures—one in woe and chains, the other proud and free—
Were met in converse deep and grave beside the western sea.

II.

" What, ne'er content, and restless still!" the proud one sternly
    cried;
" Forsooth of Freedom prattling still and parting from my side?
I hold thy chain thou busy fool, mine ire thou mayest provoke,
And bring destruction on thine head, but never shake my yoke!"

III.

Then up arose the mourning one, and raised her beauteous head,
And mild and calm, though sad in tone, "my sister," thus she
    said,
"For sister I would fain thee call, though tyrant thou hast been—
None feller, or more pitiless, hath hapless slave e'er seen.

IV.

"The Rights, the Freedom, that I seek, the Lord of Heaven gave,
That mighty Lord who never willed that earth should hold a slave!
Those rights—that Freedom thou didst take I only ask of thee,
To give *mine own* to me again, and friends we 'll ever be!"

V.

The proud one laughed in haughty scorn, and waved a falchion
    bright
O'er the enchained one's head aloft, and dared her to the fight!
The flushing cheek and kindling eye bespoke no terror there,
But with a strong convulsive grasp, she bow'd to Heaven in prayer!

VI.

Then raised her front serene again, and mildly spoke once more:
" Seven long and weary centuries of insult have passed o'er—
Of insult and of cruel wrong! and from the earliest hour,
E'en to this day, a tyrant thou hast been, in pride of power.

VII.

" But when distress and enemies came threat'ningly around,
Then soft in words, and falsely kind, thou ever hast been found!
Distress again may come to thee, and foreign dangers press,
And thou be forced to yield me all, and earn no thankfulness!"

VIII.

Again the proud one scornful laughed, and waved again her brand,
The other mutely rais'd to Heaven her chain'd and fetter'd hand—
Then swift a storm passed o'er the scene, and when its gloom was
    gone,
The tyrant form was lowly laid—the captive had her own!

THE MEN OF THE NORTH.

BY CHARLES GAVAN DUFFY.

I.

Oh! shout for the day, when the charge of the *Gael*,
Like a thunder-burst scattered the pride of the Pale;
And the strength of the stranger, like stubble, went down
Before the strong ranks of the Cross and the Crown,
                            The Men of the North.

II.

And what though our God, to whom glory and praise!
Hath not left to their children the spoil of those days;
More bright be our honour, more goodly our gain,
That he gave us stout hearts to achieve it again—
                            The Men of the North.

III.

When darkness and danger encompassed our Isle,
And the timid made cause with the venal and vile,
When her hope was the least, and her hazard the most,
Still, firm as Sliab Domangort,* she found at their post—
                            The Men of the North.

IV.

Proud homesteads of An-druim, Ard-maca, Tir-Eogain,†
Oh! triumph for ever, proclaiming your own
The citizen-soldiers, who rose to o'ercome
The Foe from without and the Tyrant at home—
                            The Men of the North.

---

* Slievedonard.
† In common spelling, Antrim, Armagh, and Tyrone.

O

V.

And when the black work of oppression began,
And Power upon reason and right set her ban,
All threats and seductions they bravely withstood
Till the cause of their country they sealed with their blood—
     The Men of the North.

VI.

Oh! joy for the day, and 'tis coming at length,
When the slumbering giant will gather his strength,
And speaking stout words, which stout hearts will maintain,
Proclaim our fair country a NATION again—
     The Men of the North.

VII.

The waters of Bann are unruffled and slow,
And though coldly and calmly our pulses may flow,
Yet as soon shall you roll back its deep, swelling tide,
As turn from their slow-chosen purpose aside
     The Men of the North.

VIII.

Then, oh! when Green Erin her trust and her might,
Shall summon to battle for God and our right—
For the home of our hearts, or the freedom of man,
May one gallant phalanx still march in the van—
     The Men of the North.

THE LOST PATH.

BY THOMAS DAVIS.

AIR—"Ᵹᴘᴀᴅ ᴍᴏ ċᴘᴏᴊᴅᴇ."

I.

SWEET thoughts, bright dreams, my comfort be,
 All comfort else has flown;
For every hope was false to me,
 And here I am alone.
What thoughts were mine in early youth!
 Like some old Irish song,
Brimful of love, and life, and truth,
 My spirit gush'd along.

II.

I hoped to right my native isle,
 I hoped a soldier's fame,
I hoped to rest in woman's smile,
 And win a minstrel's name—
Oh! little have I served my land,
 No laurels press my brow,
I have no woman's heart or hand,
 Nor minstrel honors now.

III.

But fancy has a magic power,
 It brings me wreath and crown,
And woman's love, the self-same hour
 It smites oppression down.
Sweet thoughts, bright dreams, my comfort be,
 I have no joy beside;
Oh! throng around, and be to me
 Power, country, fame, and bride.

o 2

BIDE YOUR TIME !

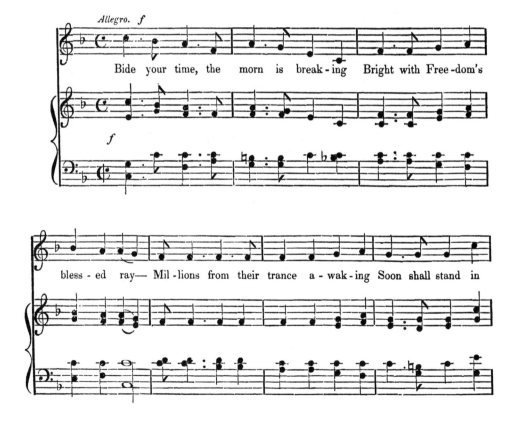

Bide your time, the morn is break - ing Bright with Free - dom's

bless - ed ray— Mil -lions from their trance a - wak - ing Soon shall stand in

stern ar - ray. Man shall fet - - ter man no long - er,

Li - - ber - - ty shall march sub - - - lime, Ev' - - ry mo - ment

makes you strong - er, Firm, un - shrink - ing, — BIDE YOUR TIME!

BIDE YOUR TIME.

BY M. J. BARRY.

I.

BIDE YOUR TIME, the morn is breaking,
  Bright with Freedom's blessed ray—
Millions, from their trance awaking,
  Soon shall stand in firm array.
Man shall fetter man no longer;
  Liberty shall march sublime:
Every moment makes you stronger—
  Firm, unshrinking, BIDE YOUR TIME!

II.

BIDE YOUR TIME—one false step taken
  Perils all you yet have done;
Undismayed—erect—unshaken—
  Watch and wait, and all is won.
'Tis not by a rash endeavour
  Men or states to greatness climb—
Would you win your rights for ever,
  Calm and thoughtful, BIDE YOUR TIME!

III.

BIDE YOUR TIME—your worst transgression
  Were to strike, and strike in vain;
He, whose arm would smite oppression,
  Must not need to smite again!
Danger makes the brave man steady—
  Rashness is the coward's crime—
Be for Freedom's battle ready,
  When it comes—but, BIDE YOUR TIME!

TWO SONNETS.

BY CHARLES GAVAN DUFFY.

I.

LITERARY LEISURE.

" Around me I behold
    The mighty minds of old ;
    My never-failing friends are they,
    With whom I converse day by day."
                                SOUTHEY.

LET my life pass in cheerful, letter'd ease,
    The world and all its schemes shut out my door;
    Rich in a competence and nothing more,
Saving the student's wealth—" Apollo's fees"—
Long rows of goodly volumes, to appease
    My early love and quenchless thirst of lore.
No Want to urge me on the path of Gain—
    No Hope to lure me in Ambition's track;
Struggles and strife, and all their savage train,
    Still from my tranquil threshold driven back;
    My only triumphs—if such toys I lack—
Some subtle nut of science burst in twain,
    Some knot unravell'd.   Thus be 't mine to live,
    And feel life fade like a long summer eve.

———

II.

THE SPIRIT OF THE TIMES.

" From pole to pole the deep electric tone
    Of Liberty is out.   Wilt thou not share ? "
                                ANON.

UP, recreant, up!   Our land hath called her sons
    From solitude and cities, courts and marts,
    To fight her fight, and lo! what eager hearts
Answer her call.   But not with blades and guns,

But arms more keen than Europe's or the Hun's—
   Reason and Truth—come they to play their parts.
Shake off the dream-world's thraldom and awake
   To see thy land become regenerate,
     And aid, if aid thou may'st, a work, so great.
The mist of prejudice, as from a lake,
Is rising from men's minds, and tyrants quake
   Reading the stormy signs that speak our coming fate.
Then up! and learn how patriot hearts may glow
With ecstacy that tame life cannot know.

THE FATE OF KING DATHI.*

I.

DARKLY their glibs o'erhang,
Sharp is their wolf-dog's fang,
Bronze spear and falchion clang—
   Brave men might shun them!
Heavy the spoil they bear—
Jewels and gold are there—
Hostage and maiden fair—
   How have they won them?

---

* " In the two last reigns, the Irish arms prevailed only on the maritime coasts of Gaul, in Brittany and Normandy ; in the present, we see them unite with their allies, and carry terror and ruin to the very foot of the Alps, where Daithi was killed by lightning * * * * * Their army, under the command of Laogaire, son to the hero Niall, and cousin-german to the deceased, made a regular retreat, bringing home with them the embalmed body of Daithi, who was interred with great funeral pomp at Roilig na Riogh,—(the burial place of the kings.)"—*O'Halloran's History of Ireland*, at the years 426-7-8.

The foreigner who is puzzled how to sound King Dati's name had best look to the rhyming of it in the last verse.

II.

From the soft sons of Gaul,
Roman, and Frank, and thrall,
Borough, and hut, and hall,
　　These have been torn.
Over Britannia wide,
Over fair Gaul they hied,
Often in battle tried—
　　Enemies mourn !

III.

Fiercely their harpers sing,
Led by their gallant king,
They will to Erin bring
　　Beauty and treasure.
Britain shall bend the knee—
Rich shall their households be—
When their long ships, the sea,
　　Homeward shall measure.

IV.

Barrow and tower shall rise,
Raits, too, of wondrous size,
Tailtean they 'll solemnize,
　　Feis-Tamra assemble.
Samin and Baal shall smile
On the rich holy isle—
After a little while
　　Œtius shall tremble ! *

---

* The consul Œtius, the shield of Italy, and terror of " the barbarian," was a cotemporary of King Dati. Feis Tamra, the Parliament of Tara. Tailtean, games held at Tailte. Co. Meath.　Samin and Baal, the moon and sun which Ireland worshipped.

P

v.

Up on the glacier's snow,
Down on the vales below,
Monarch and clansmen go—
    Bright is the morning.
Never their march they slack,
Jura is at their back,
When falls the ev'ning black,
    Hideous, and warning.

VI.

Eagles scream loud on high;
Far off the chamois fly;
Hoarse comes the torrent's cry,
    On the rocks whit'ning.
Strong are the storm's wings;
Down the tall pine it flings;
Hail-stone and sleet it brings—
    Thunder and lightning.

VII.

Little these vet'rans mind
Thundering, hail, or wind;
Closer their ranks they bind—
    Matching the storm.
The cast of a spear or more,
On, the front ranks before,
Dati, the sunburst bore—
    Haughty his form.

VIII.

Forth from the thunder-cloud
Leaps out a foe as proud—
Sudden the monarch bow'd—
    On rush the vanguard;
Wildly the king they raise—
Struck by the lightning's blaze—
Ghastly his dying gaze,
    Clutching his standard!

IX.

Mild is the morning beam,
Gently the rivers stream,
Happy the valleys seem;
    But the lone islanders—
Mark how they guard their king!
Hark, to the wail they sing!
Dark is their counselling—
    Helvetia's highlanders

X.

Gather, like ravens, near—
Shall Dati's soldiers fear?
Soon their home-path they clear—
    Rapid and daring;
On through the pass and plain,
Until the shore they gain,
And, with their spoil, again,
    Landed in Erin.

XI.

Little does Erin care
For gold or maiden fair—
" Where is King Dati?—where,
    Where is my bravest?"
On the rich deck he lies,
O'er him his sunburst flies—
Solemn the obsequies,
    Erin! thou gavest.

XII.

See ye that countless train
Crossing Roscommon's plain,
Crying, like hurricane,
    " Ululu-ai!"—
Broad is his cairn's base—
Nigh " The King's burial-place,"
Last of the Pagan race,
    Lieth King Dati!

THE PRICE OF FREEDOM.

BY D. F. M'CARTHY.

I.

Man of Ireland!—Heir of sorrow—
　Wronged, insulted, scorned, oppressed—
Wilt thou never see that morrow
　When thy weary heart may rest?
Lift thine eyes, thou outraged creature;
　Nay, look up, for *Man* thou art—
Man in form, and frame, and feature—
　Why not act Man's godlike part?

II.

Think, reflect, inquire, examine,
　Is 't for this God gave you birth—
With the spectre look of famine,
　Thus to creep along the earth?
Does this world contain no treasures
　Fit for thee, as Man, to wear?—
Does this life abound in pleasures,
　And thou askest not to share?

III.

Look! the nations are awaking—
　Every chain that bound them burst!
At the crystal fountains slaking
　With parched lips their fever thirst!
Ignorance, the demon, fleeing,
　Leaves unlocked the fount they sip—
Wilt thou not, thou wretched being,
　Stoop and cool thy burning lip?

IV.

History's lessons, if thou read 'em,
  All proclaim this truth to thee:
Knowledge is the price of freedom—
  Know thyself, and thou art free!
Know, oh! man, thy proud vocation—
  Stand erect, with calm, clear brow—
Happy! happy, were our nation
  If thou hadst that knowledge now!

V.

Know thy wretched, sad condition—
  Know the ills that keep thee so—
Knowledge is the sole physician—
  Thou wert healed, if thou didst know!
Those who crush, and scorn, and slight thee—
  Those to whom you once would kneel—
Were the foremost then to right thee,
  If thou felt as thou shouldst feel!

VI.

Not as beggars lowly bending—
  Not in sighs, and groans, and tears—
But a voice of thunder sending
  Through thy tyrant brother's ears!
Tell him he is not thy master—
  Tell him of man's common lot—
Feel life has but one disaster—
  To be a slave, and know it not!

VII.

If thou knew what knowledge giveth—
  If thou knew how blest is he
Who in Freedom's presence liveth,
  Thou wouldst die, or else be free!
Round about he looks in gladness—
  Joys in heaven, and earth, and sea—
Scarcely heaves a sigh of sadness,
  Save in thoughts of such as thee!

INNIS-EOGHAIN.*

BY CHARLES GAVAN DUFFY.

I.

GOD bless the grey mountains of dark Dun na n-gall! †
God bless Royal Aileach! the pride of them all;
For she sits evermore, like a queen on her throne,
And smiles on the valleys of Green Innis-Eogain.
    And fair are the valleys of Green Innis-Eogain,
    And hardy the fishers that call them their own—
    A race that nor traitor nor coward have known,
    Enjoy the fair valleys of Green Innis-Eogain.

II.

Oh! simple and bold are the bosoms they bear,
Like the hills that with silence and nature they share;
For our God, who hath planted their home near His own,
Breath'd his spirit abroad upon fair Innis-Eogain.
    Then praise to our Father for wild Innis-Eogain,
    Where fiercely for ever the surges are thrown—
    Nor weather nor fortune a tempest hath blown
    Could shake the strong bosoms of brave Innis-Eogain.

III.

See the bountiful Cul-daim ‡ careering along—
A type of their manhood so stately and strong—

---

* INNIS-EOGHAIN (commonly written Innishowen, and pronounced Innishone) is a wild and picturesque district in the county Donegal, inhabited chiefly by the descendants of the Irish clans permitted to remain in Ulster after the plantation of James I. The native language, and the old songs and legends of the country, are as universal as the people. One of the most familiar of these legends is, that a troop of Hugh O'Neil's horse lies in magic sleep in a cave under the hill of Aileach, where the princes of the country were formerly installed.) These bold troopers only wait to have the spell removed to rush to the aid of their country; and a man (says the legend) who wandered accidentally into the cave, found them lying beside their horses, fully armed, and holding the bridles in their hands. One of them lifted his head, and asked, " Is the time come?" but receiving no answer—for the intruder was too much frightened to reply—dropped back into his lethargy. Some of the old folk consider the story an allegory, and interpret it as they desire.

† Donegal.

‡ The Couldah, or Culdaff, is a chief river in the Innishowen mountains.

On the weary for ever its tide is bestown,
So they share with the stranger in fair Innis-Eogain.
 God guard the kind homesteads of fair Innis-Eogain,
 Which manhood and virtue have chos'n for their own ;
 Not long shall the nation in slavery groan,
 That owns the tall peasants of fair Innis-Eogain.

IV.

Like the oak of St. Bride which nor Devil nor Dane,
Nor Saxon nor Dutchman, could rend from her fane,
They have clung by the creed and the cause of their own,
Through the midnight of danger in true Innis-Eogain.
 Then shout for the glories of old Innis-Eogain,
 The stronghold that foeman has never o'erthrown—
 The soul and the spirit, the blood and the bone,
 That guard the green valleys of true Innis-Eogain.

V.

Nor purer of old was the tongue of the Gael,
When the charging ᴀbú made the foreigner quail ;
Than it gladdens the stranger in welcome's soft tone,
In the home-loving cabins of kind Innis-Eogain.
 Oh! flourish, ye homesteads of kind Innis-Eogain,
 Where seeds of a people's redemption are sown ;
 Right soon shall the fruit of that sowing have grown,
 To bless the kind homesteads of Green Innis-Eogain.

VI.

When they tell us the tale of a spell-stricken band,
All entranced, with their bridles and broadswords in hand,
Who await but the word to give Erin her own,
They can read you that riddle in proud Innis-Eogain.
 Hurra for the Spæmen of proud Innis-Eogain !—
 Long live the wild Seërs of stout Innis-Eogain !—
 May Mary, our mother, be deaf to their moan
 Who love not the promise of proud Innis-Eogain !

WE'RE PADDIES EVERMORE.

Air—*"Paddies Evermore."*

Allegretto. m.f.

The hour is past to fawn or crouch As sup-pli-ants for our

right; Let word and deed un-shrink-ing vouch The band-ed mil-lion's might; Let

them who scorn'd the foun-tain rill Now dread the tor-rent's roar; And

hear our e - cho'd cho - rus still—We're Pad - dies e - ver - more. Let

them who scorn'd the foun - tain rill Now dread the tor - rent's roar; And

hear our e - cho'd cho - rus still—We're Pad - dies e - ver - - more.

PADDIES EVERMORE.

I.

THE hour is past to fawn or crouch
  As suppliants for our right;
Let word and deed unshrinking vouch
  The banded millions' might:
Let them who scorned the fountain rill,
  Now dread the torrent's roar,
And hear our echoed chorus still,
  We're Paddies evermore.

II.

What, though they menace, suffering men
  Their threats and them despise;
Or promise justice once again,
  We know their words are lies;
We stand resolved those rights to claim
  They robbed us of before,
Our own dear nation and our name,
  As Paddies evermore.

III.

Look round—the Frenchman governs France,
  The Spaniard rules in Spain,
The gallant Pole but waits his chance
  To break the Russian chain;
The strife for freedom here begun
  We never will give o'er,
Nor own a land on earth but one—
  We're Paddies evermore.

IV.

That strong and single love to crush,
  The despot ever tried—
A fount it was whose living gush
  His hated arts defied.

'Tis fresh, as when his foot accurst
  Was planted on our shore,
And now and still, as from the first,
  We 're Paddies evermore.

v.

What reck we though six hundred years
  Have o'er our thraldom rolled,
The soul that roused O'Conor's spears,
  Still lives as true and bold;
The tide of foreign power to stem
  Our fathers bled of yore,
And we stand here to-day, like them,
  True Paddies evermore.

vi.

Where 's our allegiance?   With the land,
  For which they nobly died;
Our duty?   By our cause to stand,
  Whatever chance betide;
Our cherished hope?   To heal the woes,
  That rankle at her core;
Our scorn and hatred?   To her foes,
  Like Paddies evermore.

vii.

The hour is past to fawn or crouch
  As suppliants for our right;
Let word and deed unshrinking vouch
  The banded millions' might;
Let them who scorned the fountain rill,
  Now dread the torrent's roar,
And hear our echoed chorus still,
  We 're Paddies evermore.

SLIABH CUILINN.

OH! HAD I THE WINGS OF A BIRD.

BY D. F. M'CARTHY.

I.

Oh! had I the wings of a bird,
 To soar through the blue sunny sky,
By what breeze would my pinions be stirred?
 To what beautiful land would I fly?
Would the gorgeous East allure,
 With the light of its golden eves,
Where the tall green palm, over isles of balm,
 Waves with its feath'ry leaves?
   Ah! no!—no!—no!
    I heed not its tempting glare;
   In vain would I roam from my island home,
    For skies more fair!

II.

Would I seek a southern sea,
 Italia's shore beside,
Where the clustering grape from tree to tree
 Hangs in its rosy pride?
My truant heart be still,
 For I long have sighed to stray
Through the myrtle flowers of fair Italy's bowers,
 By the shores of its southern bay.
   But no!—no!—no!
    Though bright be its sparkling seas,
   I never would roam from my island home
    For charms like these!

III.

Would I seek that land so bright,
  Where the Spanish maiden roves,
With a heart of love and an eye of light
  Through her native citron groves?
Oh! sweet would it be to rest
  In the midst of the olive vales,
Where the orange blooms, and the rose perfumes
  The breath of the balmy gales!
      But no!—no!—no!
        Though sweet be its wooing air,
      I never would roam from my island home
        To scenes though fair!

IV.

Would I pass from pole to pole?
  Would I seek the Western skies,
Where the giant rivers roll,
  And the mighty mountains rise?
Or those treacherous isles that lie
  In the midst of the sunny deeps,
Where the cocoa stands on the glistening sands,
  And the dread tornado sweeps?
      Ah! no!—no!—no!
        They have no charms for me;
      I never would roam from my island home,
        Though poor it be!

V.

Poor!—oh! 'tis rich in all
  That flows from Nature's hand—
Rich in the emerald wall
  That guards its emerald land!

Are Italy's fields more green?
  Do they teem with a richer store
Than the bright green breast of the Isle of the West,
  And its wild luxuriant shore?
      Ah! no!—no!—no!
        Upon it Heaven doth smile.
      Oh! I never would roam from my native home,
        My own dear isle!

O'DOṄṠALL ABU.

A.D. 1597.

BY M. J. M'CANN.

I.

PROUDLY the note of the trumpet is sounding,
  Loudly the war-cries arise on the gale,
Fleetly the steed by Loc Suilig* is bounding
  To join the thick squadrons in Saimear's green vale.
      On, every mountaineer,
        Strangers to flight and fear;
    Rush to the standard of dauntless Red Hugh!†
        Bonnought and Gallowglass‡
        Throng from each mountain-pass!
On for old Erin!—O'Doṁṅall abú!

---

* Lough Swilly.

  † The famous Red Hugh O'Donnell, who aided O'Neil in defeating the best generals
and most brilliant armies of Elizabeth.

  ‡ See Note page 48.

II.

Princely O'Neil to our aid is advancing
  With many a chieftain and warrior-clan;
A thousand proud steeds in his vanguard are prancing,
  'Neath the borderers brave from the banks of the Bann :—
      Many a heart shall quail
      Under its coat of mail;
  Deeply the merciless foeman shall rue,
      When on his ear shall ring,
      Borne on the breeze's wing,
  Tirconnell's dread war-cry—O'Doṁnall abú!

III.

Wildly o'er Desmond the war wolf is howling,
  Fearless the eagle sweeps over the plain,
The fox in the streets of the city is prowling—
  All, all who would scare them are banished or slain!
      Grasp, every stalwart hand,
      Hackbut and battle-brand—
  Pay them all back the deep debt so long due:
      Norris and Clifford well
      Can of Tir-Conaill tell—
  Onward to glory !—O'Doṁnall abú !

IV.

Sacred the cause that Clann-Conaill's defending—
  The altars we kneel at and homes of our sires;
Ruthless the ruin the foe is extending—
  Midnight is red with the plunderer's fires !
      On with O'Domnall, then,
      Fight the old fight again,
  Sons of Tir-Conaill all valiant and true !
      Make the false Saxon feel
      Erin's avenging steel !
  Strike for your country !—O'Doṁnall abú !

THE RIGHT ROAD.

BY THOMAS DAVIS.

I.

Let the feeble-hearted pine,
Let the sickly spirit whine,
But to work and win be thine,
          While you 've life.
God smiles upon the bold—
So, when your flag 's unroll'd,
Bear it bravely till you 're cold
          In the strife.

II. ·

If to rank or fame you soar,
Out your spirit frankly pour—
Men will serve you and adore,
          Like a king.
Woo your girl with honest pride,
Till you 've won her for your bride—
Then to her, through time and tide,
          Ever cling.

III.

Never under wrongs despair;
Labour long, and everywhere,
Link your countrymen, prepare,
          And strike home.
Thus have great men ever wrought,
Thus must greatness still be sought,
Thus labour'd, lov'd, and fought
          Greece and Rome.

A RALLY FOR IRELAND.

MAY, 1689.

Shout it out,'till it ring, From Benmore to Cape Clear, For our Country, and King, and Re-

li - gion so dear, Ral - ly, men! ral - ly, I - rish-men! ral - ly, Ga - ther

round the dear flag, that, wet with our tears, And torn and bloody, lay hid for long years, And

R

now once a - gain in its pride re - ap - pears. See from The Cas - tle our

Green Ban - ner waves, Bear - ing fit mot - to for up - ris - ing slaves, For

"Now, or Ne - ver, Now—and for E - ver !" Bids you to bat - tle for

tri - umph or graves, Bids you to burst on the Sa - sa - nach knaves

Loudly.

Ral - - ly, then, ral - ly. I - rish - men! ral - - ly. Shout, "Now or Ne - ver,

Now, and for E - ver!" Heed not their fu - - ry how - e - - ver it raves,

Wel - come their horse - men with pikes and with staves, Close on their can - non, their

bay'nets and glaives, Down with their stand-ard wher-e - ver it waves, Fight to the last and ye

Firmly.

can - not be slaves! Fight to the last and ye can - not be slaves!

Slower and firmly.

GAILLTE.

A RALLY FOR IRELAND.

MAY, 1689.

BY THOMAS DAVIS.

I.

Shout it out, till it ring
    From Beinn-Mor to Cape Cleir,
For our country and king,
    And religion so dear.
        Rally, men! rally—
        Irishmen! rally!
Gather round the dear flag, that, wet with our tears,
And torn, and bloody, lay hid for long years,
And now, once again, in its pride re-appears.
    See! from The Castle our green banner waves,
    Bearing fit motto for uprising slaves—
            For "Now or Never!
            "Now and for Ever!"
    Bids you to battle for triumph or graves—
    Bids you to burst on the Sasanach knaves—
            Rally, then, rally!
            Irishmen, rally!
            Shout "Now or Never,
            "Now and for ever!"
    Heed not their fury, however it raves,
    Welcome their horsemen with pikes and with staves,
    Close on their cannon, their bay'nets, and glaives,
    Down with their standard wherever it waves;
    Fight to the last, and ye cannot be slaves!
    Fight to the last, and ye cannot be slaves!

II.

Gallant Sheldon is here,
And Hamilton, too,
And Tirconaill so dear,
And MacCartha, so true.
And there are Frenchmen;
Skilful and stanch men—
De Rosen, Pontée, Pusignan, and Boisseleau,
And gallant Lauzun is a coming, you know,
With Bealdearg, the kinsman of great Owen Roe.
From Sionainn to Bann, and from Lifé to Laoi,*
The country is rising for Libertie.
Tho' your arms are rude,
If your courage be good,
As the traitor fled will the stranger flee,
At another Drom-mhór, from " the Irishry."
Arm, peasant and lord!
Grasp musket and sword!
Grasp pike, staff, and skian!
Give your horses the rein!
March, in the name of his Majesty—
Ulster and Munster unitedly—
Townsman and peasant, like waves of the sea—
Leinster and Connacht to victory—
Shoulder to shoulder for Liberty,
Shoulder to shoulder for Liberty.

III.

Kirk, Schomberg and Churchill
Are coming—what then?
We'll drive them and Dutch Will
To England again;
We can laugh at each threat,
For our Parliament's met—

---

* These rivers are vulgarly named Shannon, Liffey, and Lee.

De Courcy, O'Brien, M'Domhnaill, Le Poer,
O'Neil and St. Lawrence, and others *go leor*,
The choice of the land from Athlone to the shore!
    They'll break the last link of the Sasanach chain—
    They'll give us the lands of our fathers again!
        Then up ye! and fight
        For your King and your Right,
  Or ever toil on, and never complain,
  Tho' they trample your roof-tree, and rifle your fane.
        Rally, then, rally!
        Irishmen, rally—
        Fight "Now or Never,
        "Now and for ever!"
Laws are in vain without swords to maintain;
So, muster as fast as the fall of the rain:
Serried and rough as a field of ripe grain,
Stand by your flag upon mountain and plain:
Charge till yourselves or your foemen are slain!
Fight till yourselves or your foemen are slain!

EIRE A RUIN.

AIR—Ꞷꙗблꙗn ᴀ Rúꙗn.*

I.

Long thy fair cheek was pale,
    Ꞷꙗꞃe ᴀ ꞃúꙗn—
Too well it spake thy tale,
    Ꞷꙗꞃe ᴀ ꞃúꙗn—
Fondly-nursed hopes betrayed,
Gallant sons lowly laid,
All anguish there pourtrayed,
    Ꞷꙗꞃe ᴀ ꞃúꙗn.

---

* In vulgar spelling, Eileen aroon.

II.

Long thy dear *clairseach's* string,
    Eιρe a ρúιη,
Sang but as captives sing,
    Eιρe a ρúιη,—
'Twas sorrow's broken sigh,
Blent with mirth's reckless cry,
Saddest of minstrelsy!
    Eιρe a ρúιη.

III.

Still was it thine to cope,
    Eιρe a ρúιη,—
Still against hope to hope,
    Eιρe a ρúιη,
Ever through blackest woe,
Fronting that tyrant foe,
Whom thou shalt yet lay low,
    Eιρe a ρúιη.

IV.

Though he should sue thee now,
    Eιρe a ρúιη,
Heed not his traitor vow,
    Eιρe a ρúιη;
When didst thou e'er believe,
When his false words receive,
But sorely thou didst grieve,
    Eιρe a ρúιη.

V.

Millions of hearts are thine,
    Eιρe a ρúιη;
Millions as one combine,
    Eιρe a ρúιη;
Closer in peril knit,
Patient, though passion-lit—
For such is triumph writ,
    Eιρe a ρúιη.

VI.

Then let thy *clairseach* pour,
Éire a rúin,
Wailings of grief no more,
Éire a rúin,
But strains like flash of steel,
Kindling that fire of zeal,
Which melts their chains who feel,
Éire a rúin.

SLIABH CUILINN.

TONE'S GRAVE.

BY THOMAS DAVIS.

I.

In Bodenstown Churchyard there is a green grave,
And wildly along it the winter winds rave;
Small shelter, I ween, are the ruin'd walls there,
When the storm sweeps down on the plains of Kildare.

II.

Once I lay on that sod—it lies over Wolfe Tone—
And thought how he perished in prison alone,
His friends unavenged, and his country unfreed—
"Oh, bitter," I said, "is the patriot's meed;

III.

For in him the heart of a woman combin'd
With a heroic life, and a governing mind—
A martyr for Ireland—his grave has no stone—
His name seldom nam'd, and his virtues unknown."

IV.

I was woke from my dream by the voices and tread
Of a band, who came into the home of the dead;
They carried no corpse, and they carried no stone,
And they stopp'd when they came to the grave of Wolfe Tone.

s

v.

There were students and peasants, the wise and the brave,
And an old man who knew him from cradle to grave,
And children who thought me hard-hearted; for they,
On that sanctified sod, were forbidden to play.

vi.

But the old man, who saw I was mourning there, said,
"We come, sir, to weep where young Wolfe Tone is laid,
And we're going to raise him a monument, too—
A plain one, yet fit for the simple and true."

vii.

My heart overflow'd, and I clasped his old hand,
And I bless'd him, and bless'd every one of his band;
"Sweet! sweet! 'tis to find that such faith can remain
To the cause, and the man so long vanquish'd and slain."

viii.

*   *   *   *   *   *   *   *

ix.

*   *   *   *   *   *   *   *

x.

In Bodenstown Churchyard there is a green grave,
And freely around it let winter winds rave—
Far better they suit him—the ruin and gloom,
Till Ireland, a nation, can build him a tomb.

THE ORPHAN CHILD.

BY THE REV. CHARLES J. MEEHAN.

i.

Her look it is so innocent,
  Her face so calm and mild,
You'd scarcely think that sorrow prey'd
  Upon that orphan child.

II.

Her form is to a shadow worn,
  Yet ever I espy
Much resignation, trustingly,
  Beam from her sunken eye.

III.

By looks alone she asks for aid,
  And leaves her woes unspoken:
As strangers pass she shrinks aside—
  Her little heart is broken.

IV.

Her hopes are not upon the earth,
  She only longs to die,
And often thinks of one green spot
  Where she might softly lie.

V.

And oft she seeks that little spot,
  And whispers, while she weeps,
" Oh! that I were within her arms—
  How sound my mother sleeps!"

VI.

And stretched upon the grassy turf,
  In feverish repose,
She dreams her mother speaks to her,
  And weeps the thought to lose.

VII.

God pity thee, forsaken thing!
  And, sure, thou art his care—
Heaven is the orphan's only home,
  Thou 'lt find thy mother there.

s 2

𝔘𝔞 𝔗-𝔰𝔢𝔞𝔫 𝔟𝔥𝔢𝔞𝔫 𝔟𝔥𝔬𝔠𝔥𝔡.

AIR.—Aɲ τ-ɼαeɲ beαɲ boċb.

The saint-ed isle of old, Says the ɼeαɲ beαɲ boċb, The sainted isle of old, Says the ɼeαɲ beαɲ boċb, The pa-rent and the mould Of the beau-ti-ful and bold, Has her blithe-some heart wax'd cold? Says the ɼeαɲ beαɲ boċb.

AN T-SEAN BHEAN BHOCHD.

A.D. 1176.

BY MICHAEL DOHENY.

I.

THE sainted isle of old,
    Says the ṛeaɲ beaɲ boċɒ,*
The sainted isle of old,
    Says the ṛeaɲ beaɲ boċɒ,
The parent and the mould
Of the beautiful and bold,
Has her blithesome heart waxed cold?
    Says the ṛeaɲ beaɲ boċɒ.

II.

The Saxon and the Dane,
    Says the ṛeaɲ beaɲ boċɒ,
The Saxon and the Dane,
    Says the ṛeaɲ beaɲ boċɒ,
The Saxon and the Dane,
Our immortal hills profane,
Oh! confusion seize the twain,
    Says the ṛeaɲ beaɲ boċɒ.

III.

What are the Chiefs to do?
    Says the ṛeaɲ beaɲ boċɒ;
What are the Chiefs to do?
    Says the ṛeaɲ beaɲ boċɒ.

---

* Vulgarly The Shan Van Vacht.

What should the Chieftains do,
But to treat the hireling crew,
To a touch of Brian Boru?
  Says the ꞃeaɲ beaɲ boċᴅ.

IV.

They came across the wave,
  Says the ꞃeaɲ beaɲ boċᴅ,
They came across the wave,
  Says the ꞃeaɲ beaɲ boċᴅ,
They came across the wave,
But to plunder and enslave,
And should find a robber's grave,
  Says the ꞃeaɲ beaɲ boċᴅ.

V.

Then be the trusty brand,
  Says the ꞃeaɲ beaɲ boċᴅ,
Then be the trusty brand,
  Says the ꞃeaɲ beaɲ boċᴅ,
Then be the trusty brand,
Firmly clutched in every hand,
And we'll scourge them from the land,
  Says the ꞃeaɲ beaɲ boċᴅ.

VI.

There's courage yet and truth,
  Says the ꞃeaɲ beaɲ boċᴅ,
There's courage yet and truth,
  Says the ꞃeaɲ beaɲ boċᴅ;
There's a God above us all,
And whatever may befal,
No invader shall enthrall,
  Says the ꞃeaɲ beaɲ boċᴅ.

THE SLAVES' BILL.

BY WILLIAM DRENNAN.

I.

Aye, brand our arms, nor them alone,
    But brand our brows; degraded race,
Oh, how a fear can England own
    Of men, who cannot feel disgrace?
Men! *Are* we men? We talk as such,
    Heav'ns, how we talk! but—vain alarms—
Nought masculine endures so much,
    Then brand our brows, as well as arms!

II.

This brand is not an ugly thing—
    May seem an ornament, indeed;
The shame to some would be the sting,
    But not to slaves who dare not bleed!
Six hundred weary years have pass'd,
    And which, without some newer harms
From Dear Old England! This, the last,
    Is *but an insult*—brand our arms!

III.

Yes, brand our language, faith, and name!
    Black, down Time's river let them roll;
Let Erin be a word of shame,
    And burn its mem'ry from my soul!
Oh! Erin, Erin!—never more
    That darling name let me repeat!
If such the sons my mother bore,
    West-Briton were a sound as sweet.

IV.

Aye, brand us all! yet still we crave
    A pittance at our master's door:
Then leave the wealthy Irish slave
    His bottle, club, and paramour;
And leave the wretched serf his wife—
    You may, (she has not many charms,)
Potatoes, and his paltry life;
    But, leave us not—ev'n branded arms!

V.

Mad as ye are, who reckless dare
    To mock the spirit God hath given,
Pause, ere ye drive us in despair
    To its appeal—from man to heaven!
From calmer eyes the furies glare,
    And colder bosoms vengeance warms,
Till rage finds weapons, ev'rywhere,
    For Nature's two unbranded arms!

THE BRIDE OF MALLOW.

BY THOMAS DAVIS.

I.

'TWAS dying they thought her,
And kindly they brought her
To the banks of Blackwater,
    Where her forefathers lie;
'Twas the place of her childhood,
And they hoped that its wild wood,
And air soft and mild would
    Soothe her spirit to die.

II.

But she met on its border
A lad who ador'd her—
No rich man, nor lord. or
    A coward, or slave,
But one who had worn
A green coat, and borne
A pike from Sliaḃ Mourne,
    With the patriots brave.

III.

Oh! the banks of the stream are
Than emeralds greener:
And how should they wean her
    From loving the earth,
While the song-birds so sweet,
And the waves at their feet,
And each young pair they meet,
    Are all flushing with mirth.

IV.

And she listed his talk,
And he shar'd in her walk—
And how could she baulk
    One so gallant and true?
But why tell the rest?
Her love she confest,
And sunk on his breast,
    Like the eventide dew.

V.

Ah! now her cheek glows
With the tint of the rose,
And her healthful blood flows,
    Just as fresh as the stream;

T

And her eye flashes bright,
And her footstep is light,
And sickness and blight
    Fled away like a dream.

VI.

And soon by his side
She kneels a sweet bride,
In maidenly pride
    And maidenly fears;
And their children were fair,
And their home knew no care,
Save that all homesteads were
    Not as happy as theirs.

THE GATHERING OF THE NATION.

BY J. D. FRAZER.

I.

THOSE scalding tears—those scalding tears,
    Too long have fallen in vain—
Up with the banners and the spears,
And let the gather'd grief of years
    Show sterner stuff than rain.
The lightning, in that stormy hour
    When forth defiance rolls,
Shall flash to scathe the Saxon pow'r,
But melt the links our long, long show'r
    Had rusted round our souls.

II.

To bear the wrongs we can redress!
  To make *a thing of time*—
The tyranny we can repress—
Eternal by our dastardness!
  Were crime—or worse than crime.
And we, whose *best*—and *worst* was shame,
  From first to last alike,
May take, at length, a loftier aim,
And struggle, since it is the same
  To *suffer*—or to *strike*.

III.

What hatred of perverted might
  The cruel hand inspires,
That robs the linnet's eye of sight,
To make it sing both day and night!
  Yet thus they robb'd our sires,
By blotting out the ancient lore,
  Where every loss was shown.—
Up with the flag! we stand before
The Saxons of the days of yore,
  In Saxons of our own.

IV.

Denial met our just demands!
  And hatred met our love!
Till now, by Heaven! for grasp of hands,
We'll give them clash of battle-brands,
  And gauntlet 'stead of glove.
And may the Saxon stamp his heel
  Upon the coward's front,
Who sheathes his own unbroken steel,
Until for mercy tyrants kneel,
  Who forced us to the brunt!

T 2

WHAT ARE REPEALERS?

BY EDWARD WALSH.

"Papa! what are Repealers?"—MY SON.

AIR—"*Tipperary O!*"

I.

MILLIONS who've given their gage, my boy,
Fierce war with oppression to wage, my boy,
    Till Erin, once more,
    Shall shine as of yore
The land of the hero and sage, my boy!

II.

That land was all Europe's pride, my boy
It's glory and fame were wide, my boy,
    And Roman and Dane,
    Who offer'd the chain,
By the sword of its heroes died, my boy!

III.

Her chiefs wax'd faithless and proud, my boy,
And discord's hoarse voice grow loud, my boy;
    And, record of shame,
    The stranger then came,
And liberty laid in her shroud, my boy.

IV.

The land, red rapine long swept, my boy,
And mercy and truth long slept, my boy,
    Oh! could you but know
    Such tyrants—such woe—
Your young eyes with mine had wept, my boy.

V.

But in the despot's despite, my boy,
The millions arise in their might, my boy.

And swear by the tears
And blood of past years,
To wrest from that despot their right, my boy !

VI.

They are banded, and firm, and true, my boy,
Resolved to die or to do, my boy,
The young and the old
In the cause are enroll'd,
And I 've sworn you one of them, too, my boy !

VII.

Ere this vow be unsafe in thy keeping, boy,
May your father bemoan you sleeping, boy,
Where green willows wave
Above your young grave,
And none to condole his weeping, boy !

THE GERALDINES.

BY THOMAS DAVIS.

I.

THE Geraldines, the Geraldines, 'tis full a thousand years
Since, 'mid the Tuscan vineyards, bright flashed their battle-spears;
When Capet seized the crown of France, their iron shields were
known,
And their sabre-dint struck terror on the banks of the Garonne
Across the downs of Hastings they spurred hard by William's side,
And the grey sands of Palestine with Moslem blood they dyed—
But never then, nor thence, till now, have falsehood or disgrace
Been seen to soil Fitzgerald's plume, or mantle in his face.

II.

The Geraldines, the Geraldines, 'tis true in Strongbow's van,
By lawless force, as conquerors, their Irish reign began—

And, oh! through many a dark campaign they proved their
    prowess stern,
In Leinster's plains, and Munster's vales, on king, and chief, and
    kerne;
But noble was the cheer within the halls so rudely won,
And gen'rous was the steel-gloved hand that had such slaughter
    done;
How gay their laugh, how proud their mien, you'd ask no herald's
    sign—
Among a thousand you had known the princely Geraldine.

III.

These Geraldines, these Geraldines, not long our air they breathed—
Not long they fed on venison, in Irish water seethed—
Not often had their children been by Irish mothers nursed,
When from their full and genial hearts an Irish feeling burst;
The English monarchs strove in vain, by law, and force, and bribe,
To win from Irish thoughts and ways this "more than Irish" tribe;
For still they clung to fosterage, to breithamh,* cloak, and hard—
What king dare say to Geraldine "your Irish wife discard"?

IV.

Ye Geraldines, ye Geraldines, how royally ye reigned
O'er Desmond broad, and rich Cilldare,† and English arts dis-
    dained:
Your sword made knights, your banner waved, free was your
    bugle call
By Gleann's green slopes, and Daingean's tide, from Bearbha's
    banks to Eochaill.
What gorgeous shrines, what Breithamh lore, what minstrel feasts
    there were
In and around Magh Nuadhait's keep, and palace-filled Athdare,

---

* Brehon.
† The common English spellings of the words in this verse are Kildare, **Glyn**,
Dingle, Barrow, Youghal, Maynooth, and Adare.

But not for rite or feast ye stayed, when friend or kin was pressed,
And foemen fled, when "Ꞇꝓom Ꝇbú" bespoke your lance in rest.

V.

Ye Geraldines, ye Geraldines, since Silken Thomas flung
King Henry's sword on council board, the English thanes among,
Ye never ceased to battle brave against the English sway,
Though axe and brand and treachery your proudest cut away;
Of Desmond's blood, through woman's veins passed on th' exhausted
    tide,
His title lives—a Saxon churl usurps the lion's hide;
And, though Kildare tower haughtily, there's ruin at the root,
Else why, since Edward fell to earth, had such a tree no fruit?

VI.

True Geraldines, brave Geraldines, as torrents mould the earth,
You channelled deep old Ireland's heart by constancy and worth:
When Ginckle leagured Limerick, the Irish soldiers gazed
To see if in the setting sun dead Desmond's banner blazed!
And still it is the peasants' hope upon the Currach's mere,
" They live, who'll see ten thousand men with good Lord Edward
    here"—
So let them dream till brighter days, when, not by Edward's shade,
But by some leader true as he, their lines shall be arrayed.

VII.

The Geraldines, these Geraldines, rain wears away the rock,
And time may wear away the tribe that stood the battle's shock,
But, ever, sure, while one is left of all that honored race,
In front of Ireland's chivalry is that Fitzgerald's place;
And, though the last were dead and gone, how many a field and
    town,
From Thomas Court to Abbeyfeale, would cherish their renown,
And men would say of valour's rise, or ancient power's decline,
" 'Twill never soar, it never shone, as did the Geraldine."

HYMN OF FREEDOM.

Adagio Maestoso.

God of Peace! be - - - fore Thee, Peace-ful, here we kneel,

Hum - bly to im - plore Thee For a na - tion's weal: Calm her sons' dis-

sen - sions, Bid their dis - - cord cease, End their mad con - -

ten - - tions, Hear us, God of Peace! End their mad con - - ten - - tions,

Hear us, God of Peace! Hear us, God of Peace!

HYMN OF FREEDOM.

BY M. J. BARRY.

I.

God of Peace! before thee,
  Peaceful, here we kneel,
Humbly to implore thee
  For a nation's weal;
Calm her sons' dissensions,
  Bid their discord cease,
End their mad contentions—
  Hear us, God of Peace!

II.

God of Love! low bending
  To thy throne we turn—
Let thy rays descending
  Through our island burn;
Let no strife divide us,
  But, from Heaven above,
Look on us and guide us—
  Hear us, God of Love!

III.

God of Battles! aid us;
  Let no despot's might
Trample or degrade us,
  Seeking this our right!
Arm us for the danger;
  Keep all craven fear
To our breasts a stranger—
  God of Battles! hear.

IV.

God of Right! preserve us
   Just—as we are strong;
Let no passion swerve us
   To one act of wrong—
Let no thought, unholy,
   Come our cause to blight—
Thus we pray thee, lowly—
   Hear us, God of Right!

V.

God of Vengeance! smite us
   With thy shaft sublime,
If one bond unite us
   Forged in fraud or crime!
But, if humbly kneeling,
   We implore thine ear,
For our rights appealing—
   God of Nations! hear.

THE UNION.

I.

How did they pass the Union?
   By perjury and fraud;
By slaves who sold their land for gold,
   As Judas sold his God:
By all the savage acts that yet
   Have followed England's track:
The pitchcap and the bayonet,
   The gibbet and the rack.

And thus was passed the Union,
  By Pitt and Castlereagh;
Could Satan send for such an end
  More worthy tools than they?

II.

How thrive we by the Union?
  Look round our native land:
In ruined trade and wealth decayed
  See slavery's surest brand;
Our glory as a nation gone—
  Our substance drained away—
A wretched province trampled on,
  Is all we've left to-day.
    Then curse with me the Union,
      That juggle foul and base,
    The baneful root that bore such fruit
      Of ruin and disgrace.

III.

And shall it last, this Union,
  To grind and waste us so?
O'er hill and lea, from sea to sea,
  All Ireland thunders, No!
Eight million necks are stiff to bow—
  We know our might as men—
We conquered once before, and now
  We'll conquer once again;
    And rend the cursed Union,
      And fling it to the wind—
    And Ireland's laws in Ireland's cause
      Alone our hearts shall bind!

SLIABH CUILINN.

THE PEASANT GIRLS.

I.

The Peasant Girl of merry France,
   Beneath her trellis'd vine,
Watches the signal for the dance—
   The broad, red sun's decline.
'Tis there—and forth she flies with glee
   To join the circling band,
Whilst mirthful sounds of minstrelsy
   Are heard throughout the land.

II.

And fair Italia's Peasant Girl,
   The Arno's banks beside,
With myrtle flowers that shine like pearl,
   Will braid at eventide
Her raven locks; and to the sky,
   With eyes of liquid light,
Look up and bid her lyre outsigh—
   "Was ever land so bright?"

III.

The Peasant Girl of England, see
   With lip of rosy dye,
Beneath her sheltering cottage tree,
   Smile on each passer by.
She looks on fields of yellow grain,
   Inhales the bean-flower's scent,
And seems, amid the fertile plain,
   An image of content.

IV.

The Peasant Girl of Scotland goes
   Across her Highland hill,
With cheek that emulates the rose,
   And voice the skylark's thrill.

Her tartan plaid she folds around,
  A many-coloured vest—
Type of what varied joys have found
  A home in her kind breast.

v.

The Peasant Girl of Ireland, she
  Has left her cabin home,
Bearing white wreaths—what can it be
  Invites her thus to roam?
Her eye has not the joyous ray
  Should to her years belong;
And, as she wends her languid way,
  She carols no sweet song.

vi.

Oh! soon upon the step and glance
  Grief does the work of age;
And it has been her hapless chance
  To open that dark page.
The happy harvest home was o'er,
  The fierce tithe-gatherer came;
And her young lover, in his gore,
  Fell by a murderous aim!

vii.

Then, well may youth's bright glance be gone
  For ever from that eye,
And soon will sisters weep upon
  The grave that she kneels by;
And well may prouder hearts than those,
  That there place garlands, say—
" Have Ireland's peasant girls such woes?—
  When will they pass away?"

THE DAY-DREAMER.

BY CHARLES GAVAN DUFFY.

I.

What joy was mine in that merry time,
   When I was an Outlaw bold!
Girt with my clan in the glades of Triuch,
   Or shut in my castle-hold
In council deep, with the Sages grey,
   And the deathless chiefs of old.

II.

When I wept the fate of a land betrayed
   At the feet of the Soldier-Saint;*
Or drank high hopes from our dauntless Hugh
   That cordial the hearts of the faint;
Or wove bold plots with untiring Tone
   To blot out our Isle's attaint.

III.

What deeds we vowed for the dear old land!
   What solemn words we spoke;
How never we'd cease or sleep in peace
   'Till we shattered the Stranger's yoke;
And not with a storm of windy words,
   But many a soldier stroke.

IV.

Bright days were those when the weak and poor
   Might match with the proud and strong;
For willing swords from our scabbards leapt,
   At the dawning of fraud or wrong—
To dare brave deeds like the deeds of old,
   That live in the File's† song.

---

* St. Lawrence O'Toole, or rather O'Tuathail.   † File, a bard.

V.

We'd knotted whips for the Saxon churls,
   And swords for the Norman peers,
And gyves of steel for the pampered priests
   Who were drunk with the poor man's tears—
And the Towers grim where the Robbers laired,
   We dashed them about their ears.

VI.

The Harp and *Stoc** we could wield them too,
   As true as the *sleagh*† and *skian ;*‡
And forth we sent to the listening land,
   Full many's the stirring strain,
Which scattered the slavish fear away
   That hung on its breast like a chain.

VII.

The torrent's voice in the noiseless night
   Is tame to the words we spake,
They startled the isle like a sudden stream
   That is dashed on a stagnant lake,
Till the millions rose from their shameful sleep,
   And their chains like a reed they brake.

VIII.

It stirs me still, that thrilling sight
   Of the dear old land made free,
Our Flag afloat from her castles tall,
   And the ships on the circling sea,
While the joyful sheen of their native Green
   Made the millions mad with glee.

IX.

And woe is me! was it all a dream
   That cheated my trancéd heart!
The vision-life of a sickly boy,
   The thrall of a world apart,

---

* A war trumpet.   † A spear.   ‡ A dagger.

Who launched his boat on a summer sea,
And sailed without helm or chart.

X.

Ay, woe is me ! for my heart's decay
 Since that dream of my youth hath flown,
For Care, like a midnight owl, hath sat
 By the ruin he made his own.
And gay hopes bloom, but like ivy green
 O'er the grey of the mould'ring stone !

THE BATTLE OF GLEANN-DA-LOCHA.*

A BALLAD OF THE PALE

A.D. 1580.

BY M. J. M'CANN.

I.

An autumn's sun is beaming on Dublin's Castle towers,
Whose portal fast is pouring forth the Pale's embattled powers;
And on for Wicklow's hills they urge their firm and rapid way,
And well may proud Lord Grey exult to view their stern array.

II.

For there was many a stately knight whose helm was rough with
     gold,
And spearman grim, and musketeer, in Erin's wars grown old,
Speed on for Gleann-da-Locha 'gainst Fiacha Mac Aodha,†
Who lately with his mountain bands to that wild glen withdrew.

---

* Glendaloch.   † Called in the old English books Pheagh Mac Hugh.

X

III.

And now above the rugged glen their prancing steeds they rein,
While many an eager look along its mazy depths they strain;
But where 's the marshall'd foe they seek—the camp or watch-
    fires—where?
For, save the eagle screaming high, no sign of life is there!

IV.

"Ho!" cried the haughty Deputy, "my gallant friends we 're late—
I rightly deem'd the rebel foe would scarce our visit wait!
But, onward lead the foot, Carew! perhaps, in sooth, 'twere well
That something of their flocks and herds our soldiery should tell.

V.

" I 've heard it is the traitors' wont in cave and swamp to hide,
Where'er they deem their force too weak the battle's brunt to bide;
So, mark, where'er a rebel lurks arouse him in his lair—
And death to him whose hand is known an Irish foe to spare!"

VI.

But thus the veteran Cosby spoke—"My lord, I 've known for years
The hardihood and daring of those stalwart mountaineers;
And, trust me, that our bravest would, in yonder rugged pass,
But little like the greeting of an Irish galloglass.

VII.

"For though his brawny breast may not be cased in temper'd steel,
Right sheer and heavy is the stroke his nervous arm can deal;
And, too, my lord, perhaps 'twere ill that here you first should
    learn
How truly like a mountain cat is Erin's fearless kern."

VIII.

" March!" was the sole and stern reply; and, as the leader spoke,
Horn and trump, and thundering drum, a thousand echoes woke!
And on, with martial tramp, the host, all bright in glittering mail,
Wound like a monstrous serpent far along the gloomy vale.

IX.

But, hark ! what wild defiant yell, the rocks and woods among,
Has now so fierce from every side in thrilling echoes rung ?—
O'Byrne's well-known warrison !—and hark ! along the dell,
With rapid and successive peal, the musquet's deadly knell !

X.

As wolves, that in a narrowing ring the hunter's band enclose,
So rush the baffled Saxons on the ambush of their foes ;—
And lo ! from every craggy screen, as 'twere instinct with life,
Up spring the mountain warriors to meet the coming strife.

XI.

And tall, amid their foremost band, his broadsword flashing bright,
Bold Fiacha MacAodha is seen to cheer them to the fight;—
And from the fiery chieftain's lips these words of vengeance
    passed—
" Behold the bloody Sasanach—remember Mullachmaist !" *

XII.

Now, gallant clansmen, charge them home !—not often, hand to
    hand,
In battle with your ruthless foes on terms so poised you stand ;
Ye meet not now in firm array the spearmen's serried ranks—
No whelming squadrons here can dash upon your scattered flanks !

XIII.

The keen and ponderous battle-axe with deadly force is plied,
And deep the mountain pike and skian in Saxon blood are dyed ;
And many a polish'd corselet 's pierced and many a helm is cleft—
And few of all that proud array for shameful flight are left !

XIV.

No time to breathe or rally them—so hotly are they pressed ;
For thousand maddening memories fire each raging victor's breast !
And many a father's murder, and many a sister's wrong,
Dark Gleann-da-Locha was avenged, thy echoing vale along.

---

* The massacre of Mullachmaistean was perpetrated a few years previous to the date of the event here commemorated, and was for a long time a watchword of vengeance throughout Leinster

x 2

THE BATTLE-EVE OF THE BRIGADE.

Air—*" Contented I am."*

The mess-tent is full and the glass-es are set, And the gal-lant Count Tho-mond is Pre-si-dent yet. The Vet'-ran a-rose like an

up - lift - ed lance, Cry - ing, "Com-rades! a health to the

mo - narch of France,"—With bum - pers and cheers they have

done as he bade, For King Lou - is is lov'd by THE IRISH BRIGADE.

THE BATTLE EVE OF THE BRIGADE.

BY THOMAS DAVIS.

AIR—"*Contented I am.*"

I.

THE mess-tent is full, and the glasses are set,
And the gallant Count Thomond is president yet;
The vet'ran arose, like an uplifted lance,
Crying—"Comrades, a health to the monarch of France!"
With bumpers and cheers they have done as he bade,
For King Louis is lov'd by The Irish Brigade.

II.

"A health to King James," and they bent as they quaff'd,
"Here's to George the *Elector*," and fiercely they laugh'd,
"Good luck to the girls we woo'd long ago,
Where Sionainn,* and Bearbha,† and Abhain-dubh‡ flow;"
"God prosper Old Ireland," you'd think them afraid,
So pale grew the chiefs of The Irish Brigade.

III.

"But, surely, that light cannot come from our lamp?
And that noise—are they *all* getting drunk in the camp?"
"Hurrah! boys, the morning of battle is come,
And the *generale's* beating on many a drum."
So they rush from the revel to join the parade:
For the van is the right of The Irish Brigade.

IV.

They fought as they revell'd, fast, fiery, and true,
And, though victors, they left on the field not a few;
And they, who surviv'd, fought and drank as of yore,
But the land of their heart's hope they never saw more,
For in far foreign fields, from Dunkirk to Belgrade,
Lie the soldiers and chiefs of The Irish Brigade.

---

* Shannon.   † Barrow.   ‡ Avondhu or Black-water.

THE VOW OF TIPPERARY.

BY THOMAS DAVIS.

AIR—" *Tipperary.*" *

I.

FROM Carrick streets to Shannon shore,
From Sliabh na m-Ban† to Ballindeary,
From Longford Pass to Gaillte Mór,
Come hear The Vow of Tipperary.

II.

Too long we fought for Britain's cause,
And of our blood were never chary ;
She paid us back with tyrant laws,
And thinned The Homes of Tipperary.

III.

Too long, with rash and single arm,
The peasant strove to guard his eyrie,
Till Irish blood bedewed each farm,
And Ireland wept for Tipperary.

IV.

But never more we 'll lift a hand—
We swear by God and Virgin Mary !
Except in war for Native Land,
And *that's* The Vow of Tipperary !

THE SONGS OF THE NATION.

BY EDWARD WALSH.

I.

YE songs that resound in the homes of our island—
That wake the wild echoes by valley and highland—

---

* See p. 84.   † Commonly written Slievenamon.

That kindle the cold with their forofather's story—
That point to the ardent the pathway of glory !—
        Ye send to the banish'd,
         O'er ocean's far wave,
        The hope that had vanish'd,
         The vow of the brave ;
And teach each proud despot of loftiest station,
To pale at your spell-word, sweet Songs of THE NATION !

II.

Sweet songs ! ye reveal, through the vista of ages,
Our monarchs and heroes—our minstrels and sages—
The splendour of Eamhan *—the glories of Teamhair,†
When Erin was free from the Saxon defamer—
        The green banner flying—
         The rush of the Gael—
        The Sasanach dying—
         His matron's wild wail—
These glories forgotten, with magic creation
Burst bright at your spell-word, sweet Songs of THE NATION !

III.

The minstrels who waken these wild notes of freedom,
Have hands for green Erin—if Erin should need 'em ;
And hearts for the wrong'd one, wherever he ranges,
From Zembla to China—from Sionainn to Ganges—
        And hate for his foeman,
         All hatred above—
        And love for dear woman,
         The tenderest love—
But chiefest the fair ones whose eyes' animation
Is the spell that inspires the sweet Songs of THE NATION !

---

* The Palace of the Ulster Kings, near Armagh, Latinized Emania.   † Tara.

A BALLAD OF FREEDOM.

BY THOMAS DAVIS.

I.

THE Frenchman sailed in Freedom's name to smite the Algerine,
The strife was short, the crescent sunk, and then his guile was seen,
For, nestling in the pirate's hold—a fiercer pirate far—
He bade the tribes yield up their flocks, the towns their gates
    unbar.
Right on he press'd with freemen's hands to subjugate the free,
The Berber in old Atlas glens, the Moor in Titteri;
And wider had his *razzias* spread, his cruel conquests broader,
But God sent down, to face his frown, the gallant Abdel Kader—
The faithful Abdel-Kader! unconquered Abdel-Kader!

Like falling rock,
Or fierce siroc—
No savage or marauder—
Son of a slave!
First of the brave!
Hurrah for Abdel-Kader!*

II.

The Englishman, for long long years, had ravaged Ganges' side—
A dealer first, intriguer next, he conquered far and wide,
Till, hurried on by avarice, and thirst of endless rule,
His sepoys pierced to Candahar, his flag waved in Cabul;
But still within the conquered land was one unconquered man,
The fierce Pushtani† lion, the fiery Akhbar Khan—

---

* This name is pronounced Cawder. The French say that their great foe was a slave's son. Be it so—he has a hero's and freeman's heart. " Hurrah for Abdel-Kader !"

† This is the name by which the Affghans call themselves. Affghan is a Persian name (see Elphinstone's delightful book on Cabul). Note, too, that in most of their words *a* sounds *aw*, *u* sounds *oo*, and *i* sounds *ee*.

Y

He slew the sepoys on the snow, till Sindh's* full flood they
    swam it
Right rapidly, content to flee the son of Dost Mohammed,
The son of Dost Mohammed, and brave old Dost Mohammed—
        Oh! long may they
        Their mountains sway,
    Akhbar and Dost Mohammed!
        Long live the Dost!
        Who Britain crost,
    Hurrah for Dost Mohammed!

III.

The Russian, lord of million serfs, and nobles serflier still,
Indignant saw Circassia's sons bear up against his will;
With fiery ships he lines their coast, his armies cross their streams—
He builds a hundred fortresses—his conquest done, he deems.
But, steady rifles—rushing steeds—a crowd of nameless chiefs—
The plough is o'er his arsenals!—his fleet is on the reefs!
The maidens of Kabyntica are clad in Moscow dresses—
His slavish herd, how dared they beard the mountain-bred Cher-
    kesses!
The lightening Cherkesses!—the thundering Cherkesses!
        May Elburz top
        In Azof drop,
    Ere Cossacks beat Cherkesses!
        The fountain head
        Whence Europe spread—
    Hurrah! for the tall Cherkesses!†

---

* The real name of the Indus, which is a Latinised word.

† Cherkesses or Abdyes is the right name of the, so-called, Circassians. Kabyntica
is a town in the heart of the Caucasus, of which Mount Elburz is the summit. Blu-
menbach, and other physiologists, assert that the finer European races descend from a
Circassian stock.

IV.

But Russia preys on Poland's fields, where Sobieski reigned,
And Austria on Italy—the Roman eagle chained—
Bohemia, Servia, Hungary, within her clutches, gasp;
And Ireland struggles gallantly in England's loosening grasp.
Oh! would all these their strength unite, or battle on alone,
Like Moor, Pushtani, and Cherkess, they soon would have their own.
Hurrah! hurrah! it can't be far, when from the Scindh to Sionainn*
Shall gleam a line of freemen's flags begirt by freemen's cannon!
The coming day of Freedom—the flashing flags of Freedom!
> The victor glaive—
> The mottoes brave,
> May we be there to read them!
> That glorious noon,
> God send it soon—
> Hurrah! for human Freedom!

"CEASE TO DO EVIL—LEARN TO DO WELL."

—Inscription on O'Connell's Prison.

BY D. F. M'CARTHY.

OH! thou whom sacred duty hither calls,
  Some glorious hours in freedom's cause to dwell,
Read the mute lesson on thy prison walls—
  "Cease to do evil—learn to do well."

I.

If haply thou art one of genius vast,
  Of generous heart, of mind sublime and grand,
Who all the spring-time of thy life hast pass'd
  Battling with tyrants for thy native land—
If thou hast spent thy summer as thy prime,
  The serpent brood of bigotry to quell,
Repent, repent thee of thy hideous crime—
  "Cease to do evil—learn to do well!"

---

* Shannon.

Y 2

II.

If thy great heart beat warmly in the cause
   Of outraged man, whate'er his race might be—
If thou hast preached the Christian's equal laws,
   And stayed the lash beyond the Indian sea—
If at thy call a nation rose sublime—
   If at thy voice seven million fetters fell,
Repent, repent thee of thy hideous crime—
   "Cease to do evil—learn to do well!"

III.

If thou hast seen thy country's quick decay,
   And, like a prophet, raised thy saving hand,
And pointed out the only certain way
   To stop the plague that ravaged o'er the land!—
If thou hast summoned from an alien clime
   Her banished senate here at home to dwell,
Repent, repent thee of thy hideous crime—
   Cease to do evil—learn to do well!"

IV.

Or if, perchance, a younger man thou art,
   Whose ardent soul in throbbings doth aspire,
Come weal come woe, to play the patriot's part
   In the bright footsteps of thy glorious sire!
If all the pleasures of life's youthful time
   Thou hast abandoned for the martyr's cell,
Do thou repent thee of thy hideous crime—
   "Cease to do evil—learn to do well!"

V.

Or art thou one whom early science led
   To walk with Newton through the immense of Heaven;
Who soared with Milton, and with Mina bled,
   And all thou hadst, in Freedom's cause hath given!
Oh! fond enthusiast—in the after time
   Our children's children of your worth shall tell—
England proclaims thy honesty a crime—
   "Cease to do evil—learn to do well!"

VI.

Or art thou one whose strong and fearless pen
 Roused the Young Isle, and bade it dry its tears,
And gathered round thee, ardent, gifted men,
 The hope of Ireland in the coming years;
Who dares in prose and heart-awakening rhyme
 Bright hopes to breathe, and bitter truths to tell!
Oh! dangerous criminal, repent thy crime—
 " Cease to do evil—learn to do well !"

VII.

" Cease to do evil"—ay! ye madmen, cease!
 Cease to love Ireland—cease to serve her well;
Make with her foes a foul and fatal peace,
 And quick will ope your darkest, dreariest cell.
" Learn to do well"—ay! learn to betray—
 Learn to revile the land in which you dwell—
England will bless you on your altered way—
 " Cease to do evil—learn to do well !"

Third Week of the Captivity.

FILL HIGH TO-NIGHT.

I.

Fill high to-night, in our halls of light,
 The toast on our lips shall be
" The sinewy hand, the glittering brand,
 Our homes and our altars free."

II.

Though the coward pale, like the girl may wail,
 And sleep in his chains for years,
The sound of our mirth shall pass over earth
 With balm for a nation's tears.

III.

A curse for the cold, a cup for the bold,
 A smile for the girls we love;
And for him who'd bleed, in his country's need,
 A home in the skies above.

IV.

We have asked the page of a former age
   For hope secure and bright,
And the spell it gave to the stricken slave
   Was in one strong word—" Unite."

V.

Though the wind howl free o'er a simple tree
   Till it bends beneath its frown—
For many a day it will howl away
   Ere a forest be stricken down.

VI.

By the martyr'd dead, who for freedom bled,
   By all that man deems divine,
Our patriot band for a sainted land
   Like brothers shall all combine.

VII.

Then, fill to-night, in our halls of light,
   The toast on our lips must be
" The sinewy hand, the glittering brand,
   Our homes and our altars free."

NATIONALITY.

BY THOMAS DAVIS.

I.

A NATION'S voice, a nation's voice—
   It is a solemn thing!
It bids the bondage-sick rejoice—
   'Tis stronger than a king.
'Tis like the light of many stars,
   The sound of many waves;
Which brightly look through prison-bars;
   And sweetly sound in caves.
Yet is it noblest, godliest known,
When righteous triumph swells its tone.

II.

A nation's flag, a nation's flag—
   If wickedly unrolled,
May foes in adverse battle drag
   Its every fold from fold.
But, in the cause of Liberty,
   Guard it 'gainst Earth and Hell;
Guard it till Death or Victory—
   Look you, you guard it well!
No saint or king has tomb so proud,
As he whose flag becomes his shroud.

III.

A nation's right, a nation's right—
   God gave it, and gave, too,
A nation's sword, a nation's might,
   Danger to guard it through.
'Tis freedom from a foreign yoke,
   'Tis just and equal laws,
Which deal unto the humblest folk,
   As in a noble's cause.
On nations fixed in right and truth,
God would bestow eternal youth.

IV.

May Ireland's voice be ever heard,
   Amid the world's applause!
And never be her flag-staff stirred,
   But in an honest cause!
May Freedom be her very breath,
   Be Justice ever dear;
And never an ennobled death
   May son of Ireland fear!
So the Lord God will ever smile,
With guardian grace, upon our isle.

THE SWORD.

What rights the brave? The Sword! What free's the slave? The

Sword! .What cleaves in twain The Des - pot's chain,

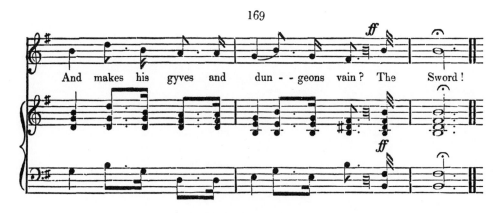

And makes his gyves and dun - - geons vain? The Sword!

CHORUS.

Allegro. *m.f.*

Then cease thy proud task ne - ver, While rests a link to se - ver,

Guard of the free, We'll che - rish thee, And keep thee bright for e - ver.

z

THE SWORD.

BY M. J. BARRY.

I.

WHAT rights the brave?
                    The sword!
What frees the slave?
                    The sword!
What cleaves in twain
The Despot's chain,
And makes his gyves and dungeons vain?
                    The sword!

CHORUS.

Then cease thy proud task never,
While rests a link to sever,
        Guard of the free,
        We'll cherish thee,
And keep thee bright for ever!

II.

What checks the knave?
                    The sword!
What smites to save?
                    The sword!
What wreaks the wrong
Unpunished long,
At last, upon the 'guilty strong?
                    The sword!

CHORUS.

Then cease thy proud task never, &c.

III.

What shelters right?
                    The sword!
What makes it might?
                    The sword!

What strikes the crown
Of tyrants down,
And answers with its flash their frown?
The sword!

CHORUS.

Then cease thy proud task never, &c.

IV.

Still be thou true,
Good sword!
We 'll die or do,
Good sword!
Leap forth to light
If tyrants smite,
And trust our arms to wield thee right,
Good sword!

CHORUS.

Yes! cease thy proud task never,
While rests a link to sever,
Guard of the free,
We 'll cherish thee,
And keep thee bright for ever!

LAMENT FOR EIBHLIN O'BRIN,

WHOM ROGER TYRREL, OF CAISEAL-CNOC,* FORCIBLY CARRIED
AWAY.

I.

SHE is gone—she is gone! where shall Dearmuid find rest,
From the grief of his spirit—the rage of his breast?
Since the child of his chieftain no more may he view,
As fair as the morning and pure as its dew.

---

* Castleknock (the castle hill), is a well-known locality, a short distance N. W. of the
Phœnix Park—it was granted by Henry the Second to Hugh Tyrrel, together with a

z 2

She is gone! Now at eve, by the Life's gay tide,
Who shall lead the aged warrior and watch by his side?
Oh! hate to thee, Tyrrel, for black is thy sin,
Who hast nipp'd in its bloomhood the flow'r of O'Brin.

II.

Young Armoric loved her, and once as she hung
O'er her harp, and the wrongs of green Erin she sung,
He vowed by her beauty, the strength of the land
He would marshal for freedom, or forfeit her hand.
Poor Eibhlin was silent; still trembling she play'd,
While the tears in her dark eye her bosom betrayed:
Ah, madd'ning the thought! that the foes of her kin,
And her country, should rob us of Eibhlin O'Brin.

III.

As here in the depths of the dark tangled wood,*
When the throstle, sweet bird! rears his promising brood,
The spoiler, to mark them, is oft wont to come
Ere he, merciless, plunders their moss-covered home;
So Tyrrel, while ruin his heart had long plann'd,
Watched Eibhlin, to see all her beauties expand,
Then, fiendlike, that heart which he never could win
He tore from the homestead of Tirlogh O'Brin.

---

moiety of the river Lifé. In the early part of the 16th century the Tyrrel of Castleknock was also named Hugh, during whose absence with Skeffington in Ulster, his
brother, Roger Tyrrel, seized Eibhlin O'Brin (or O'Byrne) near her father's residence,
and carried her to that " stronghold of iniquity" where she died by her own hand. A
part of a tower densely covered with ivy, and a wall some eight or ten feet in thickness,
still stand to verify the site of the " stronghold." A treble line of circumvallation is
nearly perfect where the writer of these lines, when freed from his task, has often
gamboled in happy ignorance of the fate of Eibhlin O'Brin, and all the other " iniquities"
of the place, *ferula* excepted.—*See Preface to Burton's Kilmainham; Dalton's
Dublin, &c.*

* O'Brin's residence was on a woody " rath" to the west of where Chapelizod now
stands.—*Burton.*

IV.

How smooth was the Life—how blooming the lawn!
When she went forth as playful and light as a fawn;
Young Armoric greets her—no more could he say,
The ambush are on him—he falls—she's away!
We missed her at twilight, and swift in her track
Our kerns rush fiercely to conquer her back;
But in vain—she's secured the strong castle within,
And the accents of woe fill the home of O'Brin.

V.

We trusted the stranger—we've dwelt on his plain,*
Our safeguard his honor—'tis black with a stain;
Yet he recks not, but laughs in the face of our wail,
For they wrong, then insult us, those lords of the Pale.
Gleann-da-Locha, thy deep sunny vallies for me,
And thy mountains that watch o'er the homes of the free,
Where chieftains, as brave as e'er battle did win,
Would bow to the beauty of Eibhlin O'Brin.

VI.

But we've lost her—up Cualann,† thy warriors awake!
Gleann-dubh, send thy bravest to fight for her sake—
O'Brin! see your name is dishonored—repay
The tyrant whose minions forced Eibhlin away;
O'Tuathail, O'Diomasaigh, your weapons unsheath—
Come down, let your war-cry be " Vengeance or death,"
Nor cease ye one moment, when once ye begin,
Till the life-blood of Tyrrel atone to O'Brin.

---

* Tirlogh O'Brin, one of the chiefs of Wicklow, had come down and fixed his residence in the Pale under the protection of the English government.—*Ibid.*

† An ancient name of the East of Wicklow.—*Ibid.*

‡ O'Toole and O'Dempsy.

A DREAM OF THE FUTURE.

BY D. F. M‘CARTHY.

I.

I DREAMT a dream, a dazzling dream, of a green isle far away,
Where the glowing west to the ocean's breast calleth the dying day;
And that island green was as fair a scene as ever man's eye did see,
With its chieftains bold, and its temples old, and its homes and its
    altars free!
No foreign foe did that green isle know—no stranger band it bore,
Save the merchant train from sunny Spain, and from Afric's golden
    shore!
And the young man's heart would fondly start, and the old man's
    eye would smile,
As their thoughts would roam o'er the ocean foam to that lone and
    " holy isle!"

II.

Years passed by, and the orient sky blazed with a newborn light,
And Bethlehem's star shone bright afar o'er the lost world's dark-
    some night;
And the diamond shrines from plundered mines, and the golden
    fanes of Jove,
Melted away in the blaze of day at the simple spell-word—Love!
The light serene o'er that island green played with its saving beams,
And the fires of Baal waxed dim and pale like the stars in the
    morning streams!
And 'twas joy to hear, in the bright air clear, from out each sunny
    glade,
The tinkling bell, from the quiet cell, or the cloister's tranquil
    shade!

III.

A cloud of night o'er that dream so bright soon with its dark wing
    came,
And the happy scene of that island green was lost in blood and
    shame;
For its kings unjust betrayed their trust, and its queens, though
    fair, were frail—

And a robber band, from a stranger land, with their war-whoops
    filled the gale;
A fatal spell on that green isle fell—a shadow of death and gloom
Passed withering o'er, from shore to shore, like the breath of the
    foul simmoom;
And each green hill's side was crimson dyed, and each stream
    rolled red and wild,
With the mingled blood of the brave and good—of mother, and
    maid, and child!

IV.

Dark was my dream, though many a gleam of hope through that
    black night broke,
Like a star's bright form through a whistling storm, or the moon
    through a midnight oak!
And many a time, with its wings sublime, and its robes of saffron
    light,
Would the morning rise on the eastern skies, but to vanish again
    in night!
For, in abject prayer, the people there still raised their fetter'd hands,
When the sense of right and the power to smite are the spirit that
    commands;
For those who would sneer at the mourner's tear, and heed not
    the suppliant's sigh,
Would bow in awe to that first great law—a banded nation's cry!

V.

At length arose o'er that Isle of woes a dawn with a steadier smile,
And in happy hour a voice of power awoke the slumbering Isle!
And the people all obeyed the call of their chief's unsceptred hand,
Vowing to raise, as in ancient days, the name of their own dear land!
My dream grew bright as the sunbeam's light, as I watched that
    Isle's career
Through the varied scene and the joys serene of many a future
    year—
And, oh! what thrill did my bosom fill, as I gazed on a pillared pile,
Where a senate once more in power watched o'er the rights of that
    lone green Isle!

DALCAIS WAR SONG.

AIR.—*Faз aɲ Bealaċ.*

Dal - cas-sia's war-rior bands now The chase fore- go, the chase fore -go, Far

nobler game demands now The spear and bow, the spear and bow. From mountain, glen, and

val -ley, In bright ar -ray, in bright ar -ray, Round E-rin's standard ral - ly! Let

cow-ards stay, let cowards stay, The SUNBURST that floats o'er us In banner'd pride, in

banner'd pride, Has e-ver wav'd be-fore us O'er Vic- to-ry's tide, o'er Vic- to-ry's tide.

2 A

DALCAIS WAR SONG.

A.D. 1013.

BY M. J. M'CANN.

I.

DALCASSIA's warrior bands, now,
   The chase forego, the chase forego;
Far nobler game demands, now,
   The spear and bow, the spear and bow—
From mountain, glen, and valley,
   In bright array, in bright array,
Round Erin's standard rally!
   Let cowards stay! let cowards stay!
The sun-burst that floats o'er us
   In banner'd pride, in banner'd pride,
Has ever waved before us
   O'er victory's tide! o'er victory's tide!

II.

Who, who, like craven falters,
   Nor bravely draws, nor bravely draws,
To guard his country's altars,
   And homes and laws! and homes and laws!
Who fears, with cause so holy,
   The pirate Dane, the pirate Dane?
Although the Saxon, lowly,
   Now brooks his chain! now brooks his chain!*
The sun-burst that floats o'er us
   In banner'd pride, in banner'd pride,
Has ever waved before us
   O'er victory's tide! o'er victory's tide!

---

* Irishmen should never forget that, at the time of the glorious victory of Clontarf,
the English, our present masters, bowed beneath the Danish yoke.

III.

Still victory's smile is beaming
   Where Morogh leads, where Morogh leads ;
And where his blade is gleaming
   The foeman bleeds ! the foeman bleeds !
Old Brian's dark eye 's glancing
   Along th' array, along th' array ;
And the steed 's impatient prancing—
   Then let 's away ! away ! away !
The sun-burst that floats o'er us
   In banner'd pride, in banner'd pride,
Has ever waved before us
   O'er victory's tide ! o'er victory's tide !

THE BURIAL.

BY THOMAS DAVIS.

WHY rings the knell of the funeral bell from a hundred village
   shrines,
Through broad Fingall, where hasten all those long and order'd
   lines ?
With tear and sigh they 're passing by, the matron and the
   maid—
Has a hero died—is a nation's pride in that cold coffin laid ?
With frown and curse, behind the hearse, dark men go tramping
   on—
Has a tyrant died, that they cannot hide their wrath till the rites
   are done ?

2 A 2

THE CHANT.

" Ululu ! ululu ! high on the wind,
There 's a home for the slave where no fetters can bind."
" Woe, woe to his slayers"—comes wildly along,
With the trampling of feet and the funeral song.

*   *   *   *   *

And now more clear
It swells on the ear;
Breathe low, and listen, 'tis solemn to hear.

*   *   *   *   *

" Ululu ! ululu ! wail for the dead.
" Green grow the grass of Fingall on his head;
" And spring-flowers blossom, ere elsewhere appearing,
" And shamrocks grow thick on the Martyr for Erin.
" Ululu ! ululu ! soft fall the dew
" On the feet and the head of the martyr'd and true."

*   *   *   *   *

For awhile they tread
In silence dread—.
Then muttering and moaning go the crowd,
Surging and swaying like mountain cloud,
And again the wail comes fearfully loud.

THE CHANT.

" Ululu ! ululu ! kind was his heart !
" Walk slower, walk slower, too soon we shall part.
" The faithful and pious, the Priest of the Lord,
" His pilgrimage over, he has his reward.

" By the bed of the sick, lowly kneeling,
" To God with the rais'd cross appealing—
" He seems still to kneel, and he seems still to pray,
" And the sins of the dying seem passing away.

" In the prisoner's cell, and the cabin so dreary,
" Our constant consoler, he never grew weary ;
" But he 's gone to his rest,
" And he 's now with the blest,
" Where tyrant and traitor no longer molest—
" Ululu ! ululu ! wail for the dead !
" Ululu ! ululu ! here is his bed."

*　　*　　*　　*　　*

Short was the ritual, simple the prayer,
Deep was the silence and every head bare ;
The Priest alone standing, they knelt all around,
Myriads on myriads, like rocks on the ground.
Kneeling and motionless—" Dust unto dust."
" He died as becometh the faithful and just—
Placing in God his reliance and trust ;"
Kneeling and motionless—" ashes to ashes"—
Hollow the clay on the coffin-lid dashes ;
Kneeling and motionless, wildly they pray,
But they pray in their souls, for no gesture have they—
Stern and standing—oh ! look on them now,
Like trees to one tempest the multitude bow ;
Like the swell of the ocean is rising their vow :

THE VOW.

" We have bent and borne, though we saw him torn from his
home by the tyrant's crew—
" And we bent and bore, when he came once more, though suffering had pierced him through ;

" And now he is laid beyond our aid, because to Ireland true—
" A martyr'd man—the tyrant's ban, the pious patriot slew.

"And shall we bear and bend for ever,
And shall no time our bondage sever,
And shall we kneel, but battle never,
    For our own soil?
"And shall our tyrants safely reign
On thrones built up of slaves and slain,
And nought to us and ours remain
    But chains and toil?
" No! round this grave our oath we plight,
To watch, and labour, and unite,
'Till banded be the nation's might—
    Its spirit steel'd,
"And then, collecting all our force,
We'll cross oppression in its course,
And die—or all our rights enforce,
    On battle field."

  * * * * *

Like an ebbing sea that will come again,
Slowly retir'd that host of men;
Methinks they'll keep some other day
The oath they swore on the martyr's clay.

THE EXTERMINATOR'S SONG.

BY JOHN CORNELIUS O'CALLAGHAN.

I.

'Tis I am the poor man's scourge,
　And where is the scourge like me?
My land, from all papists I purge,
　Who think that their votes should be free—
　Who think that their votes should be free!
For huts only fitted for brutes,
　My agent the last penny wrings;
And my serfs live on water and roots,
　While I feast on the best of good things!
　　For I am the poor man's scourge!
　　For I am the poor man's scourge!

(Chorus of the Editors of the Nation)

　Yes, *you* are the poor man's scourge!
　But of *such* the whole island we'll purge!

II.

A despot, and strong one, am I,
　Since a Drummond no longer is here,
To my " *duties*" to point ev'ry eye,
　Though of " *rights*" I wish only to hear—
　Though of " *rights*" I wish only to hear!
If conspiracies I apprehend,
　To throw off my rack-renting rule,
For a " *Special Commission*" I send
　To my friends of the old Tory school!
　　For I am the poor man's scourge!
　　For I am the poor man's scourge!

(Chorus of the Editors of the Nation)

　Yes, *you* are the poor man's scourge!
　But of *such* the whole island we'll purge!

III.

I prove to the world I'm a man,
　In a way very pleasant to show;
I corrupt all the tenants I can,
　　And of children I have a long row—
　　And of children I have a long row!
My cottiers must all cringe to me,
　Nor grudge me the prettiest lass;
Or they know very well that they'll see
　Their hovels as flat as the grass!
　　　For I am the poor man's scourge!
　　　For I am the poor man's scourge!

(Chorus of the Editors of the Nation)

Yes, *you* are the poor man's scourge!
But of *such* the whole island we'll purge!

IV.

If a Connor my right should deny,
　To "do what I like with my own!"
For the rascal I've soon a reply,
　　Into gaol for "*sedition*" he's thrown—
　　Into gaol for "*sedition*" he's thrown!
The Tariff is bringing rents down—
　Yet more cash from the farmer I'll squeeze;
And, for fear of being shot, come to town
　To drink, game, and intrigue at my ease!
　　　For I am the poor man's scourge!
　　　For I am the poor man's scourge!

(Chorus of the Editors of the Nation)

Yes, *you* are the poor man's scourge!
But of *such* the whole island we'll purge!

ANNIE, DEAR.

AIR.—*"Maids in May."*

Our moun-tain brooks were rush-ing, An-nie, Dear; The Autumn eve was

flush - ing, An - nie, Dear, But bright - er was your blush-ing, When

first your mur-murs hush-ing, I told my love out-gush-ing An-nie, Dear.

2 B

ANNIE DEAR.

BY THOMAS DAVIS.

I.

Our mountain brooks were rushing,
                Annie, dear,
The Autumn eve was flushing,
                Annie, dear;
But brighter was your blushing,
When first, your murmurs hushing,
I told my love outgushing,
                Annie, dear.

II.

Ah! but our hopes were splendid,
                Annie, dear,
How sadly they have ended
                Annie, dear;
The ring betwixt us broken,
When our vows of love were spoken,
Of your poor heart was a token,
                Annie, dear.

III.

The primrose flow'rs were shining,
                Annie, dear,
When, on my breast reclining,
                Annie, dear,
Began our Mi-na-Meala,
And many a month did follow
Of joy—but life is hollow,
                Annie, dear.

IV.

For once, when home returning,
                Annie, dear,
I found our cottage burning,
                Annie, dear;
Around it were the yeomen,
Of every ill an omen,
The country's bitter foemen,
                Annie, dear.

v.

But why arose a morrow,
    Annie, dear,
Upon that night of sorrow,
    Annie, dear?
Far better, by thee lying,
Their bayonets defying,
Than live an exile sighing,
    Annie dear.

HOPE DEFERRED.

BY THOMAS DAVIS.

AIR—"*Oh! art thou gone, my Mary dear?*"

I.

'Tis long since we were forced to part, at least it seems so to my grief,
For sorrow wearies us like time, but ah! it brings not time's relief;
As in our days of tenderness, before me still she seems to glide;
And, though my arms are wide as then, yet she will not abide.
The day-light and the star-light shine, as if her eyes were in their light,
And, whispering in the panting breeze, her love-songs come at lonely night;
While, far away with those less dear, she tries to hide her grief in vain,
For, kind to all while true to me, it pains her to give pain.

II.

I know she never spoke her love, she never breathed a single vow,
And yet I'm sure she lov'd me then, and still doats on me now;
For, when we met, her eyes grew glad, and heavy, when I left her side,
And oft she said she'd be most happy as a poor man's bride;
I toil'd to win a pleasant home, and make it ready by the spring;
The spring is past—what season now my girl unto our home will bring?
I'm sick and weary, very weary—watching, morning, night, and noon;
How long you're coming—I am dying—will you not come soon?

A NEW YEAR'S SONG.

You've brave - - ly march'd, and no - - bly met, Our
lit - - tle green isle through; But oh! my friends, there's
some - thing yet For I - - rish - men to do.

A NEW YEAR'S SONG.

BY D. F. M'CARTHY.

I.

My countrymen, awake! arise!
  Our work begins anew,
Your mingled voices rend the skies,
  Your hearts are firm and true,
You 've bravely marched, and nobly met,
  Our little green isle through;
But, oh! my friends, there 's something yet
  For Irishmen to do!

II.

As long as Erin hears the clink
  Of base ignoble chains—
As long as one detested link
  Of foreign rule remains—
As long as of our rightful debt
  One smallest fraction 's due,
So long, my friends, there 's something yet
  For Irishmen to do!

III.

Too long we 've borne the servile yoke—
  Too long the slavish chain—
Too long in feeble accents spoke,
  And ever spoke in vain—
Our wealth has filled the spoiler's net,
  And gorg'd the Saxon crew;
But, oh! my friends, we 'll teach them yet
  What Irishmen can do!

IV.

The olive branch is in our hands,
  The white flag floats above;
Peace—peace pervades our myriad bands,
  And proud forgiving love!

But, oh! let not our foes forget
  We're *men*, as Christians, too,
Prepared to do for Ireland yet
  What Irishmen should do!

v.

There's not a man of all our land
  Our country now can spare,
The strong man with his sinewy hand,
  The weak man with his prayer!
No whining tone of mere regret,
  Young Irish bards, for you;
But let your songs teach Ireland yet
  What Irishmen should do!

vi.

And wheresoe'er that duty lead,
  There—there your post should be;
The coward slave is never freed;
  The brave alone are free!
Oh! Freedom, firmly fixed are set
  Our longing eyes on you;
And though we die for Ireland yet,
  So Irishmen should do!

CELTS AND SAXONS.*

BY THOMAS DAVIS.

I.

WE hate the Saxon and the Dane,
  We hate the Norman men—
We curs'd their greed for blood and gain,
  We curse them now again.

---

* Written in reply to some very beautiful verses printed in the *Evening Mail*, deprecating and defying the assumed hostility of the Irish Celts to the *Irish* Saxons.

Yet start not, Irish born man,
  If you 're to Ireland true,
We heed not blood, nor creed, nor clan—
  We have no curse for you.

II.

We have no curse for you or your's,
  But Friendship's ready grasp,
And Faith to stand by you and your's,
  Unto our latest gasp—
To stand by you against all foes,
  Howe'er, or whence they come,
With traitor arts, or bribes, or blows,
  From England, France, or Rome.

III.

What matter that at diff'rent shrines
  We pray unto one God—
What matter that at diff'rent times
  Our fathers won this sod—
In fortune and in name we 're bound
  By stronger links than steel,
And neither can be safe nor sound
  But in the other's weal.

IV.

As Nubian rocks, and Ethiop sand
  Long drifting down the Nile,
Built up old Egypt's fertile land
  For many a hundred mile;
So Pagan clans to Ireland came,
  And clans of Christendom,
Yet joined their wisdom and their fame
  To build a nation from.

V.

Here came the brown Phœnician,
  The man of trade and toil—

Here came the proud Milesian,
  Ahungering for spoil;
And the Firbolg and the Cymry,
  And the hard, enduring Dane,
And the iron Lords of Normandy,
  With the Saxons in their train.

VI.

And oh! it were a gallant deed
  To show before mankind,
How every race and every creed
  Might be by love combined—
Might be combined, yet not forget
  The fountains whence they rose,
As, filled by many a rivulet
  The stately Sionainn flows.

VII.

Nor would we wreak our ancient feud
  On Belgian or on Dane,
Nor visit in a hostile mood
  The hearths of Gaul or Spain;
But long as on our country lies
  The Anglo-Norman yoke,
Their tyranny we'll signalize,
  And God's revenge invoke.

VIII.

We do not hate, we never curs'd,
  Nor spoke a foeman's word
Against a man in Ireland nurs'd,
  Howe'er we thought he err'd;
So start not, Irish born man,
  If you're to Ireland true,
We heed not race, nor creed, nor clan,
  We've hearts and hands for you.

2 c

THE MUNSTER WAR-SONG.

A.D. 1190.*

BY R. D. WILLIAMS.

AIR—"*And doth not a meeting.*"

I.

CAN the depths of the ocean afford you not graves,
That you come thus to perish afar o'er the waves;
To redden and swell the wild torrents that flow
Through the valley of vengeance, the dark Eatharlach.†

II.

The clangour of conflict o'erburthens the breeze,
From the stormy Sliabh Bloom to the stately Gailltees;
Your caverns and torrents are purple with gore,
Sliabh na m-Ban,‡ Gleann Colaich, and sublime Gailte Mór.

III.

The sun-burst that slumbered, embalmed in our tears,
Tipperary! shall wave o'er thy tall mountaineers!
And the dark hill shall bristle with sabre and spear,
While one tyrant remains to forge manacles here.

IV.

The riderless war-steed careers o'er the plain,
With a shaft in his flank and a blood dripping mane,
His gallant breast labours, and glare his wild eyes;
He plunges in torture—falls—shivers—and dies.

---

* This song relates to the time when the Irish began to rally and unite against their invaders. The union was, alas! brief, but its effects were great. The troops of Connaught and Ulster, under Cathal Croibh-dearg (Cathal O'Connor of the Red Hand,) defeated and slew Armoric St. Lawrence, and stripped De Courcy of half of his conquests. But the ballad relates to Munster; and an extract from Moore's (the most accessible) book will show that there was solid ground for triumph:—" Among the chiefs who agreed at this crisis to postpone their mutual feuds, and act in concert against the enemy, were O'Brian of Thomond, and MacCarthy of Desmond, hereditary rulers of North and South Munster, and chiefs respectively of the two rival tribes, the Dalcassians and Eoganians. By a truce now formed between those princes, O'Brian was left free to direct his arms against the English; and having attacked their forces at Thurles, in Fogarty's country, gave them A COMPLETE OVERTHROW, putting to the sword, add the Munster annals, a great number of knights."—*Moore's History of Ireland,* *A.D.* 1190.

† Aharlow glen, County Tipperary.   ‡ Slievenamon.

V.

Let the trumpets ring triumph! the tyrant is slain,
He reels o'er his charger deep pierced through the brain;
And his myriads are flying like leaves on the gale,
But, who shall escape from our hills with the tale?

VI.

For the arrows of vengeance are show'ring like rain,
And choke the strong rivers with islands of slain,
Till thy waves, "lordly Sionainn," all crimsonly flow,
Like the billows of hell, with the blood of the foe.

VII.

Ay! the foemen are flying, but vainly they fly—
Revenge with the fleetness of lightning, can vie;
And the septs of the mountains spring up from each rock,
And rush down the ravines like wolves on the flock.

VIII.

And who shall pass over the stormy Sliabh Bloom,
To tell the pale Saxon of tyranny's doom;
When, like tigers from ambush, our fierce mountaineers,
Leap along from the crags with their death-dealing spears?

IX.

They came with high boasting to bind us as slaves;
But the glen and the torrent have yawned for their graves—
From the gloomy Ard Fionnain to wild Teampoll Mór—*
From the Siur to the Sionainn—is red with their gore.

X.

By the soul of Heremon! our warriors may smile,
To remember the march of the foe through our isle;
Their banners and harness were costly and gay,
And proudly they flash'd in the summer sun's ray;

XI.

The hilts of their falchions were crusted with gold,
And the gems of their helmets were bright to behold;
By Saint Bride of Cildare! but they moved in fair show—
To gorge the young eagles of dark Eatharlach!

---

* Ardfinnan and Templemore.

2 c 2

THE PENAL DAYS.

Air.—"*The Wheelwright.*"

Allegretto.

Oh! weep those days, those pe - nal days, When

Ire - - land hope - less - ly com - plain'd, Oh! weep those days, the

pe - nal days, When god - less per - se - cution reign'd. When year by year, For

serf and peer, Fresh cru- el- ties were made by law, And, fill'd with hate, Our

Se - nate sate, To weld a- new each fetter's flaw! Oh! weep those days, those

pe - nal days, — Their mem' - ry still on Ire - land weighs.

THE PENAL DAYS.

BY THOMAS DAVIS.

Air—"*The Wheelwright.*"

I.

Oh! weep those days, the penal days,
    When Ireland hopelessly complained.
Oh! weep those days, the penal days,
    When godless persecution reigned;
        When, year by year,
        For serf, and peer,
    Fresh cruelties were made by law,
        And, fill'd with hate,
        Our senate sate
To weld anew each fetter's flaw.
Oh! weep those days, those penal days—
Their mem'ry still on Ireland weighs.

II.

They bribed the flock, they bribed the son,
    To sell the priest and rob the sire;
Their dogs were taught alike to run
    Upon the scent of wolf and friar.
        Among the poor,
        Or on the moor,
Were hid the pious and the true—
        While traitor knave,
        And recreant slave,
    Had riches, rank, and retinue.
And, exiled in those penal days,
Our banners over Europe blaze.

III.

A stranger held the land and tower
    Of many a noble fugitive;
No Popish lord had lordly power,
    The peasant scarce had leave to live:

Above his head
A ruined shed,
No tenure but a tyrant's will—
Forbid to plead,
Forbid to read,
Disarm'd, disfranchis'd, imbecile—
What wonder if our step betrays
The freedman, born in penal days ?

IV.

They 're gone, they 're gone, those penal days,
   All creeds are equal in our isle ;
Then grant, O Lord, thy plenteous grace,
   Our ancient feuds to reconcile.
     Let all atone
     For blood and groan,
For dark revenge and open wrong ;
     Let all unite
     For Ireland's right,
And drown our griefs in Freedom's song ;
Till time shall veil in twilight haze,
The memory of those penal days.

ENGLAND'S ULTIMATUM.

" Repeal must not be argued with. Were the Union gall it must be maintained.—
Ireland must have England as her sister, or her subjugatrix. This is our ultimatum."
—*Times.*

I.

SLAVES lie down and kiss your chains,
   To the Union yield in quiet.
Were it hemlock in your veins,
   Stand it must—*we* profit by it.

II.

English foot on Irish neck,
  English gyve on Irish sinew,
Ireland swayed at England's beck—
  So it is, and shall continue.

III.

English foot on Irish neck,
  Pine or rot, meanwhile, we care not.
Little will we pause to reck
  How you writhe, while rise you dare not.

IV.

Argue with you !—stoop to show
  Our dominions' just foundation !
Savage Celts ! and dare you so
  Task the Lords of half creation.

V.

Argue ! do not ask again,
  Proofs enough there are to sway you,
Three-and-twenty thousand men,
  Whom a word will loose to slay you.

VI.

Store of arguments besides,
  In their time we will exhibit,
Leaded thongs for rebel hides,
  Flaming thatch, and burthen'd gibbet.

VII.

Bid your fathers tell how we
  Proved our rights in bygone seasons.
Slaves ! and sons of slaves !—your knee—
  Bow to *sister* England's reasons.

SLIABH CUILINN.

THE THIRTIETH OF MAY.

I.

WHAT vast and eager numbers
  Through joyous Dublin seen;
Broad flags and arching boughs displayed,
And see! yon glittering lines arrayed
  In martial suits of green.
What now, with gleaming lance and gun,
  Doth chainless Erin need?
Long since her battle hath been won—
The wasting war of ages done—
  Her soil and people freed.

II.

Ten thousand Irish soldiers
  To-morrow cross the main:
By Dnieper shall their carbines ring,
Their charge cleave open Russia's wing—
  On 'leaguer'd Warsaw's plain;
For we who felt oppression's heel,
  Aid struggling freedom's powers,
And long as help us arm and steel,
While Irish waters float a keel,
  Shall Poland's fight be ours.

III.

They cross the sea to-morrow,
  France joins them on their track—
God's blessing on their allied swords,
And may He blast the despot's hordes,
  And sweep them howling back;
But, ere they go, a solemn call
  Leads out their files to-day—
Them and our people, one and all—
For this is Ireland's festival,
  THE THIRTIETH MORN OF MAY.

2 D

IV.

Our dear familiar music,
  Rung out by trump and drum,
A shout to Heaven's gray vaulting sent,
For through the gates of Parliament
  They come, at length they come.
Our deputies, the land's elect,
  Her choice of worth and mind—
The judges in their ermines decked,
And hierarchs of every sect
  In Christian love combined.

V.

In front of Sarsfield's statue
  In long array they form,
Senate and council, man by man,
Our Polish conscripts in the van,
  Around a countless swarm ;
From every corner of the land,
  Of every age and grade,
For who would miss a sight so grand ?—
To them whom alien tyrants banned,
  A nation's honors paid.

VI.

See here our Irish peasants,
  The yeomen of the soil,
Who share a more than kingly fate,
Free farms and homes inviolate,
  And comfort sweetening toil :
Look on their frank and happy gaze,
  The gay dress loosely worn,
The jest around the lip that plays—
Great God ! to think in other days
  What men like these have borne.

VII.

See, too, the grave mechanic,
    His wife and babes beside,
To taste the general joy come forth;
What unobtrusive sense and worth
    In those deep eyes abide!
Unlike the squalid bands that yelled
    Round England's blazing halls.
From labour, here not self-impelled,
But guided, cultured, sentinelled,
    No fruit save blessing falls.

VIII.

The artist, too, is gazing
    With visioned eye that glows—
Young students with the yearning heart
Upon that bright career to start,
    Their country's hopes disclose.
And many a stranger wafted o'er
    To witness such a day,
And mariners from every shore,
Whose masts down all the river soar,
    And crowd our glorious bay.

IX.

But all the thousand banners
    To Spring's free breezes flung,
Are stamped with one world-famous name—
Sign-post and lintel bear the same:
    It hangs on every tongue.
Nigh fifty years of wrong and ill
    Our guide and champion set;
Lord of our father's love and will,
Though long that royal heart is still,
    His spirit sways as yet.

X.

Another burst of music
　To greet them as they march,
With measured step and buoyant air,
Through many a spacious street and square,
　And many a stately arch.
Bright eyes from every window gleam—
　Fair arms a welcome wave—
For very joy the children scream,
And old men kindle up and seem
　As they would cheat the grave.

XI.

Thus march they thro' the city,
　With pomp triumphal crown'd,
And reach at length an ample green,
With trees and sparkling founts between,
　And statues scattered round;
And in the midst a column tall,
　To latest time a sign,
Beyond it, hallowed more than all,
That pile—'twas Richmond's prison wall—
　'Tis freedom's holiest shrine.

XII.

Upon it two inscriptions
　A deathless record keep—
One bidding guilt seek better ways,
The other carved of later days,
　In letters black and deep—
Black as the story they impart,
　As all that hideous past;
Deep as it sank in Ireland's heart,
HERE FOREIGN POWER, BY FOULEST ART,
　OUR COUNTRY'S SAVIOUR CAST.

XIII.

No breast but feels and worships
   The genius of the spot;
And every head is bowed and bare,
While brief but deep the freeman's prayer
   Is breathed for blessings wrought;
Till rises one above the rest—
   An honored name and good—
And round him throng, with lip compress'd,
With gleaming eye and swelling breast,
   The silent multitude.

XIV.

Once more, once more, my brothers,
   We meet in solemn rite,
High thought and purpose stern, to draw,
With hate of foreign lords and law,
   And nerve for Ireland's fight—
In grateful mem'ry of the dead
   Who wrought and suffered here,
And chief, of him whose name is spread
Wide earth around—the despot's dread,
   The freeman's rallying cheer.

XV.

Of him who found his country
   Down-stricken, gagged, and chained;
Who, battling still, untired, unawed,
From triumph on to triumph trod,
   In bloodless warfare gained.
Peace was his idol—truth his sword,
   And that they knew full well
Who dared a monarch so adored,
With countless armies at his word,
   To lock in prison-cell.

XVI.

Had he but raised one finger,
    One signal whisper dealt,
To those strong millions raging ripe,
Typhoon or earthquake were a type
    Of what our isle had felt;
For all the hoarded hate of old
    By that last deed was fed,
And had the convict slipped his hold,
Their fury, bursting uncontrolled,
    Had made the green sod red.

XVII.

And England might have cluster'd
    Her pow'rs by land and sea;
But hosts like ocean, wave on wave,
Though every furrow were a grave
    Subdued could never be—
Impassioned, outraged, reckless men,
    With freedom for their meed;
Nor were there wanting spirits then,
Of mind more trained and deeper ken,
    To marshal and to lead.

XVIII.

But his great soul was melted
    With pity as he viewed,
In that dark future, carnage rife
And spectres dread, of torch and knife,
    In kindred blood imbued;
For yet by bigot feuds insane
    Our hapless isle was tost,
And war had seen such horrors reign,
He well might doubt if earthly gain
    Could balance such a cost.

XIX.

And, oh! next Heaven, be rendered
　To him thanksgiving deep,
Who stilled the gathering tempest then,
That victory might come agen,
　So glorious and so cheap—
Be his the praise that Europe's seas
　This day our vessels fill:
The merchant's wealth, the peasant's ease,
And more ennobling gifts than these,
　And blessings richer still.

XX.

Th' inspiring sense of Freedom,
　Electric in our veins—
The daring heart, and soaring mind,
Yon free flag dancing to the wind—
　These be our priceless gains.
Well we with Genoa's son may say,
　That response true, as brave:
Better to live man's life one day
Than sleep a hundred years away
　A brute, or stone, or slave.

XXI.

The swords which guard that Freedom,
　Thank God, are stainless still;
They were not forged to crush the weak,
To hunt down patriot hearts, or wreak
　A plunderer's guilty will;
But wheresoever, near or far,
　Invaded justice pines,
Where right maintains unequal war,
There Ireland's banner, like a star
　Of hope and succour, shines.

XXII.

And ye, young pilgrim warriors,
  Whose lifted glances tell
Of valour's pride, and zeal, that fear,
Were Death, in bloody terrors, near,
  In vain would seek to quell.
Go, let the Phalanx of the West,
  In storm of battle be
A thunderbolt in Russia's breast,
Till rescued Poland raise her crest
  Enthroned amid the free.

XXIII.

Then, oh! may she and Erin
  Be knit together long
In virtue's quarrel side by side,
With souls by sorrow purified,
  And quenchless hate of wrong;
In joy and freedom, sisters dear,
  As once in thrall and woe!
When he, the mighty captive here,
Deep poured her griefs in every ear,
  And curses on her foe.

XXIV.

Oh, prison-walls of Richmond,
  Whatever time may stain,
So long as man in honored place
Shall hold the champions of his race,
  Your memory shall remain;
And Ireland—cramped her heart must be
  By worse than English sway,
When she shall cease this dawn to see,
In grateful pride and festal glee,
  The Thirtieth Morn of May.

                          SLIABH CUILINN.

OH! FOR A STEED.

Oh! for a steed, a rushing steed, and a blaz-ing sci - mi - - - tar, To
and dear Poland gather'd a - - round, To

hunt from beauteous It - a - - ly the Aus - tri - an's red hus - sar, To mock their boasts, And
smite her cir-cle of sa-vage foes and smash them up - on the ground, Nor hold my hand While

strew their hosts And scat-ter their flags a - far, And scat-ter their flags a - - - - far.
on the land A fo-reign-er foe was found, A fo - - reigner foe was found.

2 E

OH! FOR A STEED.

BY THOMAS DAVIS.

I.

Oh! for a steed, a rushing steed, and a blazing scimitar,
To hunt from beauteous Italy the Austrian's red hussar;
To mock their boasts,
And strew their hosts,
And scatter their flags afar.

II.

Oh! for a steed, a rushing steed, and dear Poland gather'd around,
To smite her circle of savage foes, and smash them upon the ground;
Nor hold my hand
While, on the land,
A foreigner foe was found.

III.

Oh! for a steed, a rushing steed, and a rifle that never failed,
And a tribe of terrible prairie men, by desperate valour mailed,
Till "stripes and stars,"
And Russian czars,
Before the Red Indian quailed.

IV.

Oh! for a steed, a rushing steed, on the plains of Hindostan,
And a hundred thousand cavaliers, to charge like a single man,
Till our shirts were red,
And the English fled
Like a cowardly caravan.

V.

Oh! for a steed, a rushing steed, with the Greeks at Marathon,
Or a place in the Switzer phalanx, when the Morat men swept on,
Like a pine-clad hill
By an earthquake's will
Hurl'd the vallies upon.

VI.

Oh! for a steed, a rushing steed, when Brian smote down the
    Dane,
Or a place beside great Aodh O'Neill, when Bagenal the bold was
    slain,
            Or a waving crest
            And a lance in rest,
        With Bruce upon Bannoch plain.

VII.

Oh! for a steed, a rushing steed, on the Currach of Cilldar,
And Irish squadrons skilled to do, as they are ready to dare—
            A hundred yards,
            And Holland's guards
        Drawn up to engage me there.

VIII.

Oh! for a steed, a rushing steed, and any good cause at all,
Or else, if you will, a field on foot, or guarding a leaguered wall
            For freedom's right;
            In flushing fight
        To conquer if then to fall.

THE VOICE AND PEN.

BY D. F. M'CARTHY.

I.

Oh! the orator's voice is a mighty power
    As it echoes from shore to shore—
And the fearless pen has more sway o'er men
    Than the murderous cannon's roar.
What burst the chain far o'er the main,
    And brightens the captive's den?
'Tis the fearless voice and the pen of power—
    Hurrah! for the Voice and Pen!
                Hurrah!
    Hurrah! for the Voice and Pen!

II.

The tyrant knaves who deny our rights,
   And the cowards who blanch with fear,
Exclaim with glee, " no arms have ye—
   Nor cannon, nor sword, nor spear!
Your hills are ours; with our forts and tow'rs
   We are masters of mount and glen"—
Tyrants, beware! for the arms we bear,
   Are the Voice and the fearless Pen!
               Hurrah!
   Hurrah! for the Voice and Pen!

III.

Though your horsemen stand with their bridles in hand,
   And your sentinels walk around—
Though your matches flare, in the midnight air,
   And your brazen trumpets sound;
Oh! the orator's tongue shall be heard among
   These listening warrior men,
And they 'll quickly say, " why should we slay
   Our friends of the Voice and Pen?"
               Hurrah!
   Hurrah! for the Voice and Pen!

IV.

When the Lord created the earth and sea,
   The stars and the glorious sun,
The Godhead *spoke*, and the universe woke,
   And the mighty work was done!
Let a word be flung from the orator's tongue,
   Or a drop from the fearless pen,
And the chains accursed asunder burst,
   That fettered the minds of men!
               Hurrah!
   Hurrah! for the Voice and Pen!

V.

Oh! these are the swords with which we fight,
   The arms in which we trust;
Which no tyrant hand will dare to brand,
   Which time cannot dim or rust!
When these we bore, we triumphed before,
   With these we'll triumph again—
And the world will say, " no power can stay
   The Voice and the fearless Pen!"
                 Hurrah!
Hurrah! for the Voice and Pen!

FONTENOY.

BY THOMAS DAVIS.

I.

THRICE, at the huts of Fontenoy, the English column failed,
And, twice, the lines of Saint Antoin, the Dutch in vain assailed;
For town and slope were guarded with fort and artillery,
And well they swept the English ranks, and Dutch auxiliary.
As vainly, through De Barri's wood, the British soldiers burst—
The French artillery drove them back, diminished, and dispersed.
The bloody Duke of Cumberland beheld with anxious eye,
And ordered up his last reserve, his latest chance to try.
On Fontenoy, on Fontenoy, how fast his gen'rals ride!
And mustering come his chosen troops, like clouds at eventide.

II.

Six thousand English veterans, in stately column tread,
Their cannon blaze in front and flank, Lord Hay is at their head;
Steady they step a-down the slope—steady they climb the hill;
Steady they load—steady they fire, moving right onward still,

Betwixt the wood and Fontenoy, as through a furnace blast,
Through rampart, trench, and palisade, and bullets show'ring fast;
And on the open plain above they rose, and kept their course,
With ready fire and steadiness—that mocked at hostile force,
Past Fontenoy, past Fontenoy, while thinner grow their ranks—
They break, as broke the Zuyder Zee through Holland's ocean
　　banks.

III.

More idly than the summer flies, French tirailleurs rush round;
As stubble to the lava tide, French squadrons strew the ground;
Bomb-shell, and grape, and round-shot tore, still on they marched
　　and fired—
Fast, from each volley, grenadier and voltigeur retired.
"Push on, my household cavalry," King Louis madly cried:
To death they rush, but rude their shock—not unavenged they
　　died.
On through the camp the column trod—King Louis turns his rein:
"Not yet, my liege," Saxe interposed, "the Irish troops remain;"
And Fontenoy, famed Fontenoy, had been a Waterloo,
Were not these exiles ready then, fresh, vehement, and true.

IV.

"Lord Clare," he says, "you have your wish, there are your
　　Saxon foes,"
The Marshal almost smiles to see, so furiously he goes!
How fierce the look these exiles wear, who're wont to be so gay,
The treasured wrongs of fifty years are in their hearts to-day,
The treaty broken, ere the ink wherewith 'twas writ could dry,
Their plundered homes, their ruined shrines, their women's part-
　　ing cry,
Their priesthood hunted down like wolves, their country over-
　　thrown—
Each looks, as if revenge for all rested on him alone.

On Fontenoy, on Fontenoy, nor ever yet elsewhere,
Rushed on to fight a nobler band than these proud exiles were.

v.

O'Brien's voice is hoarse with joy, as, halting, he commands,
" Fix bay'nets"—" charge."—Like mountain storm, rush on these
    fiery bands!
Thin is the English column now, and faint their volleys grow,
Yet, must'ring all the strength they have, they make a gallant
    show.
They dress their ranks upon the hill to face that battle-wind—
Their bayonets the breakers' foam; like rocks, the men behind!
One volley crashes from their line, when, through the surging
    smoke,
With empty guns clutched in their hands, the headlong Irish
    broke.
On Fontenoy, on Fontenoy, hark to that fierce huzzah,
" Revenge! remember Limerick! dash down the Sasanach!"

vi.

Like lions leaping at a fold, when mad with hunger's pang,
Right up against the English line the Irish exiles sprang.
Bright was their steel, 'tis bloody now, their guns are filled with
    gore;
Through shattered ranks, and severed files, and trampled flags
    they tore.
The English strove with desp'rate strength, paused, rallied,
    staggered, fled—
The green hill side is matted close with dying and with dead.
Across the plain, and far away passed on that hideous wrack,
While cavalier and fantassin dash in upon their track.
On Fontenoy, on Fontenoy, like eagles in the sun,
With bloody plumes the Irish stand—the field is fought and won!

UP! FOR THE GREEN.

AIR.—"*The Wearing of the Green.*"

'Tis the green,—oh! the green is the co - lor of the true, And we'll

back it 'gainst the o - range, and we'll raise it o'er the blue; For the

co-lor of our Fatherland a - lone should here be seen, 'Tis the co - lor of the martyr'd dead, our

own im-mor-tal green. Then up! for the green, boys, and up! for the green; Oh! 'tis

down in the dust, and a shame to be seen; But we've hands, oh! we've hands, boys, full

strong e-nough, I ween, To res-cue and to raise a-gain our own im-mor-tal green!

2 F

UP FOR THE GREEN!

A SONG OF THE UNITED IRISHMEN.

A.D. 1796.

I.

'TIS the green—oh, the green is the colour of the true,
And we 'll back it 'gainst the orange, and we 'll raise it o'er the blue!
For the colour of our Fatherland alone should here be seen—
'Tis the colour of the martyr'd dead—our own immortal green
    Then up for the green, boys, and up for the green!
    Oh, 'tis down to the dust, and a shame to be seen;
    But we 've hands—oh, we 've hands, boys, full strong enough,
        I ween,
    To rescue and to raise again our own immortal green!

II.

They may say they have power 'tis vain to oppose—
'Tis better to obey and live, than surely die as foes;
But we scorn all their threats, boys, whatever they may mean;
For we trust in God above us, and we dearly love the green.
    So, we 'll up for the green, and we 'll up for the green!
    Oh, to *die* is far better than be curst as we have been;
    And we 've hearts—oh, we 've hearts, boys, full true enough
        I ween,
    To rescue and to raise again our own immortal green!

III.

They may swear as they often did, our wretchedness to cure;
But we 'll never trust John Bull again, nor let his lies allure.
No, we won't—no, we won't, Bull, for now nor ever more!
For we 've hopes on the ocean, and we 've trust on the shore.
    Then up for the green, boys, and up for the green!
    Shout it back to the Sasanach, "We 'll *never* sell the green!"
    For our TONE is coming back, and with men enough, I ween,
    To rescue, and avenge us and our own immortal green.

IV.

Oh, remember the days when their reign we did disturb,
At ꞮꞭꞮꞮꞮꞮꞮꞮꞮ* and ꞮꞭꞮꞮꞮ †—Blackwater and ꞮꞭꞮꞮꞮꞮꞮꞮ; ‡
And ask this proud Saxon if our blows he did enjoy,
When we met him on the battle-field, of France—at Fontenoy.
    Then we 'll up for the green, boys, and up for the green !
    Oh, 'tis *still* in the dust, and a shame to be seen ;
    But we 've hearts and we 've hands, boys, full strong enough,
      I ween,
To rescue and to raise again our own unsullied green !

FERMOY.

MY LAND.

BY THOMAS DAVIS.

I.

She is a rich and rare land ;
Oh ! she 's a fresh and fair land ;
She is a dear and rare land—
This native land of mine.

II.

No men than her's are braver—
Her women's hearts ne'er waver ;
I 'd freely die to save her,
And think my lot divine.

III.

She 's not a dull or cold land ;
No ! she 's a warm and bold land ;
Oh ! she 's a true and old land—
This native land of mine.

IV.

Could beauty ever guard her,
And virtue still reward her,
No foe would cross her border—
No friend within it pine !

V.

Oh, she 's a fresh and fair land ;
Oh, she 's a true and rare land !
Yes, she 's a rare and fair land—
This native land of mine.

---

* Limerick.   † Mispelled Thurles.   ‡ Benburb.

OH! THE MARRIAGE.

AIR—*"The Swaggering Jig."*

Oh! the mar-riage, the marriage, With Love, and mo buacaıl for me, The

la - dies that ride in a car - riage Might en - vy my marriage to me. For

Eó - ɡaṅ is straight as a tow - er, And ten - der and lov - ing and true; He

told me more love in an hour Than the squires of the coun-ty could do.Then

oh! the mar-riage, the mar-riage,With love, and mo buaċaıl for me,The

la - dies that ride in a car-riage Might en-vy my mar-riage to me.

OH! THE MARRIAGE.

BY THOMAS DAVIS.

AIR—"*The Swaggering Jig.*"

I.

Oh! the marriage, the marriage,
  With love and *mo bhuachail* for me,
The ladies that ride in a carriage
  Might envy my marriage to me;
For Eoghan* is straight as a tower,
  And tender and loving and true,
He told me more love in an hour
  Than the Squires of the county could do.
          Then, Oh! the marriage, &c.

II.

His hair is a shower of soft gold,
  His eye is as clear as the day,
His conscience and vote were unsold
  When others were carried away—
His word is as good as an oath,
  And freely 'twas given to me—
Oh! sure 'twill be happy for both
  The day of our marriage to see.
          Then, Oh! the marriage, &c.

III.

His kinsmen are honest and kind,
  The neighbours think much of his skill,
And Eoghan's the lad to my mind,
  Though he owns neither castle nor mill.
But he has a tilloch of land,
  A horse, and a stocking of coin,
A foot for the dance, and a hand
  In the cause of his country to join.
          Then, Oh! the marriage, &c.

---

* *Vulgo* "Owen;" but that is, properly, a name among the Cymry (Welsh.)

IV.

We meet in the market and fair—
   We meet in the morning and night—
He sits on the half of my chair,
   And my people are wild with delight.
Yet I long through the winter to skim,
   Though Eoghan longs more I can see,
When I will be married to him,
   And he will be married to me.
        Then, Oh! the marriage, the marriage,
          With love and *mo bhuachail* for me,
        The ladies that ride in a carriage
          Might envy my marriage to me.

THE PLACE WHERE MAN SHOULD DIE.

BY M., J. BARRY.

I.

How little recks it where men lie,
   When once the moment's past
In which the dim and glazing eye
   Has looked on earth its last—
Whether beneath the sculptured urn
   The coffined form shall rest,
Or, in its nakedness, return
   Back to its mother's breast.

II.

Death is a common friend or foe,
   As different men may hold;
And at his summons each must go—
   The timid and the bold!

But when the spirit, free and warm,
    Deserts it, as it must,
What matter where the lifeless form
    Dissolves again to dust?

III.

The soldier falls, 'mid corses piled,
    Upon the battle-plain,
Where reinless war-steeds gallop wild
    Above the mangled slain;
But, though his corse be grim to see,
    Hoof-trampled on the sod,
What recks it, when the spirit free
    Has soared aloft to God!

IV.

The coward's dying eyes may close
    Upon his downy bed,
And softest hands his limbs compose,
    Or garments o'er them spread;
But ye, who shun the bloody fray,
    Where fall the mangled brave,
Go—strip his coffin-lid away,
    And see him—in his grave!

V.

'Twere sweet, indeed, to close our eyes
    With those we cherish, near,
And wafted upwards, by their sighs,
    Soar to some calmer sphere.
But, whether on the scaffold high,
    Or in the battle's van,
The fittest place where man can die
    Is, where he dies for man!

SAINT LAURENCE'S ADDRESS TO THE IRISH PRINCES AT PEACE WITH THE INVADER.

BY CHARLES GAVAN DUFFY.

[Laurence, properly Lorcan O'Tuathail (*vulgŏ* O'Toole), one of the truest and boldest patriots GOD ever granted to the necessities of a people, was Archbishop of Dublin at the period of the English Invasion. From the first hour of their usurpation he was the head and soul of all the effective opposition offered to the Foreigners. After the landing of the second gang of Adventurers, he went among the Princes of the country, and by his solitary exertions, organized a formidable League against them. He afterwards addressed himself to the task of winning the Princes, who had made submission to the enemy, back to their natural allegiance. The address which he may be supposed to have delivered upon that occasion is the subject of the present Ballad. The great influence St. Laurence possessed with the Dynasts arose partly from his belonging to their rank by birth, but much more from his wise, pious, and exalted character, and ascetic life. He died in France (some assert in exile for his patriotism), and in course of time was canonised and chosen Patron Saint of Dublin. Ireland produced no man who served her more faithfully, or whose services have been more shamefully forgotten.]

A.D. 1171.

I.

PRINCES, Tanists, Chiefs of Eirinn, wherefore meet we here to-
    day?
Come ye but to raise the *calloid*,* o'er your country's lifeless clay?
Come ye here to whine your sorrow, for the ill yourselves have
    wrought,
Or to swear you'll buy redemption, at the price it may be bought?

II.

Once your names were names of honour in the citied-camps of
    Gaul—
Once the iron tribe of Odin did not blush to bear your thrall†—
Once the proud Iberian boasted how your royal race begun ;
But your glory hath gone from you, swiftly as a setting sun.

---

* Ꞓꜳlló⁊ꝺ, a Funeral Elegy.

† Many of the Danes who remained in Ireland after the battle of Cluantarbh (Clontarf) took service under the Irish Princes.

2 G

III.

And throughout our desolation, mark you not God's holy hand
Smiting us with subtle vengeance, for our sins against the land?—
Frantic feuds and broken pactions, selfish ends and sordid lust,
And, the blackest vice of vices, treason to our sacred trust!

IV.

Where be all the feifs He gave you—well to govern, well to
    guard?
Bartered to the Godless Spoiler—and behold your just reward:
Desolation shall pursue you, and shall pierce you through and
    through,
Till, where women's tears are raining, Princely rage shall thunder
    too!

V.

When the Stranger came a stranger, still you gave the stranger's
    meed—
Shelter when he came an Exile—succour when he came in need—
When he came a Student, learning, and the right of book and
    board—
Princes! when he came a Robber, had you not the axe and sword?

VI.

And was peace the fruit of treason?   Let our kinsmen, fled or
    dead,
Chainless plunder, lust and murder, teach you how submission
    sped;
Nay, behold yon vale! a convent lay like love embosomed there,
Where the weary found a shelter, and the wounded needful care;

VII.

And the prayers of holy maidens streamed to Heaven night and
    day,
Like a healing incense burning all infectious sin away:
So it flourished till the spoiler, Christless, more than Hun or
    Jew,
Came—and now the wolf and Saxon share the wreck between
    the two.

VIII.

Oh! may God, our Lord, assoil me, if at times, in high disdain,
Seeing this, I prayed that Brian had not wholly crushed the
Dane.
Well the savage pirate guarded all the spoil his crimes amass'd,
And the Isle, from sea to centre, trust me, *he* had held it fast.

IX.

When ye shrink to monks, 'tis seeming, monks should fill your
princely place;
And a peaceful priest proclaims you traitors black with foul
disgrace.
Tell me not of leagues and treaties; treaties sealed in faith as
true
As Black Raymond's on the bloody feast of Saint Bartholomew!*

X.

But their King will be your Father? Yea, and grant you many
a grace—
Gyves and fetters from the donjons of his own begotten race!
Oh! disdain this scheme to mesh you in a net of knavish words,
Thank him, as his sons have thanked him—thank him with your
naked swords.

XI.

Still you doubt! Then, royal Norman, reeking red with holy
blood,
Come and lead to newer slaughters all your sacrilegious brood;

---

* One of the most infamous butcheries recorded in history was committed by the
English invader on ST. BARTHOLOMEW'S DAY. Strongbow, who first set foot in
Ireland that very day, appointed his confederate, *Raymond Le Gros*, to attack
Waterford, which after a resolute resistance, was taken; whereupon (to use the words
of Leland, the Protestant Historian) "*the whole city was made a scene of promiscuous
carnage, without mercy or distinction.*" That is to say, they murdered the citizens for
protecting their own city from a gang of pirates, landed only a few hours on the soil.

2 G 2

Come in triumph— here are Bishops, worn to stone with fast and
    prayer,
None shall question why you send them Becket's bloody shroud
    to share.

XII.

Nay, my children, if you doom us to the Martyr's heavy crown,
With your own dishonoured weapons strike your priests and
    Prelates down;
Better thus than by the Stranger, better thus than being cursed
With that hideous daily torture, living on to know the worst.

XIII.

And the loyal wives that love you, with a fond and gen'rous truth,
And the daughters who surround you with the sunshine of their
    youth—
Drag them to the carnal tyrant as he swoops upon your shore,
Meekly you must do his pleasure, nor deny him ever more.

XIV.

Oh! forgive my rash injustice; Heber's blood is wroth at wrong,
And I see you burn to grapple all the ills we bore so long;
And you'll league like royal brothers, till from joyful shore to
    shore
Princely rage indeed shall thunder, women's tears shall rain no
    more.

XV.

Yes, like brothers; let the Psalters link his name with fixt dis-
    grace,
Who, when Eirinn waves her banner, strikes for region, clann, or
    race;
Not for Desmond, not for Uladh; not for Ir or Eoghan's seed,*
But for ocean-girdled Eirinn must our kingly Chieftains bleed.

---

* *Desmond,* or Deas Mumhain, South Munster; *Uladh,* Ulster; *Ir,* a son of *Mileadh*
(Milesius), and head of many illustrious Irish families; *Eibhear* and *Eireamhón* (Heber
and Heremon) his other sons who reigned in Ireland; *Eoghan* (Owen), descendant of
Eibhear, and head of a race, located chiefly in North Munster.

XVI.

Muran's self-denying justice, Daithi's world-embracing fame,
Fodhla's wisdom, Cormac's counsel, holy Patrick's sacred name; *
And our own dear land that gave us kindly culture, state, and
    gold—
Oh! my children, need you stronger spell-words for the true and
    bold?

XVII.

Thus you match and over-match them, be they harnessed breasts
    and backs—
Never Norman forged a cuirass could resist an Irish axe;
And be sure your fiery clansmen soon shall mock at their array,
As the cowards clad in iron and a-horse to ride away! †

XVIII.

And the dull and slavish Saxons, whipped and leashed by Norman
    hands,
Trained to wreak the wrongs they suffered on the breast of kindred
    lands;
Trained like mastiffs in the shambles, at a beck to rend and bite,
As the wolves before the beagles, you shall track their bloody
    flight.

---

  * Perhaps it may be necessary to inform some readers that *Muran*, the son of a usurper of the Irish crown abandoned his claim in favour of the legitimate heir, and became chief judge of Ireland, and illustrious for his equity—his miraculous collar is famous in song and story; *Daithi*, the last of our Pagan Kings, carried the Irish arms through Gaul and Helvetia in the fifth century, and last year puzzled excessively the successors of *Muran* in the Queen's Bench, on the trial of " O'Connell and others." *Ollamh Fodhla*, the great law-giver of our ancestors, earned the reputation of profound wisdom by his laws and institutions; his head adorns the Hall of the Four Courts and the Volunteer's card of the Repeal Association. *Cormac* was King and Bishop of Cashel, and a poet of celebrity; some of his writings are still extant. *Padruic* or *Padraic* is the Irish spelling of our Apostle's name.

  † Is it necessary to remind the reader that the English adventurers were defended by armour and fought on horseback, while the Irish were without armour, and generally fought on foot?

XIX.

Pause not till each Dun and Tower planted by the Strangers' hand
Blazes like a Viking's beacon, guiding them from out the land;
Till the last of all the pirates to their galleys shall have fled,
Shuddering at the dire *gal-tromba* * as the Trumpet of the Dead.

XX.

Thus shall you be free for ever—thus the promised day shall come,
When the Children of the Soldier † guard a proud, untrammell'd
    home;
Thus your memory of the present, like the Prophet's joy shall
    seem,
Who, oppressed with fearful danger, waked to find 'twas but a
    dream.

THE WILD GEESE.

BY M. J. BARRY.

" Friday morning several flocks of wild geese were observed passing over this city
in a very noisy mood. Their appearance presages an unusually severe winter."—
Limerick Chronicle.

I.

THE wild geese—the wild geese—'tis long since they flew
O'er the billowy ocean's bright bosom of blue,
For the foot of the false-hearted stranger had curst
The shore, on whose fond breast they'd nestled at first;

---

* The war-trumpet of the Irish.
† "Children of the Soldier," *i. e.* of *Milesius*, whose name *Mileadh*, is also the
Irish for a soldier or champion.

And they sought them a home, afar off o'er the sea,
Where their pinions, at least, might be chainless and free.

II.

The wild geese—the wild geese—sad, sad was the wail
That followed their flight on the easterly gale;
But the eyes that had wept o'er their vanishing track
Ne'er brightened to welcome the wanderers back,
The home of their youth was the land of the slave,
And they died on that shore far away o'er the wave.

III.

The wild geese—the wild geese—their coming once more
Was the long-cherished hope of that desolate shore,
For the loved ones behind knew it yet would be free,
If they flew on their white pinions back o'er the sea;
But vainly the hope of those lonely ones burned,
The wild geese—the wild geese, they never returned.

IV.

The wild geese—the wild geese—hark! heard ye that cry?
And marked ye that white flock o'erspreading the sky?
Can ye read not the omen? Joy, joy to the slave,
And gladness and strength to the hearts of the brave;
For wild geese are coming, at length, o'er the sea,
And Eirinn, green Eirinn, once more shall be free!

---

* The recruits for the Irish Brigade were generally conveyed to France in the smugglers which brought foreign wines and brandy to our west coast, and were entered on the ship's books as " wild geese." Hence this became the common name for them among the country people.

OUR HOPES.

Let them mock at our hopes as i - dle dreams, We'll cling to them clos - er

still, With the pas-sion of youth for its dar -ling schemes, And the vi -gour of man-ly

will,   All feelings and thoughts through the heart that glide, With us in one stream are

met ; Nor e - ver that tide shall   turn a - side Till it   bear us   to free -dom

yet. Nor e - ver that tide shall   turn a -side Till it   bear us   to   free-dom yet.

2 H

OUR HOPES.

I.

LET them mock at our hopes as idle dreams,
　　We'll cling to them closer still,
With the passion of youth for its darling schemes,
　　And the vigour of manly will.
All feelings and thoughts through the breast that glide,
　　With us in one stream are met;
Nor ever that tide shall turn aside
　　Till it bear us to freedom yet.
　　　　Nor ever that tide shall turn aside
　　　　　Till it bear us to freedom yet.

II.

Do we dream the things we have heard and read,
　　The things we have seen, and know;
The famine where God a feast hath spread,
　　And the millions bowed down in woe;
The wrongs that have kindled our cheeks in rage,
　　The griefs that have left them wet;
And the one black page from age to age?—
　　We'll open another yet.
　　　　And the one black page from age to age?—
　　　　　We'll open another yet.

III.

Do we dream what freedom can work for man,
　　Or the glorious change 'twill bring,
When the foreign shackle, our blight and ban,
　　From sinew and heart we fling;
When the hope, the food that he rears to share,
　　Will sweeten the toiler's sweat?
Be of cheer, sad heir of thraldom and care,
　　Blithe homes are before us yet.
　　　　Be of cheer, sad heir of thraldom and care,
　　　　　Blithe homes are before us yet.

IV.

Oh! many a nobler heart than ours
    Hath perished that dream to gain;
And many a mind of Godlike powers
    Was wasted—not all in vain!
They 've left us a treasure of pity and wrath—
    A spur to our cold blood set—
And we 'll tread their path with a spirit that hath
    Assurance of triumph yet.
        And we 'll tread their path with a spirit that hath
            Assurance of triumph yet.

SLIABH CUILINN.

BLIND MARY.

BY THOMAS DAVIS.

AIR—" *Blind Mary.*"

I.

THERE flows from her spirit such love and delight,
That the face of Blind Mary is radiant with light—
As the gleam from a homestead through darkness will show,
Or the moon glimmer soft through the fast falling snow.

II.

Yet there 's a keen sorrow comes o'er her at times,
As an Indian might feel in our northerly climes;
And she talks of the sunset, like parting of friends,
And the starlight, as love, that nor changes nor ends.

III.

Ah! grieve not, sweet maiden, for star or for sun,
For the mountains that tow'r, or the rivers that run—
For beauty, and grandeur, and glory, and light,
Are seen by the spirit, and not by the sight.

IV.

In vain for the thoughtless are sunburst and shade,
In vain for the heartless flow'rs blossom and fade,
While the darkness that seems your sweet being to bound
Is one of the guardians, an Eden around.

2 H 2

LAMENT FOR THE MILESIANS.

AIR—Ḃṙuac ṅa Caṙṙaiʒe ḃáiṅe.

Oh! proud were the chieftains of green Iṅiṙḟail, Aʼṙ cṙuaʒ ʒaṅ oiḋ-ṙ ʼṅ-a ḃ-ḟaṙṙaḋ; The stars of our sky, and the salt of our soil, Aʼṙ

τρυαξ ζαη οιδ - ιη 'η-α b-ϝαρραδ. Their hearts were as soft as a

child in the lap, Yet they were "the men in the gap," And

now that the cold clay their limbs doth enwrap, Α'ρ τρυαξ ζαη οιδ-ιη 'η-α b-ϝαρραδ.

LAMENT FOR THE MILESIANS.

BY THOMAS DAVIS.

I.

Oh! proud were the chieftains of proud Innis-Fail,
  A's truagh gan oidhir 'n-a bh-farradh!*
The stars of our sky and the salt of our soil,
  A's truagh gan oidhir 'n-a bh-farradh!
Their hearts were as soft as a child in the lap,
Yet they were " the men in the gap"—
And now that the cold clay their limbs doth enwrap,
  A's truagh gan oidhir 'n-a bh-farradh!

II.

'Gainst England, long battling, at length they went down,
  A's truagh gan oidhir 'n-a bh-farradh!
But they 've left their deep tracks on the road of renown,
  A's truagh gan oidhir 'n-a bh-farradh!
We are heirs of their fame, if we 're not of their race,
And deadly and deep our disgrace,
If we live o'er their sepulchres, abject and base,
  A's truagh gan oidhir 'n-a bh-farradh!

III.

Oh! sweet were the minstrels of kind Innis-Fail!
  A's truagh gan oidhir 'n-a bh-farradh!
Whose music, nor ages nor sorrow can spoil,
  A's truagh gan oidhir 'n-a bh-farradh!
But their sad stifled tones are like streams flowing hid,
Their caoine and their pibroch were chid,
And their language, "that melts into music," forbid,
  A's truagh gan oidhir 'n-a bh-farradh!

---

* A'r τρυαᵹ ᵹαη οιδιρ 'η-α b-ϝαρραδ, " That is pity, without heir in
their company," i. e. What a pity that there is no heir of their company. See the poem
of Giolla Iosa Mor Mac Firbisigh in *The Genealogies, Tribes, and Customs of the Ui
Fiachrach*, or *O'Dubhda's Country*, printed for the Irish Arch. Soc. p. 230, line 2,
and note d. Also *O'Reilly's Dict. voce.* ϝαρραδ.

IV.

How fair were the maidens of fair Innis-Fail!
    A 's truagh gan oidhir 'n-a bh-farradh!
As fresh and as free as the sea-breeze from soil,
    A 's truagh gan oidhir 'n-a bh-farradh!
Oh! are not our maidens as fair and as pure,
Can our music no longer allure?
And can we but sob, as such wrongs we endure,
    A 's truagh gan oidhir 'n-a bh-farradh!

V.

Their famous, their holy, their dear Innis-Fail,
    A 's truagh gan oidhir 'n-a bh-farradh!
Shall it still be a prey for the stranger to spoil,
    A 's truagh gan oidhir 'n-a bh-farradh!
Sure, brave men would labour by night and by day
To banish that stranger away,
Or, dying for Ireland, the future would say
    A 's truagh gan oidhir 'n-a bh-farradh!

VI.

Oh! shame—for unchanged is the face of our isle,
    A 's truagh gan oidhir 'n-a bh-farradh!
That taught them to battle, to sing, and to smile,
    A 's truagh gan oidhir 'n-a bh-farradh!
We are heirs of their rivers, their sea, and their land,
Our sky and our mountains as grand—
We are heirs—oh! we 're not of their heart and their hand,
    A 's truagh gan oidhir 'n-a bh-farradh!

RESISTANCE.

BY M. J. BARRY.

I.

WHEN tyrants dare to trample down
    The rights of those they rule,

When toiling men must meet the frown
　　Of every lordling fool,
When laws are made to crush the weak,
　　And lend the strong assistance,
When millions, vainly, justice seek,
　　Their duty is—Resistance!

II.

When tyrant force aids tyrant laws,
　　When brothers sever'd stand,
When failure *must* be his who draws
　　On power the freeman's brand,
True men will bid the millions pray
　　For God's divine assistance,
And calmly bide a better day,
　　Their duty still—Resistance!

III.

When times of better hope arise,
　　And feuds are laid aside,
When men have grown too calm and wise
　　For traitors to divide,
When first to aid a people's right
　　There springs into existence
Its surest stay, a people's might,
　　The hour *is* for—Resistance!

IV.

No empty boast be ours to-day,
　　No braggart word or tone,
Enough to feel we know the way
　　That men should win their own.
Our hope and trust for Fatherland
　　Now gleam *not* in the distance;
Let tyrants dare unsheath the brand,
　　That hour will teach—Resistance!

MUNSTER.

I.

Ye who rather
Seek to gather
Biding thought than fleeting pleasure;
  In the South what wonders saw ye?
  From the South what lesson draw ye?
Wonders, passing thought or measure—
Lessons, through a life to treasure.

II.

Ever living,
Nature, giving
Welcome wild, or soft caress—
  Scenes that sink into the being
  Till the eye grows full with seeing,
And the mute heart can but bless
Him that shaped such loveliness.

III.

Dark and wide ill
Rivers idle,
Wealth unwrought of sea and mine—
  Bays where Europe's fleets might anchor—
  Scarce Panama's waters blanker,
Ere Columbus crossed the brine,
Void of living sound or sign.

IV.

God hath blest it,
Man opprest it—
Sad the fruits that mingling rise—
  Fallow fields, and hands to till them,
  Hungry mouths, and grain to fill them
But a social curse denies
Labour's guerdon, want's supplies.

v.

Sunlight glances,
Life that dances
In the limbs of childhood there—
Glowing tints, that fade and sicken
In the pallid, famine-stricken
Looks, that men and women wear,
Living types of want and care.

vi.

Faith and patience,
'Mid privations—
Genial heart, and open hand;
But, what fain the eye would light on,
Pleasant homes to cheer and brighten
Such a race and such a land—
These, alas! their lords have banned.

vii.

These things press on
Us the lesson,
Much may yet be done and borne;
But the bonds that thus continue
Paralysing limb and sinew,
From our country *must* be torn;
Then shines out young Munster's morn.

SLIABH CUILINN.

EMMET'S DEATH.

I.

" HE dies to day," said the heartless judge,
    Whilst he sate him down to the feast,
And a smile was upon his ashy lip,
    As he uttered a ribald jest;
For a demon dwelt, where his heart should be,
    That lived upon blood and sin,
And oft, as that vile judge gave him food
    The demon throbbed within.

II.

" He dies to-day," said the gaoler grim,
  Whilst a tear was in his eye ;
" But why should I feel so grieved for *him* ?
  " Sure I 've seen many die :
" Last night 1 went to his stony cell
  " With his scanty prison fare—
" He was sitting at a table rude
  " Plaiting a lock of hair !
" And he looked so mild, with his pale, pale face,
  " And he spoke in so kind a way,
" That my old breast heav'd with a smothering feel,
  " And I knew not what to say !"

III.

" He dies to-day," thought a fair sweet girl—
  She lacked the life to speak ;
For sorrow had almost frozen her blood,
  And white were her lip and cheek—
Despair had drank up her last wild tear,
  And her brow was damp and chill,
And her friends oft felt her heart with fear,
  For its ebb was all but still.

IV.

The lover upon the gallows tree !
  The maid, with her plighted troth,
Dying with grief on a bier-like bed !
  Oh, God ! have mercy on both.

*　　*　　*　　*　　*

V.

That judge is gone to his last abode,
  A pest has passed from the earth,
But a scathing path, wherever he trode,
  Has blackened the peasant's hearth
And his memory lives, as darkness does,
  Without a moon or a star !
Or a light—save such as mercy shows
  At the mouth of a treacherous bar !

VI.

But, the martyr's name, like a holy spell,
 That is murmur'd alone, in pray'r,
As long, in the land that he lov'd, shall dwell,
 As a pure heart lingers there.
Nay, wail him not; with the harp's sad string,
 Let him sleep with the mournful past;
His spirit is here, like an earth-pent spring,
 And will sparkle to light at last!

VII.

And SHE is gone—the fond and the fair!—
 The last of this bloodful doom!
Ah! she wither'd as fast as the braided hair
 That was over *his* heart, in the tomb!
* * * * * *

VIII.

How should the lover's vow be given?
 Where should brave men meet?—
With the truth of her who is high in heaven!
 With his nameless grave at their feet!

THE TRUE IRISH KING.*

BY THOMAS DAVIS.

I.

THE Cæsar of Rome has a wider demesne,
And the Ard-Righ of France has more clans in his train;
The sceptre of Spain is more heavy with gems,
And our crowns cannot vie with the Greek diadems;

---

* See Appendix L to O'Donovan's "Hy-Fiachra," p. 245, &c.

But kinglier far before heaven and man
Are the Emerald fields, and the fiery-eyed clan,
The sceptre, and state, and the poets who sing,
And the swords that encircle A TRUE IRISH KING !

II.

For, he must have come from a conquering race—
The heir of their valour, their glory, their grace :
His frame must be stately, his step must be fleet,
His hand must be trained to each warrior feat,
His face, as the harvest moon, steadfast and clear,
A head to enlighten, a spirit to cheer,
While the foremost to rush where the battle-brands ring,
And the last to retreat is A TRUE IRISH KING !

III.

Yet, not for his courage, his strength, or his name,
Can he from the clansmen their fealty claim.
The poorest, and highest, choose freely to-day
The chief, that to-night, they 'll as truly obey ;
For loyalty springs from a people's consent,
And the knee that is forced had been better unbent—
The Sasanach serfs no such homage can bring
As the Irishmen's choice of A TRUE IRISH KING !

IV.

Come, look on the pomp when they "make an O'Neill;"
The muster of dynasts—O'h-Again, O'Shiadhail,
O'Cathain, O'h-Anluain, O'Bhrislein and all,
From gentle Aird Uladh to rude Dun na n-gall ;
" St. Patrick's *comharba*," * with bishops thirteen,
And ollamhs and breithamhs, and minstrels, are seen,
Round Tulach-Og† Rath, like the bees in the spring,
All swarming to honour A TRUE IRISH KING !

---

* Successor—coṁaṙba Ṗhaḋṅaiʒ—the Archbishop of Armagh.
† In the county Tyrone, between Cookstown and Stewartstown.

V.

Unsandalled he stands on the foot-dinted rock,
Like a pillar-stone fix'd against every shock.
Round, round is the Rath on a far-seeing hill,
Like his blemishless honour, and vigilant will.
The grey-beards are telling how chiefs by the score
Have been crowned on " The Rath of the Kings" heretofore,
While, crowded, yet ordered, within its green ring,
Are the dynasts and priests round THE TRUE IRISH KING!

VI.

The chronicler read him the laws of the clan,
And pledged him to bide by their blessing and ban ;
His skian and his sword are unbuckled to show
That they only were meant for a foreigner foe ;
A white willow wand has been put in his hand—
A type of pure, upright, and gentle command—
While hierarchs are blessing, the slipper they fling,
And O'Cathain proclaims him A TRUE IRISH KING!

VII.

Thrice looked he to Heaven with thanks and with prayer—
Thrice looked to his borders with sentinel stare—
To the waves of Loch N-Eathach, the heights of Strath-bhan ;
And thrice on his allies, and thrice on his clan—
One clash on their bucklers !—one more !—they are still—
What means the deep pause on the crest of the hill ?
Why gaze they above him ?—a war-eagle's wing !
" 'Tis an omen !—Hurrah ! for THE TRUE IRISH KING !"

VIII.

God aid him !—God save him !—and smile on his reign—
The terror of England—the ally of Spain.
May his sword be triumphant o'er Sasanach arts !
Be his throne ever girt by strong hands, and true hearts !
May the course of his conquest run on till he see
The flag of Plantagenet sink in the sea,
And minstrels for ever his victories sing,
And saints make the bed of THE TRUE IRISH KING !

THE BANKS OF THE LEE.

BY THOMAS DAVIS.

AIR—"*A Trip to the Cottage.*"

I.

OH! the Banks of the Lee, the Banks of the Lee,
And love in a cottage for Mary and me,
There's not in the land a lovelier tide,
And I'm sure that there's no one so fair as my bride.

She's modest and meek,
There's a down on her cheek,
And her skin is as sleek
As a butterfly's wing—
Then her step would scarce show
On the fresh-fallen snow,
And her whisper is low,
But as clear as the spring.

Oh! the Banks of the Lee, the Banks of the Lee,
And love in a cottage for Mary and me,
I know not how love is happy elsewhere,
I know not how any but lovers are there!

II.

Oh! so green is the grass, so clear is the stream,
So mild is the mist, and so rich is the beam,
That beauty should ne'er to other lands roam,
But make on the banks of our river its home.

When, dripping with dew,
The roses peep through,
'Tis to look in at you,
They are growing so fast,
While the scent of the flowers
Must be hoarded for hours,
'Tis poured in such showers
When my Mary goes past.

Oh! the Banks of the Lee, the Banks of the Lee,
And love in a cottage for Mary and me—
Oh, Mary for me, Mary for me,
And 'tis little I'd sigh for the Banks of the Lee!

THE GREEN FLAG.

AIR.—"O'Connell's March."

Boys, fill your glasses, Each hour that pass-es Steals, it may be, on our last night's cheer;

Day soon shall come, boys, With fife and drum, boys, Break-ing shrilly on the sol-dier's ear.

Drink, the faith-ful hearts that love us, Mid to-morrow's thickest fight While our green flag

floats a-bove us, Think, boys, 'tis for them we smite. Down with each mean flag,

None but the Green Flag Shall in triumph be a - bove us seen; Think on its glory

Long shrin'd in sto - ry, Charge for Érin and her Flag of Green.

THE GREEN FLAG.

A.D. 1647.

BY M. J. BARRY.

I.

Boys! fill your glasses,
Each hour that passes
Steals, it may be, on our last night's cheer.
The day soon shall come, boys,
With fife and drum, boys,
Breaking shrilly on the soldier's ear.
Drink the faithful hearts that love us—
'Mid to-morrow's thickest fight,
While our green flag floats above us,
Think, boys, 'tis for them we smite.
Down with each mean flag,
None but the green flag
Shall in triumph be above us seen:
Oh! think on its glory,
Long shrined in story,
Charge for Eire and her Flag of Green!

II.

Think on old Brian,
War's mighty lion,
'Neath that banner 'twas he smote the Dane,
The Northman and Saxon,
Oft turned their backs on
Those who bore it o'er each crimson'd plain.
Beal-an-atha-Buidhe beheld it
Bagenal's fiery onset curb,
Scotch Munroe would fain have fell'd it;
We, boys, followed him from red Beinnburb.

Down with each mean flag,
None but the green flag
Shall above us be in triumph seen :
Oh ! think of its glory,
Long shrined in story,
Charge with Eoghan for our Flag of Green !

III.

And if at eve, boys,
Comrades shall grieve, boys,
O'er our corses, let it be with pride,
When thinking that each, boys,
On that red beach, boys,
Lies the flood-mark of the battle's tide.
See—the first faint ray of morning
Gilds the east with yellow light :
Hark ! the bugle note gives warning—
One full bumper to old friends to-night.
Down with each mean flag,
None but the green flag
Shall above us be in triumph seen ;
Oh ! think on its glory,
Long shrined in story,
Fall or conquer for our Flag of Green !

WHO SPEAKS OR STRIKES.

BY D. F. M'CARTHY.

AIR—" *Fag-an-Bealach.*"

I.

COME fill up to the brim, boy,
Your glass with me, your glass with me,
And drink success to him, boy,
Whoe'er he be, whoe'er he be,

2 K 2

Who does his best endeavour
  With heart and hand, with heart and hand,
To free, and free for ever,
  His native land, his native land.
Then let us drink to-night, boy,
  As each one likes, as each one likes,
The man in Freedom's fight, boy,
  Who speaks or strikes, who speaks or strikes!

II.

Amid the ranks of glory,
  Who leads the van? who leads the van?
The answer for all story
  Is *such* a man, is *such* a man; ·
Whose words like mighty rivers
  Spread o'er the plain, spread o'er the plain,
Or whose bright sword-blade shivers
  The tyrant's chain, the tyrant's chain.
Then let us drink to-night, boy,
  As each one likes, as each one likes—
The man in Freedom's fight, boy,
  Who speaks or strikes, who speaks or strikes!

III.

Oh! what is death or danger,
  To him the slave—to him the slave,
Whose country by the stranger
  Is made one grave—is made one grave?
The glories it is keeping
  Oh! ne'er forget—oh! ne'er forget:
They are not dead, but sleeping—
  We'll wake them yet—we'll wake them yet.
Then let us drink to-night, boy,
  As each one likes—as each one likes—
The man in Freedom's fight, boy,
  Who speaks or strikes—who speaks or strikes.

THE ISRAELITE LEADER.

I.

A HEBREW youth, of thoughtful mien
   And dark impassioned eye,
Once stood beside the leafy sheen
   Of an oak that towered high;
Ever, amid man's varied race,
   Such port and glance are found,
Unerring signs by which to trace
   The slave's first upward bound.

II.

Ay! Liberty's good son, though he
   Yet bears the tyrant brand—
Not distant far the hour can be
   For such to arm and band.
His father's heaped-up corn was near,
   To tend it seemed his care;
But—souls like his to Heaven are dear—
   An Angel sought him there.

III.

Under the shade of that tall oak
   A stranger met his eyes,
And glorious were the words he spoke,
   Of Israel's quick uprise;
Deep, thrilling words—they instant made
   That young heart overflow,
As the strong leap of the cascade
   Heaves up the tide below.

IV.

He spread a feast for the harbinger
   Who such good tidings bore,
But—fire from Heaven consumed it there—
   He saw that guest no more;

And when the first deep awe had passed,
  Of such strange visitant,
Upsprung his hopes for Israel fast,
  As eagles from their haunt.

v.

And the pale youth who but that morn,
  (So meek of heart was he,)
Stood winnowing his father's corn,
  At midnight, like a sea,
When tameless is its stormy roar,
  To Baal's high altar rushed,
And it was overturned before
  The next bright orient blushed.

vi.

An Altar to the Living God
  Upon the ruin stood,
And groves, where Baal's Priests had trod,
  Were rooted from the wood—
And God's good sword with Gideon went
  For ever from that day,
Till, of the hosts against him sent,
  Not one was left to slay.

vil

Oh ! names like his bright beacons are
  To realms that Kings oppress,
Hailing with radiant light from far
  Their signals of distress.
When a crushed Nation humbly turns
  From sin that was too dear,
Not long the proud Oppressor spurns,
  Deliverance is near.

A———.

LOVE'S LONGINGS.

BY THOMAS DAVIS.

I.

To the conqueror his crowning,
 First freedom to the slave,
And air unto the drowning
 Sunk in the ocean's wave—
And succour to the faithful,
 Who fight their flag above,
Are sweet, but far less grateful
 Than were my lady's love.

II.

I know I am not worthy
 Of one so young and bright;
And yet I would do for thee
 Far more than others might;
I cannot give you pomp or gold,
 If you should be my wife,
But I can give you love untold,
 And true in death or life.

III.

Methinks that there are passions
 Within that heaving breast
To scorn their heartless fashions,
 And wed whom you love best.
Methinks you would be prouder
 As the struggling patriot's bride,
Than if rank your home should crowd, or
 Cold riches round you glide.

IV.

Oh! the watcher longs for morning,
 And the infant cries for light,
And the saint for heaven's warning,
 And the vanquished pray for might;
But their prayer, when lowest kneeling,
 And their suppliance most true,
Are cold to the appealing
 Of this longing heart to you.

RECRUITING SONG

OF

THE IRISH BRIGADE.

Air.—*"The White Cockade."*

Presto. *f*

Oh! is there a youth-ful gal - lant here On fire for fame, un-

know - ing fear, Who in the char - ge's mad ca - reer On

Æl - pe's foes would bend his spear. Come let him wear the

White Cock - ade And learn the sol - dier's glo - rious trade, 'Tis

of such stuff a he - ro's made, Then let him join The Bold Bri - gade.

RECRUITING SONG FOR THE IRISH BRIGADE.

BY MAURICE O'CONNELL, M. P.

I.

Is there a youthful gallant here
On fire for fame—unknowing fear—
Who in the charge's mad career
On Erin's foes would flesh his spear?
  Come, let him wear the White Cockade,
  And learn the soldier's glorious trade,
  'Tis of such stuff a hero's made,
  Then let him join the Bold Brigade.

II.

Who scorns to own a Saxon Lord,
And toil to swell a stranger's hoard?
Who for rude blow or gibing word
Would answer with the Freeman's sword?
  Come, let him wear the White Cockade, &c.

III.

Does Erin's foully slandered name
Suffuse thy cheek with generous shame—
Would'st right her wrongs—restore her fame?—
Come, then, the soldier's weapon claim—
  Come, then, and wear the White Cockade, &c.

IV.

Come, free from bonds your father's faith,
Redeem its shrines from scorn and scathe,
The Hero's fame, the Martyr's wreath,
Will guild your life or crown your death.
  Then, come, and wear the White Cockade, &c.

v.

To drain the cup—with girls to toy,
The serf's vile soul with bliss may cloy;
But would'st thou taste a manly joy?—
Oh! it was ours at Fontenoy!
   Come, then, and wear the White Cockade, &c.

vi.

To many a fight thy fathers led,
Full many a Saxon's life-blood shed;
From thee, as yet, no foe has fled—
Thou wilt not shame the glorious dead?
   Then, come, and wear the White Cockade, &c.

vii.

Oh! come—for slavery, want and shame,
We offer vengeance, freedom, fame,
With Monarchs, comrade rank to claim,
And, nobler still, the Patriot's name.
      Oh! come and wear the White Cockade,
      And learn the soldier's glorious trade;
      'Tis of such stuff a hero's made—
      Then come and join the Bold Brigade.

ST. PATRICK'S DAY.

BY M. J. BARRY.

AIR—" St. Patrick's Day."

1.

Oh, blest be the days when the green banner floated
   Sublime o'er the mountains of free Innisfail;
When her sons to her glory and freedom devoted,
   Defied the invader to tread her soil.
         When back o'er the main
         They chased the Dane,
And gave to religion and learning their spoil,

When valour and mind
Together combined—
But wherefore lament o'er those glories departed,
  Her star shall yet shine with as vivid a ray ;
For ne'er had she children more brave or true-hearted,
  Than those she now sees on St. Patrick's day.

II.

Her sceptre, alas ! passed away to the stranger,
  And treason surrendered what valour had held,
But true hearts remained amid darkness and danger,
  Which spite of her tyrants would *not* be quelled.
Oft, oft, through the night
Flashed gleams of light,
Which almost the darkness of bondage dispelled ;
But a star now is near,
Her heaven to cheer,
Not like the wild gleams which so fitfully darted,
  But long to shine down with its hallowing ray,
On daughters as fair, and on sons as true-hearted,
  As Erin beholds on St. Patrick's Day.

III.

Oh ! blest be the hour, when begirt by her cannon,
  And hail'd as it rose by a nation's applause,
That flag waved aloft o'er the spire of Dungannon,
  Asserting for Irishmen Irish laws.
Once more shall it wave
O'er hearts as brave,
Despite of the dastards who mock at her cause ;
And like brothers agreed,
Whatever their creed,
Her children, inspired by those glories departed,
  No longer in darkness desponding will stay,
But join in her cause, like the brave and true-hearted,
  Who rise for their rights on St. Patrick's day.

STEP TOGETHER.

Allegro Fermo.

Step to-ge-ther—boldly tread, Firm each foot, e - rect each head; Fix'd in front be ev'-ry glance,

Tramping Left,—Right.

Forward at the word, advance. Serried files that foes may dread, Like the deer on mountain heather, Tread light,

Left, right,—Left, right,— Steady, boys, and step to-gether! Steady, boys, and STEP TOGETHER!

Tramping Left,—Right.

STEP TOGETHER.

BY M. J. BARRY.

I.

Step together—boldly tread,
Firm each foot, erect each head,
Fix'd in front be every glance—
Forward, at the word advance—
Serried files that foes may dread—
Like the deer on mountain heather,
Tread light,
Left, right—
Steady, boys, and step together!

II.

Step together—be each rank
Dressed in line, from flank to flank,
Marching so that you may halt
'Mid the onset's fierce assault,
Firm as is the rampart's bank,
Raised the iron rain to weather—
Proud sight!
Left, right—
Steady, boys, and step together!

III.

Step together—be your tramp
Quick and light, no plodding stamp.
Let its cadence quick and clear
Fall, like music, on the ear;
Noise befits not hall or camp,
Eagles soar on silent feather—
Tread light,
Left, right—
Steady, boys, and step together!

IV.

Step together—self-restrained,
Be your march of thought as trained,
Each man's single pow'rs combin'd
Into one battalion'd mind,
Moving on with step sustain'd,
Thus prepared we reck not whether
Foes smite,
Left, right—
We can think and strike together!

PATIENCE.

I.

Be patient, O, be patient! put your ear against the earth—
Listen there how noiselessly the germ o' the seed has birth;
How noiselessly and gently it upheaves its little way,
Till it parts the scarcely-broken ground and the blade stands forth
to day.

II.

Be patient, O, be patient! for the germs of mighty thought
Must have their silent undergrowth, must underground be
wrought;
But, as sure as ever there's a power that makes the grass appear,
Our land shall smile with Liberty, the blade-time shall be here.

III.

Be patient, O, be patient! go and watch the wheat-ears grow,
So imperceptibly that ye can mark nor change nor throe,
Day after day, day after day, till the ear is fully grown,
And then again, day after day, till the ripen'd field is brown.

IV.

Be patient, O, be patient! though yet our hopes are green,
The harvest-fields of Freedom shall be crown'd with sunny sheen.
Be ripening! be ripening! mature your silent way,
Till the whole broad land is tongued with fire on Freedom's
harvest-day.

SPARTACUS.

THE GREEN ABOVE THE RED.

BY THOMAS DAVIS.

Air—"*Irish Molly, O!*"

I.

FULL often when our fathers saw the Red above the Green,
They rose in rude but fierce array, with sabre, pike, and skian,
And over many a noble town, and many a field of dead,
They proudly set the Irish Green above the English Red.

II.

But in the end, throughout the land, the shameful sight was seen—
The English Red in triumph high above the Irish Green;
But well they died in breach and field, who, as their spirits fled,
Still saw the Green maintain its place above the English Red.

III.

And they who saw, in after times, the Red above the Green,
Were withered as the grass that dies beneath a forest screen;
Yet often by this healthy hope their sinking hearts were fed,
That, in some day to come, the Green should flutter o'er the Red.

IV.

Sure 'twas for this Lord Edward died, and Wolfe Tone sunk
        serene—
Because they could not bear to leave the Red above the Green;
And 'twas for this that Owen fought, and Sarsfield nobly bled—
Because their eyes were hot to see the Green above the Red.

V.

So, when the strife began again, our darling Irish Green
Was down upon the earth, while high the English Red was seen;
Yet still we held our fearless course, for something in us said,
"Before the strife is o'er you'll see the Green above the Red."

VI.

And 'tis for this we think and toil, and knowledge strive to glean,
That we may pull the English Red below the Irish Green,
And leave our sons sweet Liberty, and smiling plenty spread
Above the land once dark with blood—*the Green above the Red!*

VII.

The jealous English tyrant now has bann'd the Irish Green,
And forced us to conceal it like a something foul and mean;
But yet, by Heavens! he'll sooner raise his victims from the dead
Than force our hearts to leave the Green, and cotton to the Red!

VIII.

We'll trust ourselves, for God is good, and blesses those who lean
On their brave hearts, and not upon an earthly king or queen;
And, freely as we lift our hands, we vow our blood to shed
Once and for evermore to raise the Green above the Red!

SWEET AND SAD.

A PRISON SERMON.

BY THOMAS DAVIS.

I.

'TIS sweet to climb the mountain's crest,
And run, like deer-hound, down its breast—
'Tis sweet to snuff the taintless air,
And sweep the sea with haughty stare;

2 M

And, sad it is, when iron bars
Keep watch between you and the stars,
And sad to find your footstep stayed
By prison-wall, and palisade;
   But 'twere better be
     A prisoner for ever,
   With no destiny
     To do, or to endeavour—
   Better life to spend
     A martyr or confessor,
   Than in silence bend
     To alien and oppressor.

II.

'Tis sweet to rule an ample realm,
Through weal and woe to hold the helm,
And sweet to strew, with plenteous hand,
Strength, health, and beauty, round your land;
And sad it is to be unprized,
While dotards rule, unrecognized,
And sad your little ones to see
Writhe in the gripe of poverty;
   But 'twere better pine
     In rags and gnawing hunger,
   While around you whine
     Your elder and your younger—
   Better lie in pain,
     And rise in pain to-morrow,
   Than o'er millions reign,
     While those millions sorrow.

III.

'Tis sweet to own a quiet hearth,
Begirt by constancy and mirth.

'Twere sweet to feel your dying clasp
Returned by friendship's steady grasp;
And, sad it is, to spend your life,
Like sea-bird in the ceaseless strife—
Your lullaby the ocean's roar—
Your resting-place a foreign shore;
　　But 'twere better live,
　　　Like ship caught by Lofoden,
　　Than your spirit give
　　　To be by chains corroden;
　　Best of all to yield
　　　Your latest breath, when lying
　　On a victor field,
　　　With the green flag flying!

iv.

Human joy and human sorrow,
Light or shade from conscience borrow—
The tyrant's crown is lined with flame,
Life never paid the coward's shame—
The miser's lock is never sure—
The traitor's home is never pure;
While seraphs guard, and cherubs tend
The good man's life and brave man's end;
　　But their fondest care
　　　Is the patriot's prison,
　　Hymning through its air—
　　　"Freedom hath arisen,
　　Oft from statesmen's strife,
　　　Oft from battle's flashes,
　　Oft from hero's life,
　　　Oftenest from his ashes!"

THE WELCOME.

AIR.—"An Buaċailín buiḋe."

Come in the ev'n-ing, or come in the morn-ing, Come when you're look'd for or come with-out warning, Kiss-es and wel-come you'll find here be-fore you, And the oft'n - er you come here the more I'll a-dore you. Light is my heart since the

day we were plight-ed, Red is my cheek, that they told me was blight-ed, The

green of the trees looks far green-er than e-ver, And the

lin-nets are sing-ing "true lov-ers don't se-ver."

THE WELCOME.

BY THOMAS DAVIS.

I.

Come in the evening, or come in the morning,
Come when you 're looked for, or come without warning,
Kisses and welcome you 'll find here before you,
And the oftener you come here the more I 'll adore you.
   Light is my heart since the day we were plighted,
   Red is my cheek that they told me was blighted ;
   The green of the trees looks far greener than ever,
   And the linnets are singing, " true lovers ! don't sever."

II.

I 'll pull you sweet flowers, to wear if you choose them ;
Or, after you 've kissed them, they 'll lie on my bosom.
I 'll fetch from the mountain its breeze to inspire you ;
I 'll fetch from my fancy a tale that won't tire you.
   Oh ! your step's like the rain to the summer-vex'd farmer,
   Or sabre and shield to a knight without armour ;
   I 'll sing you sweet songs till the stars rise above me,
   Then, wandering, I 'll wish you, in silence, to love me.

III.

We 'll look through the trees at the cliff, and the eyrie,
We 'll tread round the rath on the track of the fairy,
We 'll look on the stars, and we 'll list to the river,
Till you ask of your darling what gift you can give her.
   Oh ! she 'll whisper you, " Love as unchangeably beaming,
   And trust, when in secret, most tunefully streaming,
   Till the starlight of heaven above us shall quiver,
   As our souls flow in one down eternity's river."

IV.

So come in the evening, or come in the morning,
Come when you 're looked for, or come without warning,

Kisses and welcome you'll find here before you,
And the oftener you come here the more I'll adore you!
   Light is my heart since the day we were plighted,
   Red is my cheek that they told me was blighted;
   The green of the trees looks far greener than ever,
   And the linnets are singing, "true lovers! don't sever!'

WHY, GENTLES, WHY?

AIR—" *Why, Soldiers, why?* "

I.

   WHY, gentles, why,
Should we so melancholy be?
   Why, gentles, why?
We know that all must die—
    He—you—and I!
    Life at the best
    Is but a jest—
Hopes brightly shine but to fly!
    Rejoice, then, that rest—
    Deep, quiet, blest—
Stands ever nigh!

II.

   Why, tell me, why
Should we so melancholy be?
   Why, tell me, why
Bursts th' unbidden sigh,
While tears dim the eye?
    Why crave for rest;
    And even when happiest
Find gloomy thoughts ever nigh?
    'Tis that, while we live,
    Nought full content can give,
Known but on high!

                    L. N. F.

A NATION ONCE AGAIN.

And then I pray'd I yet might see Our fet-ters rent in twain, And Ire-land, long a pro-vince, be A NA-TION once a-gain; And Ire-land, long a pro-vince, be A NA-TION ONCE A-GAIN.

2 N

A NATION ONCE AGAIN.

BY THOMAS DAVIS.

I.

WHEN boyhood's fire was in my blood
  I read of ancient freemen,
For Greece and Rome who bravely stood,
  THREE HUNDRED MEN and THREE MEN.*
And then I prayed I yet might see
  Our fetters rent in twain,
And Ireland, long a province, be
  A NATION ONCE AGAIN.

II.

And, from that time, through wildest woe,
  That hope has shone, a far light;
Nor could love's brightest summer glow,
  Outshine that solemn starlight;
It seemed to watch above my head
  In forum, field, and fane,
It's angel voice sang round my bed,
  "A NATION ONCE AGAIN."

III.

It whispered, too, that "freedom's ark
  And service high and holy,
Would be profan'd by feelings dark
  And passions vain or lowly;
For freedom comes from God's right hand,
  And needs a godly train;
And righteous men must make our land
  A NATION ONCE AGAIN."

---

* The Three Hundred Greeks who died at Thermopylæ, and the Three Romans
who kept the Sublician Bridge.

IV.

So, as I grew from boy to man
  I bent me to that bidding—
My spirit of each selfish plan
  And cruel passion ridding;
For, thus I hoped some day to aid—
  Oh! can *such* hope be vain?—
When my dear country should be made
  A NATION ONCE AGAIN.

THE SONG OF THE POOR.

I.

HARP of Erin, freshly pealing!
  Harp, by patriot genius strung!
Scatter wide each finer feeling,
  Let not strife alone be sung.
Pleased, enchanted, have I heard thee
  High-born valour's praise impart,
But a nobler theme ne'er stirred thee
  Than the Irish *peasant's* heart!

II.

Let the hero's brow be braided,
  Let the victor's crest be raised;
But the *poor* man strives unaided,
  But the *poor* man sinks unpraised.
Yet, whilst woes and wrongs importune,
  And gaunt death uprears his dart,
Where's the field of feller fortune
  Than the Irish peasant's heart?

III.

Well he bears him in the quarrel,
  Never knight of high degree,
For a meed of gold or laurel,
  Shew'd a firmer front than he.

If, for wife and children only,
    Blinding tears will sometimes start,
What, in all its conflict lonely,
    Guides the Irish peasant's heart?

IV.

'Neath a despot's frigid scanning,
    From a height he deems secure,
'Neath a bigot's saintly fanning,
    Execratingly demure,
Still we see one sacred feeling
    Solitary light impart,
Where his *Soggarth* lowly kneeling
    Schools the Irish peasant's heart.

V.

Take, oppressed ones, for your guidance,
    Take the patience prompted there;
Verdant pledge of grief's subsidence
    Dovelike *peace* will soonest bear.
Layers-down of law neglected,
    Legal drawlers stand apart;
List your *convict's* code, respected
    By each Irish peasant's heart.

VI.

" Tranquil wait the birth of time !
    Temp'rate, word and action be !
Whosoe'er commits a crime,
    Wrongs his cause, himself, and me.
Sage endurance conquers fate,
    Let oppression wince and start"—
Dangerous doctrine, men of state,
    For the Irish peasant's heart !

VII.

Harp of Erin, strongly waking!
    Harp, by patriot virtue strung!
Freedom's hand thy chords is shaking,
    Freedom's hymn is o'er them sung.
Sound it ever! never sparing
    Tyrant's rage or bigot's art;
But a peaceful promise bearing
    To the Irish peasant's heart.

CATE OF ARAGLEN.

Air—"*An Cailin Ruadh.*"

I.

When first I saw thee, Cate, that summer ev'ning late,
Down at the orchard gate of Araglen,
I felt I 'd ne'er before seen one so fair, a-stór,
I fear'd I 'd never more see thee agen—
I stopped and gazed at thee, my footfall luckily
Reach'd not thy ear, tho' we stood there so near;
While from thy lips a strain, soft as the summer rain,
Sad as a lover's pain, fell on my ear.

II.

I 've heard the lark in June, the harp's wild plaintive tune,
The thrush, that aye too soon gives o'er his strain—
I 've heard in hush'd delight the mellow horn at night,
Waking the echoes light of wild Loch Lein;
But neither echoing horn, nor thrush upon the thorn,
Nor lark at early morn, hymning in air,
Nor harper's lay divine, e'er witch'd this heart of mine,
Like that sweet voice of thine, that ev'ning there.

III.

And when some rustling, dear, fell on thy listening ear,
You thought your brother near, and nam'd his name,
I could not answer, though, as luck would have it so,
His name and mine, you know, were both the same—
Hearing no answering sound, you glanced in doubt around,
With timid look, and found it was not he ;
Turning away your head, and, blushing rosy red,
Like a wild fawn you fled, far far from me.

IV.

The swan upon the lake, the wild rose in the brake,
The golden clouds that make the west their throne,
The wild ash by the stream, the full moon's silver beam,
The ev'ning star's soft gleam, shining alone ;
The lily rob'd in white—all, all are fair and bright ;
But ne'er on earth was sight so bright, so fair,
As that one glimpse of thee, that I caught then, machree,
It stole my heart from me that ev'ning there.

V.

And now you're mine alone, that heart is all my own—
That heart that ne'er hath known a flame before.
That form of mould divine, that snowy hand of thine—
Those locks of gold are mine, for evermore.
Was lover ever seen, as blest as thine, Caitilin ?
Hath lover ever been more fond, more true ?
Thine is my ev'ry vow ! for ever dear, as now !
Queen of my heart be thou ! *mo cailin ruadh !*

DOMHNALL GLEANNACH.

THE PILLAR TOWERS OF IRELAND.

BY D. F. M'CARTHY.

I.

THE pillar towers of Ireland, how wondrously they stand
By the lakes and rushing rivers through the valleys of our land;
In mystic file, through the isle, they lift their heads sublime,
These grey old pillar temples—these conquerors of time!

II.

Beside these grey old pillars, how perishing and weak
The Roman's arch of triumph, and the temple of the Greek,
And the gold domes of Byzantium, and the pointed Gothic spires—
All are gone, one by one, but the temples of our sires!

III.

The column, with its capital, is level with the dust,
And the proud halls of the mighty and the calm homes of the just;
For the proudest works of man, as certainly, but slower,
Pass like the grass at the sharp scythe of the mower!

IV.

But the grass grows again when in majesty and mirth,
On the wing of the Spring comes the Goddess of the Earth;
But for man in this world no springtide e'er returns
To the labours of his hands or the ashes of his urns!

V.

Two favorites hath Time—the pyramids of Nile,
And the old mystic temples of our own dear isle—
As the breeze o'er the seas, where the halcyon has its nest,
Thus Time o'er Egypt's tombs and the temples of the West!

VI.

The names of their founders have vanished in the gloom,
Like the dry branch in the fire or the body in the tomb;

But to-day, in the ray, their shadows still they cast—
These temples of forgotten Gods—these relics of the past!

VII.

Around these walls have wandered the Briton and the Dane—
The captives of Armorica, the cavaliers of Spain—
Phœnician and Milesian, and the plundering Norman Peers—
And the swordsmen of brave Brian, and the Chiefs of later years!

VIII.

How many different rites have these grey old temples known?
To the mind what dreams are written in these chronicles of stone!
What terror and what error, what gleams of love and truth,
Have flashed from these walls since the world was in its youth?

IX.

Here blazed the sacred fire—and, when the sun was gone,
As a star from afar to the traveller it shone;
And the warm blood of the victim have these grey old temples
      drunk,
And the death-song of the Druid and the matin of the Monk.

X.

Here was placed the holy chalice that held the sacred wine,
And the gold cross from the altar, and the relics from the shrine,
And the mitre shining brighter with its diamonds than the East,
And the crozier of the Pontiff and the vestments of the Priest!

XI.

Where blazed the sacred fire, rung out the vesper bell—
Where the fugitive found shelter became the hermit's cell;
And Hope hung out its symbol to the innocent and good,
For the cross o'er the moss of the pointed summit stood!

XII.

There may it stand for ever, while this symbol doth impart
To the mind one glorious vision, or one proud throb to the heart;
While the breast needeth rest may these grey old temples last,
Bright prophets of the future, as preachers of the past!

AID YOURSELVES AND GOD WILL AID YOU.

I.

SIGNS and tokens round us thicken,
Hearts throb high and pulses quicken,
Comes the morn, though red and lurid,
   Clouds and storms around it hung;
Still, it is that morn assured,
   Long ye've prayed for, sought, and sung.
Soon those clouds may break, and render
To your noon its genial splendour,
Or in gloom more hopeless vest it—
On your heads the end is rested,
Front to front ye've now arrayed you,
AID YOURSELVES AND GOD WILL AID YOU.

II.

Awful, past all human telling,
Is the change upon you dwelling;
Act but now the fool or craven,
   And, like Canaan doomed of yore,
" Slave of slaves" shall be engraven
   On your foreheads evermore.
Crouching to your masters' mercies,
Drugged with slavery's cup like Circè's,
Scorn and by-word of the nations,
Curse of coming generations,
Blackest shame will overshade you—
AID YOURSELVES AND GOD WILL AID YOU.

III.

Hence, oh, hence! such foul surmises,
Truer far a vision rises,
Men in freedom's ranks battalion'd,
   Countless as the bristling grain,
Firm as ardent, wise as valiant,
   All to venture—all sustain;
Men of never-sinking patience,
Tried and taught by stern privations,

2 o

From their path nor lured nor driven,
Till their every bond is riven—
Every wrong dispersed like May dew—
AID YOURSELVES AND GOD WILL AID YOU.

IV.

No! a heart-roused people's action
Cannot die like storms of faction.
Long a mute but master feeling
   In the millions' breast was nursed,
Till—a magic voice appealing—
   Forth it came, the thunder-burst.
'Gainst it now they plant their barriers,
Guard their keeps, and arm their warriors,
Lavish all their futile forces,
Power's most stale and vile resources,
Yet awhile to crush, degrade you—
AID YOURSELVES AND GOD WILL AID YOU.

V.

Blind misrule, and free opinion,
Armed lies and truth's dominion,
In a battle still recurring
   Ever have these foes been set,
Here their deadliest strife is stirring—
   Who can doubt the issue yet?
Watch and wait, your hour abiding,
Nought your goal one moment hiding,
Fearing not, nor too confiding,
Trusting in your Leader's guiding,
His who ne'er forsook, betrayed you—
AID YOURSELVES AND GOD WILL AID YOU.

VI.

But, should all be unavailing,
Reason, truth, and justice failing,
Every peaceful effort blighted,
   Every shred of freedom reft—
Then—oh, are we crushed or frighted
   While one remedy is left!

Back, each slave that faints or falters,
On, true heart that never alters,
On, stout arm, no terrors weaken,
Bruce's star and Tell's your beacon;
Strike—that stroke, is many a day due,
AID YOURSELVES AND GOD WILL AID YOU.

SLIABH CUILINN.

THE VICTOR'S BURIAL.
BY THOMAS DAVIS.

I.

WRAP him in his banner, the best shroud of the brave—
Wrap him in his *onchu*,* and take him to his grave—
Lay him not down lowly, like bulwark overthrown,
But, gallantly upstanding, as if ris'n from his throne,
With his *craiseach*† in his hand, and his sword on his thigh,
With his war-belt on his waist, and his *cathbarr*‡ on high—
Put his *fleasg*§ upon his neck—his green flag round him fold,
Like ivy round a castle wall—not conquered, but grown old—
    Wirasthrue! Oh, Wirasthrue! Oh, Wirasthrue! ochone!
    Weep for him! Oh! weep for him, but remember, in your moan,
        That he died, in his pride,
        With his foes about him strown.

II.

Oh! shrine him in Beinn-Edair ‖ with his face towards the foe,
As an emblem that not death our defiance can lay low—
Let him look across the waves from the promontory's breast,
To menace back The East, and to sentinel The West;
Sooner shall these channel waves the iron coast cut through,
Than the spirit he has left, yield, Easterlings! to you—
Let his coffin be the hill, let the eagles of the sea
Chorus with the surges round, the *tuireamh*¶ of the free!
    Wirasthrue! Oh, Wirasthrue! Oh, Wirasthrue! ochone!
    Weep for him! Oh! weep for him, but remember, in your moan,
        That he died, in his pride,
        With his foes about him strown!

---

* Flag.   † Spear.   ‡ Helmet.   § Collar.   ‖ Howth.   ¶ A Masculine Lament.

WATCH AND WAIT.

Air.—*"Paddy! Will you now?"*

Allegro spiritoso. **f**

Sad-ly as a muf-fled drum, Toll the hours of long pro-ba-tion;

Let them toll, The sta-ble soul Can work and wait to build a na-tion, Curse or groan

Ne-ver-more shall own, But our sti-fled hearts are pa-tient,—As a stone.

WATCH AND WAIT.

BY CHARLES GAVAN DUFFY.

I.

SADLY, as a muffled drum,
  Toll the hours of long probation;
Let them toll, the stable soul
  Can work and wait to build a nation.
      Curse or groan
      Never more shall own
  But our stifled hearts are patient
      As a stone.

II.

Yes, as patient as a stone,
  Till we 're struck in hate or ire;
Then the dint will fall on *flint*
  And send them back a stream of fire!
      Wait, boys, wait
      Ready for your fate,
  Prompt as powder to the linstock
      Soon or late!

III.

Let us gather love and help,
  Won from native friends and foemen;
How little loath, the hearts of both,
  We read in many a glorious omen.
      No, boys, no;
      Let no word or blow
  Brand a native Irish brother
      As our foe.

IV.

Holy Freedom's pealing voice
  Willing slaves hath never woken;
Ireland's trance was ignorance,
  And KNOWLEDGE all her spells hath broken.
      Hell and night
      Vanish from her sight,
  As when God pronounced aforetime
      Be there light!

v.

Cherish well this sacred flame,
    Feed its lamp with care and patience;
From God it came, its destined aim,
    To burst the fetters off the nations.
        Now, boys, now,
        Why should we bow,
When the promised day is dawning,
        And that's *now*.

vi.

Brothers, if this day should set,
    Another yet must crown our freedom;
That will come, with roll of drum,
    And trampling files with MEN to lead them.
        Who can save
        Renegade or slave,
Fortune only twines her garlands
        For the brave!

OUR COURSE.

BY J. D. FRAZER.

i.

WE look'd for guidance to the *blind!*
    We sued for counsel to the *dumb!*
Fling the vain fancy to the wind—
    Their hour is past, and *ours* is come;
They gave, in that propitious hour,
    Nor kindly look, nor gracious tone;
But heaven has not denied us power
    To do their duty, and our own.

ii.

And is it true, that tyrants throw
    Their shafts among us, steeped in gall;
And every arrow, swift or slow,
    Points foremost still, ascent or fall.

Still sure to wound us, tho' the aim
  Seem ta'en remotely, or amiss?
And men with spirits feel no shame
  To brook so dark a doom as this!
III.
Alas! the nobles of the land
  Are like our long-deserted halls;
No living voices, clear and grand,
  Respond when foe or freedom calls,
But ever and anon ascends
  Low moaning, when the tempest rolls;
A tone, that desolation lends
  Some crevice of their ruined souls.
IV.
So be it—yet shall we prolong
  Our prayers, when deeds would serve our need;
Or wait for woes, the swift and strong
  Can ward by strength, or 'scape by speed?
The vilest of the vile of earth
  Were nobler than our proud array,
If, suffering bondage from our birth,
  We will not burst it when we may!
V.
And has the bondage not been borne
  Till all our softer nature fled—
Till tyranny's dark tide had worn
  Down to the stubborn rock its bed?
But if the current, cold and deep,
  That channel through all time retain,
At worst, by heaven! it shall not sweep
  Unruffled o'er our hearts again.
VI.
Up for the land—'tis ours—'tis ours—
  The proud man's sympathies are all
Like silvery clouds, whose faithless showers
  Come froz'n to hailstones in their fall.
Our freedom and the sea-bird's food
  Are hid beneath deep ocean waves!
And who should search and sound the flood,
  If not, the sea-birds, and the slaves?

CLARE'S DRAGOONS.

Air.—"*Viva La.*"

Allegro. **f**

When on Ra-millies' blood-y field, The baf-fled French were forc'd to yield, The vic-tor Sax-on back-ward reel'd Be-fore the charge of Clare's Dra-goons.

mez.p.

The flags we conquer'd in that fray Look lone in Ypres' choir, they say, We'll

win them com - pa - ny to - day, Or brave -ly die, like Clare's Dra -goons.

Vi - va la for Ire-land's wrong, And vi - va la for Ire- land's right,

Vi - va la in bat - tle throng, For a Span-ish steed and sa - bre bright.

2 P

CLARE'S DRAGOONS.

BY THOMAS DAVIS.

I.

When, on Ramillies' bloody field,
The baffled French were forced to yield,
The victor Saxon backward reeled
   Before the charge of Clare's Dragoons.
The Flags, we conquered in that fray,
Look lone in Ypres' choir they say,
We'll win them company to-day,
   Or bravely die like Clare's Dragoons.

CHORUS.

Viva la for Ireland's wrong!
   Viva la for Ireland's right!
Viva la in battled throng,
   For a Spanish steed, and sabre bright!

II.

The brave old lord died near the fight,
But, for each drop he lost that night,
A Saxon cavalier shall bite
   The dust before Lord Clare's Dragoons.
For, never, when our spurs were set,
And never, when our sabres met,
Could we the Saxon soldiers get
   To stand the shock of Clare's Dragoons.

CHORUS.

Viva la the New Brigade!
   Viva la the Old One, too!
Viva la the rose shall fade,
   And the Shamrock shine for ever new!

III.

Another Clare is here to lead,
The worthy son of such a breed;
The French expect some famous deed,
    When Clare leads on his bold Dragoons.
Our colonel comes from Brian's race,
His wounds are in his breast and face,
The beᴀꞃnᴀ bᴀeᵹᴀꞁl * is still his place,
    The foremost of his bold Dragoons.

CHORUS.

Viva la the New Brigade!
    Viva la the Old One, too!
Viva la the rose shall fade,
    And the Shamrock shine for ever new!

IV.

There's not a man in squadron here
Was ever known to flinch or fear;
Though first in charge and last in rere,
    Have ever been Lord Clare's Dragoons;
But, see! we'll soon have work to do,
To shame our boasts, or prove them true,
For hither comes the English crew,
    To sweep away Lord Clare's Dragoons.

CHORUS.

Viva la for Ireland's wrong!
    Viva la for Ireland's right!
Viva la in battled throng,
    For a Spanish steed and sabre bright!

V.

Oh! comrades think how Ireland pines,
Her exiled lords, her rifled shrines,
Her dearest hope, the ordered lines,y
    And bursting charge of Clare's Dragoons.

---

* The Gap of Danger.

2 P 2

Then fling your Green Flag to the sky,
Be Limerick your battle-cry,
And charge, till blood floats fetlock-high,
    Around the track of Clare's Dragoons.

CHORUS.

Viva la the New Brigade!
  Viva la the Old One, too!
Viva la the rose shall fade,
    And the Shamrock shine for ever new!

THE PRETTY GIRL MILKING HER COW.

BY M. J. BARRY.

AIR—" Laiḷiɳ ᴅeaʀ cʀúiceaᴅ ɳa m-bo."

I.

'Twas eve, and the stars began peeping,
  Though sunset still crimson'd the west,
When sounds through the hushed air came creeping,
  That ruffled the peace of my breast:
My form in the twilight concealing,
  I sat myself down on my plough,
While sang, full of sweetness and feeling,
  A pretty girl milking her cow.

II.

" Sweet land, that my forefathers bled for,
  When strangers to trample thee thought,
Ah! what was their valiant blood shed for?
  Far better they never had fought.
Their sons think no more on thy glory,
  Like slaves to the tyrant they bow,
And I can but weep at thy story,
  And sing it while milking my cow.

III.

"It is not that riches I sigh for,
  I only repine at thy shame—
Thy glory and freedom I'd die for,
  And smile upon death as he came.
I'd prize the bold hand that would right thee,
  And spurn him with diadem'd brow
Whose base heart would injure and slight thee,
  Though a poor maiden milking her cow.

IV.

"Oh! blest be the sons of the stranger,
  Who, nursed on thy beautiful breast,
With thine shared the strife and the danger
  For thee, bleeding Queen of the West!
When the child of thy foe would befriend thee,
  Nor wrong to thy bosom allow,
Why should not the blessing attend thee,
  Of the poor maiden milking her cow?"

V.

She ceased, as the shadows fell deeper,
  And homeward returned with her pail,
But I felt like some strangely waked sleeper,
  At the tones of that eloquent wail.
Oh! sure if thy sons but relented,
  Sweet land! 'twere not late, even now,
To wash out the woes so lamented
  By the fair maiden milking her cow.

THE PATRIOT BRAVE.

BY R. D. WILLIAMS.

I.

I DRINK to the valiant who combat
  For freedom by mountain or wave,
And may triumph attend, like a shadow,
  The swords of the patriot brave!

Oh! never was holier chalice
  Than this at our festivals crown'd,
The heroes of Morven, to pledge it,
    And gods of Valhalla float round.
      Hurrah for the patriot brave!
      A health to the patriot brave!
And a curse and a blow be to liberty's foe,
    Whether tyrant, or coward, or knave.

II.

Great spirits who battled in old time
  For the freedom of Athens, descend!
As low to the shadow of Brian
  In fond hero-worship we bend.
From those that in far Alpine passes
  Saw Daithi struck down in his mail,
To the last of our chiefs' galloghlasses,
  The saffron-clad foes of the Pale.
    Let us drink to the patriot brave—
    Hurrah for the patriot brave!
But a curse and a blow be to liberty's foe,
    And more chains for the satisfied slave.

III.

Oh, Liberty! hearts that adore thee
  Pour out their best blood at thy shrine,
As freely as gushes before thee
  This purple libation of wine.
For us, whether destined to triumph,
  Or bleed as Leonidas bled,
Crushed down by a forest of lances,
  On mountains of foreigner dead,
    May we sleep with the patriot brave!
    God prosper the patriot brave!
But may battle and woe hurry liberty's foe
    To a bloody and honourless grave!

THE FALL OF THE LEAVES.

BY THE REV. C. MEEHAN.

I.

THEY are falling, they are falling, and soon, alas! they 'll fade,
The flowers of the garden, the leaves of dell and glade;
Their dirge the winds are singing in the lone and fitful blast,
And the leaves and flowers of summer are strewn and fading fast.
Ah! why then have we loved them, when their beauties might
    have told
They could not linger long with us, nor stormy skies behold?
Fair creatures of the sunshine! your day of life is past,
Ye are scattered by the rude winds, fallen and fading fast:
And, oh! how oft enchanted have we watched your opening bloom,
When you made unto the day-God your offerings of perfume!
How vain are our imaginings that joy will always last—
'Tis like to you, ye sweet things, all dimmed and faded fast.
The glens where late ye bloomed for us are leafless now and lorn,
The tempest's breath hath all their pride and all their beauty shorn.

II.

'Twas ever so, and so shall be, by fate that doom was cast—
The things we love are scarcely seen till they are gone and past.
Ay, ye are gone and faded, ye leaves and lovely flowers,
But when spring comes you'll come again to deck the garden's
    bowers;
And beauty, too, will cull you, and twine ye in her hair—
What meeter, truer, emblem can beauty ever wear?
But never, here, oh! never, shall we the loved ones meet,
Who shone in youth around us and like you faded fleet;
Full soon affliction bowed them, and life's day-dawn o'ercast,
They 're bloooming now in heaven, their day of fading's past!
Ye withered leaves and flowers! oh! may you long impart
Monition grave and moral stern unto this erring heart—
Oh! teach it that the joys of earth are short-lived, vain, and frail,
And transient as the leaves and flowers before the wintry gale!

THE REPEALERS' TRUMPET CALL.

Four Trumpets.

Band.

2 Q

CATE OF CEANN-MARE.*

BY D. F. M'CARTHY.

I.

OH ! many bright eyes full of goodness and gladness,
　Where the pure soul looks out, and the heart loves to shine,
And many cheeks pale with the soft hue of sadness,
　Have I worshipped in silence and felt them divine !
But hope in its gleamings, or love in its dreamings,
　Ne'er fashioned a being so faultless and fair
As the lily-cheeked beauty, the rose of the Ruachtach,†
　The fawn of the valley, sweet Cate of Ceann-mare!

II.

It was all but a moment, her radiant existence,
　Her presence, her absence, all crowded on me ;
But time has not ages and earth has not distance
　To sever, sweet vision, my spirit from thee !
Again am I straying where children are playing—
　Bright is the sunshine and balmy the air,
Mountains are heathy, and there do I see thee,
　Sweet fawn of the valley, young Cate of Ceann-mare !

III.

Thy own bright arbutus hath many a cluster
　Of white waxen blossoms like lilies in air ;
But, oh ! thy pale cheek hath a delicate lustre,
　No blossoms can rival, no lily doth wear.
To that cheek softly flushing, to thy lip brightly blushing,
　Oh ! what are the berries that bright tree doth bear ?
Peerless in beauty, the rose of the Ruachtach,
　That fawn of the valley, sweet Cate of Ceann-mare !

---

* Properly Ceann-mara,—head of the Sea.　　　† Commonly written Roughty.

IV.

Oh ! beauty, some spell from kind nature thou bearest,
   Some magic of tone or enchantment of eye,
That hearts that are hardest from forms that are fairest,
   Receive such impressions as never can die !
The foot of the fairy though lightsome and airy,
   Can stamp on the hard rock the shape it doth wear !
Art cannot trace it, nor ages efface it—
   And such are thy glances, sweet Cate of Ceann-mare !

V.

To him who far travels how sad is the feeling—
   How the light of his mind is o'ershadowed and dim,
When the scenes he most loves, like the river's soft stealing,
   All fade as a vision and vanish from him !
Yet he bears from each far land a flower for that garland,
   That memory weaves of the bright and the fair ;
While this sigh I am breathing *my* garland is wreathing,
   And the rose of that garland is Cate of Ceann-mare !

VI.

In lonely Lough Quinlan,* in summer's soft hours,
   Fair islands are floating that move with the tide,
Which, sterile at first, are soon covered with flowers,
   And thus o'er the bright waters fairy-like glide !
Thus the mind the most vacant is quickly awakened,
   And the heart bears a harvest that late was so bare,
Of him who in roving finds objects in loving,
   Like the fawn of the valley—sweet Cate of Ceann-mare !

---

* Dr. Smith, in his History of Kerry, says—" Near this place is a considerable fresh water lake, called Lough Quinlan, in which are some small floating islands much admired by the country people. These islands swim from side to side of the lake, and are usually composed at first of a long kind of grass, which being blown off the adjacent grounds about the middle of September, and floating about, collect slime and other stuff, and so yearly increase till they come to have grass and other vegetables grown upon them."

VII.

Sweet Cate of Ceann-mare! though I ne'er may behold thee—
　Though the pride and the joy of another you be—
Though strange lips may praise thee and strange arms enfold thee!
　A blessing, dear Cate, be on them and on thee!
One feeling I cherish that never can perish—
　One talisman proof to the dark wizard care—
The fervent and dutiful love of the beautiful,
　Of which *thou* art a type, gentle Cate of Ceann-mare!

A LAY SERMON.

BY CHARLES GAVAN DUFFY.

I.

Brother, do you love your brother?
　Brother, are you all you seem?
Do you live for more than living?
　Has your Life a law, and scheme?
Are you prompt to bear its duties,
　As a brave man may beseem?

II.

Brother, shun the mist exhaling
　From the fen of pride and doubt;
Neither seek the house of bondage
　Walling straitened souls about;
Bats! who, from their narrow spy-hole,
　Cannot see a world without.

III.

Anchor in no stagnant shallow—
　　Trust the wide and wond'rous sea,
Where the tides are fresh for ever,
　　And the mighty currents free;
There, perchance, oh! young Columbus,
　　Your New World of truth may be.

IV.

Favor will not make deserving—
　　(Can the sunshine brighten clay?)
Slowly must it grow to blossom,
　　Fed by labour and delay,
And the fairest bud of promise
　　Bears the taint of quick decay.

V.

You must strive for better guerdons;
　　Strive to *be* the thing you'd seem;
Be the thing that God hath made you,
　　Channel for no borrowed stream;
He hath lent you mind and conscience;
　　See you travel in their beam!

VI.

See you scale life's misty highlands
　　By this light of living truth!
And with bosom braced for labour,
　　Breast them in your manly youth;
So when age and care have found you,
　　Shall your downward path be smooth.

VII.

Fear not, on that rugged highway,
　　Life may want its lawful zest;
Sunny glens are in the mountain,
　　Where the weary feet may rest,
Cooled in streams that gush for ever
　　From a loving mother's breast.

VIII.

" Simple heart and simple pleasures,"
　　So they write life's golden rule;
Honor won by supple baseness,
　　State that crowns a cankered fool,
Gleam as gleam the gold and purple
　　On a hot and rancid pool.

IX.

Wear no show of wit or science,
　　But the gems you 've won, and weighed;
Thefts, like ivy on a ruin,
　　Make the rifts they seem to shade :
Are you not a thief and beggar
　　In the rarest spoils arrayed?

X.

Shadows deck a sunny landscape,
　　Making brighter all the bright :
So, my brother! care and danger
　　On a loving nature light,
Bringing all its latent beauties
　　Out upon the common sight.

XI.

Love the things that God created,
　　Make your brother's need your care;
Scorn and hate repel God's blessings,
　　But where love is, *they* are there;
As the moonbeams light the waters,
　　Leaving rock and sand-bank bare.

XII.

Thus, my brother, grow and flourish,
　　Fearing none, and loving all;
For the true man needs no patron,
　　He shall climb, and never crawl;
Two things fashion their own channel—
　　The strong man and the waterfall.

THE BATTLE OF LIMERICK.

August 27, 1690.

BY THOMAS DAVIS.

Air—" *Garryowen.*"

I.

Oh, hurrah! for the men, who, when danger is nigh,
Are found in the front, looking death in the eye.
Hurrah! for the men who kept Limerick's wall,
And hurrah! for bold Sarsfield, the bravest of all.
　　King William's men round Luimneach lay,
　　His cannon crash'd from day to day,
　　Till the southron wall was swept away
　　　　At the city of Luimneach lionnglas.*
'Tis afternoon, yet hot the sun,
When William fires the signal gun,
And, like its flash, his columns run
　　　　On the city of Luimneach lionnglas.

---

* " Limerick of the azure river," see " The Circuit of Ireland," p. 47.

II.

Yet, Hurrah! for the men, &c.

> The breach gaped out two perches wide,
> The fosse is filled, the batteries plied;
> Can the Irishmen that onset bide
>   At the city of Luimneach lionnglas.
> Across the ditch the columns dash,
> Their bay'nets o'er the rubbish flash,
> When sudden comes a rending crash
>   From the city of Luimneach lionnglas.

III.

Then, hurrah! for the men, &c.

> The bullets rain in pelting shower,
> And rocks and beams from wall and tower;
> The Englishmen are glad to cower
>   At the city of Luimneach lionnglas;
> But, rallied soon, again they pressed,
> Their bay'nets pierced full many a breast,
> Till they bravely won the breach's crest
>   At the city of Luimneach lionnglas.

IV.

Yet, hurrah! for the men, &c.

> Then fiercer grew the Irish yell,
> And madly on the foe they fell,
> Till the breach grew like the jaws of hell—
>   Not the city of Luimneach lionnglas.
> The women fought before the men,
> Each man became a match for ten,
> So back they pushed the villains then,
>   From the city of Luimneach lionnglas.

V.

Then hurrah ! for the men, &c.

> But Brandenburgh the ditch has crost,
> And gained our flank at little cost—
> The bastion's gone—the town is lost;
>> Oh ! poor city of Luimneach lionnglas.
> When, sudden, Sarsfield springs the mine—
> Like rockets rise the Germans fine,
> And come down dead, 'mid smoke and shine,
>> At the city of Luimneach lionnglas !

VI.

So, hurrah ! for the men, &c.

> Out, with a roar, the Irish sprung,
> And back the beaten English flung,
> Till William fled, his lords among,
>> From the city of Luimneach lionnglas.
> 'Twas thus was fought that glorious fight,
> By Irishmen, for Ireland's right—
> May all such days have such a night
>> As the Battle of Luimneach lionnglas.

THE BISHOP OF ROSS.

BY DR. MADDEN, AUTHOR OF THE "LIVES OF THE UNITED
IRISHMEN."

I.

THE tramp of the trooper is heard at Macroom ;*
  The soldiers of Cromwell are spared from Clonmel,†
And Broghill—the merciless Broghill—is come
  On a mission of murder which pleases him well.

---

* Magh Cromha.   † Cluain Meala.

2 R

II.

The wailing of women, the wild *ululu*,
    Dread tidings from cabin to cabin convey ;
But loud tho' the plaints and the shrieks which ensue,
    The war-cry is louder of men in array.

III.

In the park of Macroom there is gleaming of steel,
    And glancing of lightning in looks on that field,
And swelling of bosoms with patriot zeal,
    And clenching of hands on the weapons they wield.

IV.

MacEgan !* a prelate like Ambrose of old,
    Forsakes not his flock when the spoiler is near,
The post of the pastor's in front of the fold
    When the wolf 's on the plain and there 's rapine to fear.

V.

The danger is come, and the fortune of war
    Inclines to the side of oppression once more ;
The people are brave—but they fall, and the star
    Of their destiny sets in the darkness of yore.

VI.

MacEgan survives in the Philistine hands
    Of the lords of the pale, and his death is decreed ;
But the sentence is stayed by Lord Broghill's command,
    And the prisoner is dragged to his presence with speed.

VII.

To Carraig-an-Droichid † this instant, he cried,
    Prevail on your people in garrison there
To yield, and at once in our mercy confide,
    And your life, I will pledge you my honor, to spare.

---

* MacAodhagain in proper spelling.

† Commonly written Carrigadrohid, (the Rock of the Bridge,) three miles east of Macroom, Co. Cork. The Castle is built on a steep rock in the river Lee by the M'Cartys.

VIII.

" *Your mercy ! your honor !* " the prelate replied,
    " I well know the worth of—my duty I know ;
Lead on to the Castle, and there by your side,
    With the blessing of God, what is meet will I do."

IX.

The orders are given, the prisoner is led
    To the Castle, and round him are menacing hordes ;
Undaunted—approaching the walls, at the head
    Of the troopers of Cromwell, he utters these words :

X.

" Beware of the Cockatrice—trust not the wiles
    Of the serpent—for perfidy skulks in its folds !
Beware of Lord Broghill, the day that he smiles,
    His mercy is murder !—his word never holds.

XI.

" Remember 'tis writ in our annals of blood,
    Our countrymen never relied on the faith
Of truce, or of treaty, but treason ensued—
    And the issue of every delusion was death !"

XII.

Thus nobly the patriot prelate sustained
    The ancient renown of his chivalrous race,
And the last of old Eoghan's descendants obtained
    For the name of Ui—mani new lustre and grace.

XIII.

He died on the scaffold, in front of those walls
    Where the blackness of ruin is seen from afar ;
And the gloom of its desolate aspect recals
    The blackest of Broghill's achievements in war !

2 R 2

OUR OWN AGAIN.

Let the cow-ard shrink a - side,—Here's for our own a-gain; Let the brawl-ing slave de - ride,—We'll have our own a-gain! Let the ty - rant bribe and lie,—March,—threat-en,— for - ti - fy,—Loose his law - yer and his spy, Yet we'll have our own a - gain.

Let him soothe in silk-en tone, Scold from a foreign throne; Let him come with bu-gles blown,—

We shall have our own a-gain! Let us to our pur-pose bide; We'll have our

own a-gain! Let the game be fair-ly tried,—Here's for our own a-gain!

OUR OWN AGAIN.

BY THOMAS DAVIS.

I.

Let the coward shrink aside,
  We 'll have our own again;
Let the brawling slave deride,
  Here 's for our own again—
Let the tyrant bribe and lie,
March, threaten, fortify,
Loose his lawyer and his spy,
  Yet we 'll have our own again.
Let him soothe in silken tone,
Scold from a foreign throne;
Let him come with bugles blown,
  We shall have our own again.
Let us to our purpose bide,
  We 'll have our own again—
Let the game be fairly tried,
  We 'll have our own again.

II.

Send the cry throughout the land,'
  " Who 's for our own again?"
Summon all men to our band,
  Why not our own again?
Rich, and poor, and old, and young,
Sharp sword, and fiery tongue—
Soul and sinew firmly strung,
  All to get our own again.
Brothers thrive by brotherhood—
Trees in a stormy wood—
Riches come from Nationhood—
  Sha'n't we have our own again?
Munster's woe is Ulster's bane!
  Join for our own again—
Tyrants rob as well as reign,
  We 'll have our own again.

III.

Oft our fathers' hearts it stirr'd,
    " Rise for our own again!"
Often pass'd the signal word,
    " Strike for own again!"
Rudely, rashly, and untaught,
Uprose they, ere they ought,
Failing, though they nobly fought,
    Dying for their own again.
Mind will rule and muscle yield,
In senate, ship, and field—
When we 've skill our strength to wield,
    Let us take our own again.
By the slave, his chain is wrought,
    Strive for our own again.
Thunder is less strong than thought,
    We 'll have our own again.

IV.

Calm as granite to our foes,
    Stand for our own again;
Till his wrath to madness grows,
    Firm for our own again.
Bravely hope, and wisely wait,
Toil, join, and educate;
Man is master of his fate;
    We 'll enjoy our own again.
With a keen constrained thirst—
Powder's calm ere it burst—
Making ready for the worst,
    So we 'll get our own again.
Let us to our purpose bide,
    We 'll have our own again.
God is on the righteous side,
    We 'll have our own again.

WAR SONG.—A.D. 1597.

WAR SONG, A. D. 1597.

I.

Rise from your slumbers, sons of the brave,
　Eire demands your blow;
Grasp, at her summons, buckler and glaive,
　Onward to meet the foe!
Hark! to the blast of the war-trump shrill!
　This day your right ensures;
Up from each valley! down from each hill!
　Freedom or Death be your's.

II.

Think on the fields where your fathers bled;
　Think how they smote the Dane!
Shame not the graves of your glorious dead;
　Strike for your rights again!
Freedom and Vengeance both bid you rise,
　Start at their stirring call;
Strangers usurp all the blessings you prize—
　On! like a waterfall.

III.

On! with your chieftains, O'Domhnall, O'Neill!
　On! with the brave Maguire!
Break through the folds of the Sasanach mail,
　Heed not his noisy fire.
Crash through his ranks, as the lightning goes
　Right through the blackest cloud—
Red is his flag, that so haughtily glows,
　Redder shall be his shroud!

A PATRIOT'S HAUNTS.

BY WILLIAM MULCHINOECK.

I love the mountain rude and high,
Its bare and barren majesty,
And in its peopled solitude
I love to stand in musing mood,

2 s

And bring, by fancy's magic power,
Bright dreams to charm the passing hour ;
To fill the green and heathy glen
With hosts of stalwart fighting men,
With banners flaunting, fair, and free,
Fit for a new Thermopylæ ;
And in the dark and narrow pass
I place a young Leonidas.
With joy I mark the phantom fight,
And hear the shouts for native right ;
And thus, until the shades of night
Proclaim time's quick and restless flight,
In fancy, freedom's war I see,
And tread a land by slaves made free.

   I love to mark the billows rise,
And fling their spray into the skies—
To mark the bold impetuous shock
They deal upon the rugged rock ;
Until, where'er its side they lave,
Their power is shown in many a cave.
I match the rock to tyranny,
The waves to slaves and man made free ;
For know, 'twas unity like this,
That Greece put forth at Salamis,
And thus the Romans, side by side,
From Carthage tore her crest of pride ;
And yet, where slaves are found, I ween
New Fabii may still be seen,
Whose hearts though bold enough, I trow,
Sees not the fitting moment now—
Can find not yet the unity
That made the Doric children free,
That made the haughty Samnite fly
The anger of a Roman eye.

   Doubters ascend a mountain-height,
With healthy pulse and sinew light—
Cowards ! upon the foaming tide
Cast you your glances, far and wide,

And, in the dark hill, say with me,
"There's many a sure Thermopylæ,
And o'er each bay's profound abyss,
True hearts could make a Salamis."

A HEALTH.

BY J. D. FRAZER.

I.

HURRAH! our feuds are drowned at last;
  Hurrah! let tyrants tremble;
The fronted foemen of the past
  In brotherhood assemble.
Fill up—and with a lofty tongue
  As ever spoke from steeple,
From shore to shore *his* health be rung—
  The leader of the people.

II.

In mighty triumphs, singly won,
  The nation has a token
That mightier deeds will yet be done—
  The last strong fetter broken;
Since hearts of nerve and hands of strength,
  Once banded to resist him,
Unfurl his flag, and share at length
  The glory to assist him.

III.

Up with the wine from boss to brim,
  And be his voice the loudest,
Who rears, at risk of life or limb,
  Our country's flag the proudest.
"*The leader of the people*"—grand,
  Yet simple wisdom guide him!
And glory to the men who stand,
  Like sheathed swords, beside him!

ORANGE AND GREEN WILL CARRY THE DAY.

AIR.—"*The Protestant Boys.*"

Ire-land! re-joice, and Eng-land! de-plore, Fac-tion and feud are pass-ing a-way.

'Twas a low voice, but 'tis a loud roar, "O-range and Green will car-ry the day."

O-range! O-range! Green and O-range! Pitt-ed to-ge-ther in ma-ny a fray!

Li-ons in fight! And, link'd in their might, O-range and Green will car-ry the day.

m.f.

O-range!·O-range! Green and O-range! Wave them to-ge-ther o'er mountain and bay;

Cres — — —

cen — — — — do. — — — *ff*

Orange and Green! Our King and our Queen! " Orange and Green will car-ry the day!"

ff

ORANGE AND GREEN WILL CARRY THE DAY.

BY THOMAS DAVIS.

I.

Ireland! rejoice, and England! deplore—
Faction and feud are passing away.
'Twas a low voice, but 'tis a loud roar,
    "Orange and Green will carry the day."
        Orange! Orange!
        Green and Orange!
Pitted together in many a fray—
        Lions in fight!
        And link'd in their might,
Orange and Green will carry the day.
        Orange! Orange!
        Green and Orange!
Wave them together o'er mountain and bay.
        Orange and Green!
        Our King and our Queen!
    "Orange and Green will carry the day!"

II.

Rusty the swords our fathers unsheath'd—
William and James are turn'd to clay—
Long did we till the wrath they bequeath'd;
    Red was the crop, and bitter the pay!
        Freedom fled us!
        Knaves misled us!
Under the feet of the foemen we lay—
        Riches and strength
        We'll win them at length,
For Orange and Green will carry the day!
        Landlords fool'd us;
        England ruled us,
Hounding our passions to make us their prey;
        But, in their spite,
        The Irish "Unite,"
And Orange and Green will carry the day!

III.

Fruitful our soil where honest men starve;
  Empty the mart, and shipless the bay;
Out of our want the Oligarchs carve;
  Foreigners fatten on our decay!
        Disunited,
        Therefore blighted,
Ruined and rent by the Englishman's sway;
        Party and creed
        For once have agreed—
Orange and Green will carry the day!
        Boyne's old water,
        Red with slaughter!
Now is as pure as an infant at play;
        So, in our souls,
        Its history rolls,
And Orange and Green will carry the day!

IV.

English deceit can rule us no more,
  Bigots and knaves are scattered like spray—
Deep was the oath the Orangeman swore,
  " Orange and Green must carry the day!"
        Orange! Orange!
        Bless the Orange!
Tories and Whigs grew pale with dismay,
        When, from the North,
        Burst the cry forth,
  " Orange and Green will carry the day;"
        No surrender!
        No Pretender!
Never to falter and never betray—
        With an Amen,
        We swear it again,
Orange and Green shall carry the day!

PAST AND PRESENT.

"Where are the monster meetings, the myriads of Tara and Mullaghmast?"-
English Press passim.

I.

WHERE are the marshall'd hosts that met
　　Last year the Island over?
Here are they calm, but ready yet,
　　Like warriors couched in cover—
With zeal as ardent, rage as deep,
　　As bitter wrongs to feed them;
As stalwart limbs—let fools go sleep,
　　And dream of stifled freedom.

II.

A lull—the tempest lulls, and then
　　The blast the forest scatters;
The thunder peals are stilled—again
　　The bolt the turret shatters;
And low the brandished hatchet sings
　　For mightier stroke uplifted:
Round—round it swings, then down it rings,
　　And toughest blocks are rifted.

III.

There is a sullen under-hum
　　Will swell to a tornado;
A day shall come will render dumb
　　Our English lords' bravado—
When Irish parties, hand in hand,
　　And shoulder up to shoulder,
Shall take their stand on Irish land,
　　And buried feuds shall moulder.

IV.

Who chafes or falters at delay,
　　Faint-hearted and short-seeing?
What is it all?—a winter's day,
　　'Mid ages of ill-being;

Ah! thus our fathers were undone!
　They sickened and seceded—
Had they but battled constant on,
　Our battle were not needed.

v.

God knows his times—one thing know we,
　Our ills, and what will end them,
That these our fetters loosed must be,
　Or should we file, or rend them?
Shall we sit looking at our gyves,
　Who talked so loud a year hence?
Shall we who frankly staked our *lives*,
　Grudge earnest perseverance?

vi.

We'll hoard our might and gather more—
　We'll draw our brothers nigh us—
We'll give our minds, from wisdom's store,
　A firmer, manlier bias—
We'll rouse the nation near and far,
　From Rathlin to Cean-mara,
Then show them where the masses are
　Of Mullaighmast and Tara.

Sliabh Cuilinn.

A HIGHWAY FOR FREEDOM.

BY CLARENCE MANGAN.

Air—"*Boyne Water.*"

I.

" My suffering country shall be freed,
　And shine with tenfold glory!"
So spake the gallant Winkelried,
　Renowned in German story.
" No tyrant, even of kingly grade,
　Shall cross or darken my way!"
Out flashed his blade, and so he made
　For Freedom's course a highway!

II.

We want a man like this, with power
  To rouse the world by *one* word;
We want a Chief to meet the hour,
  And march the masses onward.
But Chief or none, through blood and fire,
  My Fatherland lies *thy* way!
The men must fight who dare desire
  For Freedom's course a highway!

III.

Alas! I can but idly gaze
  Around in grief and wonder;
The PEOPLE's will alone can raise
  The People's shout of thunder.
Too long, my friends, you faint for fear,
  In secret crypt and bye-way;
At last be Men!   Stand forth, and clear
  For Freedom's course a highway!

IV.

You intersect wood, lea, and lawn,
  With roads for monster waggons,
Wherein you speed like lightning, drawn
  By fiery iron dragons.
So do! Such work is good, no doubt;
  But why not seek some nigh way
For *Mind* as well?   Path also out
  For Freedom's course a highway!

V.

Yes! up! and let your weapons be
  Sharp steel and self-reliance!
Why waste your burning energy
  In void and vain defiance,
And phrases fierce but fugitive?
  'Tis deeds, not words, that *I* weigh—
Your swords and guns alone can give
  To Freedom's course a highway!

INDEX

TO THE

IRISH PHRASES USED IN THIS WORK.

Jam. Scot. Dict. Catarines and Katharines; Rich. Thesaur.
refers us to Bochart; Dict. Scoto-Celt.; *O'B. O'R.* &c.
See ʒall-óʒlaċ.

Ⅎ.

G.

L.

M.

Marcaiġeaċt na Bóiñe, *Marcaigheacht na Boinne*, Cavalcade of the Boinn, vulgò, Boyne, ... 32
Má seaḋ, *Ma seadh*, vulgò, Musha, If it be, (i.e. má is é,) ... ...
Máire, *Maire*, Mary, ... 111—189
A Ṁuire a's truaġ, *A Mhuire a's truagh*, vulgò, wirrasthrue, Oh! Mary, who art merciful. This form (with u) appears to be peculiar to addresses to the Virgin Mary, ... 48—238
Mí na meala, *Mi na meala*, month of honey; honey-moon, ... 186
Mo ḃuaċail, *Mo bhuachail*, My boy, ... 222—223
Mo ċraoiḃín aoiḃiñ áluiñ óg, *Mo chraoibhin aoibhinn aluinn og*, My pleasant,[2] beautiful,[3] young,[4] little branch,[1] ... ... 92—94
Mo ċailín ruaḋ, *Mo chailin ruadh*, My red[2] [haired] girl[1], ... 278
Mo cailin in the text is an error,
Mo ṁúirnín, *Mo mhuirnin*, my darling, ... 81

O.

Oċón, *Ochon*, vulgò, Ochone, ... 283
Ollaṁ, *Ollamh*, a doctor; teacher; learned man, Poss. ollaṁan, Nom.Plu. ollaṁna, Poss. ollaṁan; Ollaṁ Fóḋla, the learned man of Ireland, 229—245
Onċu, *Onchu*, interpreted in the text, "a flag," 283
Onċu, a leopard, onċon, a standard; ensign,—*O'R.* This word, and meirge, Nom. Plu. meirgeaḋa, standards, referred to in the notes to the Ui Fiachrach, p. 471, are rather obsolete; brataċ is more usual; *f.* Poss. brataiġe, Nom. Plu. brataċa.

R.

Raṫ, *Rath*, a fort, *f.* Poss. ráṫa, Subjective ráiṫ, Nom. Plu. ráṫana, ... 65—105—172—245—276
Rosg caṫa, *Rosg catha*, An address of (for) battle, rosg, *m.* Poss. roisge; caṫ, *m.* Poss. caṫa, ... 29—32
The interpretation in the text, "Eye of Battle," is incorrect.

S.

Sagart, *Sagart*, vulgò, soggarth, a priest, *m.* Poss. sagairt, see the Latin *sacerdos, sacerdotis.* ... ...
Scian, *Scian*, a Dagger; or knife, *f.* Poss. sceine, Nom. Plu. sceana, ... 151
Seamróg, *Seamrog*, vulgò, Shamrock, *f.* Poss. Seamróige, ... 290
Siñ féin, *Sinn fein*, We ourselves, ... 182
Sleaġ, *Sleagh*, a Spear, *m.* Poss. sleaġa, ... 31
Stoc, *Stoc*, a Trumpet, *m.* Poss. stoic, ... 152
Stór, *Stor*, a Treasure, *m.* Poss. stóir, Voc. a stór, vulgò, Asthore, oh! treasure, ... 14—277

T.

Tuireaḋ, tuireaṁ, *tuireadh, tuireamh*, a lament, ... 283

INDEX

He expressly calls him Brian Bóirbe, from a town, Boruṁa, Poss. Bóirbe, near which was Ceaṅ cora, vulgò, Kincora, *(the head of the weir,)* his royal residence. See O'Briain.
Brigid, *Brighid*, vulgò, Bride, Bridget, Poss. Briġde, ... 111—195

C.

Caitlín, *Caitlin*, N.B. Caitilin in text, ... 278
Caṫal, *Cathal*, vulgò, Cahill, &c. (and, as a christian name, sometimes Charles! with which it has no connexion), *m.* Poss. Caṫail, ... 3—26
Caṫal croiḃ ḋearg, Cathal of the red' hand', ... 194
Cormac, *Cormac*, Poss. Cormaic, ... 229

D.

Daṫi, *Dathi*, vulgò, Dathy, ... 104—229—294
This name is sometimes spelt Daithi but incorrectly. The very ancient names are not spelt by the rule, caol le caol agus leaṫan le leaṫan, and besides, that would *not* be the form of change, for the first syllable is pronounced broad.
Diarmuid, *Diarmuid*, vulgò, Dermod, Dermott, &c., Poss. Diarmada, ...
Doṁnall, Doṁnall Gleaṅaċ, ... 278
See Mac Doṁnaill, O'Doṁnaill, &c.

E.

Eiḃear, *Eibhear*, vulgò Heber, Poss. Eiḃir, ... 228
It is hard to account for the addition of the H, as the native prefix h- occurs only in a few inflexions.
Eiḃlín, *Eibhlin*, vulgò, Eveleen, Eileen, Aileen, &c. and sometimes Ellen! 127
Eiḃlín a rúin, Eibhlin, oh! secret (love or treasure.) Eiḃlín, *f.* Poss. Eiḃlíne; rún, *m.* Poss. rúin. See also 127, ... 15—117
Eireaṁón, *Eireamhon*, vulgò, Heremon, Poss. Eireaṁóin, ... 195
The H here is superfluous as in "Heber,"
Eoġan, *Eoghan*, vulgò, Owen, ...126—222—228—251—264—307
Eoġan ruaḋ, Red Eoghan, vulgò, Owen Roe, ...
The Poss. is Eoġain, as in Tír Eoġain, &c. 251

F.

Feiḋ.im, *Feidhlim*, vulgò, Phelim, ... 26
Fiaċa, *Fiacha*, Mac Aoḋa O'Braiṅ, vulgò, Pheagh Mac Hugh O'Byrne, 153
Finġin, *Finghin*, the Fair-born or purely-begotten,... 79
Firbis, *Firbis*, Poss. Firbisiġ, ... 238
Fóġartaċ, *Fogartach*, vulgò, Fogarty, ... 194
This, like most of the corrupted Irish names, is taken from the possessive case of the original word. Fóġartaċ, *m.* Poss. Fóġartaiġ, *Fogartaigh.* The English termination *y* has a resemblance to the Irish iġ. When the O', (or Ua,) Mac, or Ní, is used, the patronymic is always to be subjoined in the possessive case: thus, O'Fóġartaiġ, Ní'Fhóġartaiġ.

G.

Ꝺoƀᴀɴ, *Goban*, vulgò, Gobbin, Poss. Ꝺoƀᴀɪɴ, ... 27
. Ꝺoƀᴀɴ Ꙅᴀoꝗ was a celebrated architect.

J.

Ɪꝗ, *Ir*, Indecl. He was a son of Ϻɪʟeᴀꝺ. . The cʟᴀɴᴀ Ɍᴜᴀꝗᴀɪꝺe of Ꙍʟᴀꝺ,
derive descent from him. 228

L.

Ʌᴀoᵹᴀɪꝗe, *Laoghaire*, vulgò, Leary; Son of Niall of the Nine Hostages, 104
Ʌoꝗcᴀɴ, *Lorcan*, vulgò, Lawrence, a name with which the true Irish name
has no connexion. See, Ꙩ'Ꞇᴜᴀᴄᴀɪʟ. ... ... 151—225

M.

Ϻᴀc, *Mac*, vulgò, Mc, and Mꞌ, a son.
   Singular, Nom. mᴀc, Poss. mɪc, Subjective, mᴀc,   Voc. ᴀ ṁɪc.
   Plural,   Nom. mɪc, Poss. mᴀc, Subjective, mᴀcᴀɪƀ, Voc. ᴀ ṁᴀcᴀ.
      This is used as the initial syllable of many Highland Scotch,
      as well as Irish surnames. "Ut initialis syllaba cognoninum
      Scoticorum et Hibernicorum multorum, Mac, usurpatur;
      sic, Macdonald, i. e. son of Donald; Donaldi filius." Dict.
      Scoto-Celt.
      See the Welsh, Mab, a male, a boy, a son; and ab, ap, a son, used
      in expressing the names of men, as, Gruffyd ab Cynan; in
      the common usage of surnames the Welsh have left out the
      a and joined the *b* with the name following if it begin with
      a vowel, as, Belis for Ab Elis, or *p* if it begin with H or R,
      as, Parry, for Ap Harry; Pugh, for Ap Hugh; Pritchard,
      for Ap Richard; Probart, for Ap Robert.
Ϻᴀc Ꙍoꝺᴀ, *Mac Aodha*, See Ꙍoꝺ, ... 153
Ϻᴀc Ꙍoꝺᴀᵹᴀɪɴ, *Mac Aodhagain*, vulgò, Mac Egan, Keegan, Egan, &c.
   The son of Aodhagan, ... 73—306
      This joining of the final c of Ϻᴀc with the initial vowel of
      the patronymic following is a common mode of corruption.
Ϻᴀc Ʌᴀɴᴀ, *Mac Cana*, vulgò, Mc Cann, ... 118
Ϻᴀc Ʌᴀꝗᴄᴀɪᵹ, *Mac Carthaigh*, vulgò, Mc Carthy, Mc Carty, Carty, &c.,
   Son of Ʌᴀꝗᴄᴀᴄ, ... 73—126—194—306
Ϻᴀc Ꝺomɴᴀɪʟʟ, *Mac Domhnaill*, vulgò, Mc Donnell, Mc Donald, &c., The
   son of Domhnall, ...
Ϻᴀc Ꝫᴀɴᴀ, (or Ꝫᴀɴꝺᴀ, for the ɴꝺ has the power of double ɴ,) *Mac Eanna*,
   vulgò, Mc Kenna, Kenna, The son of Eanna, ... 28
Ϻᴀc Ƒɪꝗƀɪꝗɪᵹ, *Mac Firbisigh*, the Son of Ƒɪꝗƀɪꝗ, which see, ... 238
   Ꝺɪoʟʟᴀ Ɪoꝗᴀ Ϻoꝗ, means The great' Servant' of Jesus'.
Ϻᴀc Ꝺᴀƀᴀɴ, *Mac Gabhan*, vulgò, Mc Gowan, Gavan, Smith, &c. from
   Ꝺᴀƀᴀ, *Gabha*, m. a smith, Poss. Ꝺᴀƀᴀɴ. Theris also Ꙩ'Ꝺᴀƀᴀɴ. ... 3
Ϻᴀc Ϻᴀᴄᵹᴀṁɴᴀ, *Mac Mathghamhna*, vulgò, Mc Mahon, Mahon, Mahony,
   &c. The son of Ϻᴀᴄᵹᴀṁᴀɪɴ. See *O'B.* 6

2 U

Mac Miaḋaċain, *Mac Miadhachain*, vulgò, Mc Meechan, Meehan, &c. ... 83
Mac Murċaḋa, *Mac Murchadha*, vulgò, Mc Morrogh, Son of Murċaḋ, ...
Mileaḋ, *Mileadh*. vulgò, Milesius, Poss. Miliḋ, ... 228—236
Móran, *Moran*, ... } 229
Iḋ Mórain, The chain or collar of Moran, ... }
Murċaḋ, *Murchadh*, vulgò, Morrogh, Murogh, Poss. Murċaḋa, but in the present day it is commonly Murċaiḋ; whence Morphy, Murphy, &c. 179

N.

Ni, *Ni*, indecl. a daughter,

Whether the men of the tribe are called after their ancestor by the prefix O' or Mac, the women are uniformly designated by the prefix Ni. So in the Scotch Highlands Mac is for the men of the clann, Nic, for the women; "Nic, contr. for Nighean; used as a syllable of surnames, when a female is spoken of; cognominum syllaba, filiam denotans, cum de fœmina loquitur quis; C. S." (i.e. Common Speech,) Dict. Scoto-Celt. So, in Irish,

Ni, for niġ, niġean, inġean, inġin, a daughter,

Hence is seen the reason why in the Irish-speaking parts of the country the wife never changes her family name. In Irish, the O', Mac and Ni, like all other things, have meaning; and it would be ridiculous to suppose, that Maire ni Ḃriain, (daughter of Brian,) on marrying Padruig O'Néill, (the male descendant of Niall,) thereby became a Ni Néill, (or daughter of Niall.)

Ni Ḃriain, Eiblin Ni Ḃriain, not O'Brin, as in the text,... 171
Niall, *Niall*, vulgò, Neill. 104

This latter is the Poss. Néill, and properly used in Mac Neill, O'Neill, &c. but not separately.

O.

O', *O'*, a grandson or male descendant,

Singular, Nom. O', (ant. ua,) Poss. ui, Subjective, O, Voc. a ui,
Plural, Nom. ui, Poss. ua, Subjective, uiḃ,

This is the most usual prefix to Irish surnames though not used in the Scotch Highlands; but the root is perfectly known in the common language of both countries. Thus, "Ogha, a grandchild; nepos; *Scot.* O, Oe, Oye, *Jam.*" See, Dict. Scoto-Celt. "Ua, *s. m.* et *f.* a descendant, grandchild, proles, nepos, Llh. et O'R. vide Ogha." *Ibid.*

As a preposition, in the same sense, both simply and in composition, o and ua, from, out of, (i. e. proceeding from,) is equally used in both. O, from, is one of the instances in which the *Welsh* prepositions bear an analogy to ours.

In the plural ui, grandsons, male descendants, the word is applied to whole tribes or clann, and sometimes (incorrectly)

to the country inhabited by them; in which sense a most ridiculous corruption has been introduced, viz. " Hy—" as Hy Niall, &c. This cannot be too strenuously condemned nor too soon changed. This "Hy" is composed of two letters, neither of them in the original; and the one, ꜧ-, is never used in Irish save as a prefix, and the other, *y*, is not used at all! Besides, even those who conceive that corruptions obtain some sanction to a further continuance from an understood usage have no such support here, for Ui Neill, would be as generally understood as Hy Niall, to say nothing of the gross blundering.

See the words, *Ɔ, Ua, ꞁb*, in *O'B.* and *O'R.* applied to a country, a district, a tribe of people; see especially, *O'B.* at the end of the letter *Ɔ.* They seem to be nothing but the inflections of the same word, the initials being omitted in the first and third instances.

Ó'h-Uȝaꞁn, *O'h-Again,* vulgò, O'Hagan, ... 245
Ó'h-Ullubꞃaꞁn, *O'h-Allubhrain,* vulgò, O'Halloran, Halloran, &c. ... 104
Ó'h-Unluaꞁn, *O'h-Anluain,* vulgò, O'Hanlon, Hanlon, &c. 245
Ó'Bꞃaꞁñ, *O'Brainn,* vulgò, O'Byrne, Byrne, &c. ... ... 153—172
Ó'Bꞃiaꞁn, *O'Briain,* vulgò, O'Brien, Brien, &c. ... ... 127—194—215
Ó'Bꞁꞃlêꞁn, *O'Brislein,* descendant of Bꞁꞃleaꞁn, ... ■... ... 245
Ó'Caᴄaꞁn, *O'Cathain,* vulgò, O'Kane, Kane, Keane, Kean, &c. ... 245—246
Ó'Ceallaᴄaꞁn, *O'Ceallachain,* vulgò, O'Callaghan, Callaghan, &c.
    The name of the writer, John Cornelius O'Callaghan, should
      be written, Seaaꞁ Conᴄubaꞁ Ó'Ceallaᴄaꞁn, ... 183
Ó'Conaꞁll, *O'Conaill,* vulgò, O'Connell, &c.

    The names of Daniel, Maurice, and John, should be written,

Doṁnaꞁl Ó'Conaꞁll, THE LIBERATOR, ... 10—163
Nuꞁꞃceaꞃᴄac Ó'Conaꞁll, } His Sons, { ... ... 229—248
Seaaꞁ Ó'Conaꞁll, ... } { 258
Ó'Conallaꞁn, *O'Conallain,* ... ... 41—95
    The name of the Grammarian referred to is, Eóȝaꞁ Ó'Conallaꞁn.... 1
Ó'Conᴄubaꞁn, *O'Conchubhair,* vulgò, O'Connor, O'Conor, Connor, &c. 72—112
Ó'Dꞁomuꞃaꞁȝ, *O'Diomusaigh,* vulgò, O'Dempsey, Dempsey, Nom. Dꞁomuꞃaᴄ, 173
Ó'Doṁnaꞁll, *O'Domhnaill,* vulgò, O'Donnell, ... 119
Ó'Donobaꞁn, *O'Donobhain,* vulgò, O'Donovan, Donovan, &c. 243
Ó'Dubanaꞁȝ, *O'Dubhanaigh,* vulgò, Doheny, ... 57—134
Ó'Dubba, *ODubhda,* vulgò, O'Dowd and O'Dowda, descendant of Dubba, 238
Ó'Dubᴄaꞁȝ, *O'Dubhthaigh,* vulgò, Duffy, Nom. Dubᴄaᴄ, ... 3—26
    The name of the writer referred to is Caᴄal mac Gabaꞁn
    (or Ó'Gabaꞁn) Ó'Dubᴄaꞁȝ.
Ó'ꝼeaꞃȝaꞁll, *O'Fearghaill,* vulgò, O'Ferrell, O'Farrell, Ferrall, Farrell, &c. 6
Ó'ꝼóȝaꞃᴄaꞁȝ, *O'Fogartaigh,* vulgò, Fogarty. See ꝼóȝaꞃᴄaᴄ,

O'Maḋaḋain, (or O'Maḋaiḋin,) in Connacht; O'Maḋagain in Mumha; vulgò, O'Madden, Madden, &c.... 305
O'Mórḋa, *O'Mordha*, vulgò, O'Moore, Moore, &c. ... 39—67—194
O'Néill, *O'Neill*, See Niall, ... 127—245

There are three of the name referred to, viz.

Eógan ruaḋ O'Néill, ... 5
Aoḋ O'Néill, ...29—47—110—211
Doṁnall O'Néill, ... 57

O'Raġallaiġ, *O'Raghallaigh*, vulgò, O'Reilly, ...
O'Suilleaḃáin, *O'Suilleabhain*, vulgò, O'Sullivan, Sullivan, &c. 78

The derivations of the name Suilleḃán from súil aṁáin, *only eye*; or sug leaḃain, *juice of elder*, can satisfy no one, and only tend to show that the Milesian names are still to be traced.

O'Siaḋail, *O'Siadhail*, vulgò, O'Shiel, Shiel, &c. 245
O'Sionnaċáin, *O'Sionnachain*, vulgò, O'Shanaghan, Shannon, &c. ... 49
O'Tuaṫail, *O'Tuathail*, vulgò, O'Toole, Toole, Tuthill, male descendant of Tuaṫal, ... 151—173—225

What a base corruption from a splendid origin is "Toole." If one wanted to designate another as a wretch, could he go much lower than to cry, "Oh! Tool!" As to having the "th" in O'Tuathail not pronounced like an "h," it ought to be recollected that the "Magraths" have not suffered that indignity. Men might as easily avoid the absurd division of "Tut-hill."

Only think of the abomination, that in this Anglicising Eastern Metropolis of Ireland, a chapel about to be dedicated to the Patron Saint of Dublin, the Venerable and Heroic Lorcán O'Tuaṫail, is daily dubbed in the newspapers, by the name of Lawrence O'Toole!!!

P.

Padruig, *Padruig*, vulgò, Patrick, indecl. ... 14—28—75—229—245—259

R.

Ruaiḋri, *Ruaidhri*, vulgò, Rory, indecl. 39

S.

Saṁuin, *Samhuin*, Poss. Saṁna, ... 105
Séamus, *Seamus*, James, Poss. Séamuis, Voc. a Shéamuis, ... 95

T.

Toirḋealḃaċ, *Toirdhealbhach*, vulgò, Torlogh, Tirlogh, Turlogh, (Terence, which has nothing to do with it.) Poss. Toirḋealḃaiġ; some Munster dialects make Toirḋealḃaiġ. 172

See ḋealḃaċ, *resembling*, and Toir-ḋealḃaċ, in *O'B.* He supposes the name to mean, "one resembling the god Thor." But see tor, *m.* a tower; Poss. toir; tower-like.

INDEX

TO THE

NAMES OF PLACES MENTIONED IN THIS WORK.

B.

Baιle-aη-δοιηe, *Baile-an-doire*, vulgò, Ballinderry, ... 159

> Baιle, *m.* Sing. indecl., a town, village, home; Plu. baιlτe; Latin, *villa*; French, *ville*; Greek, πολισ. Δοιηe, *f.* Sing. indecl., a grove. The corruptions of these words—Bally, Derry, &c.—figure everywhere on our maps.

Baηa, *Banna*, vulgò, the Bann, *f.* indecl. i. e. Baη-amaη, the White River according to some, ... 98—26—126

Beaη-τιαιʒe, *Beann-traighe*, vulgò, Bantry, ... 60—89

> Beaη, head, Τιαιʒ, *f.* Poss. τιαʒa, or τιαιʒe, a strand, properly at low water. See the Welsh traeth, strand, and trai, decrease, ebb-tide. Hence -tra, and -troy, as well as -try, in many corrupted names.

Beal-aη-aτa-buιδe *Beal-an-atha-buidhe*, vulgò, Ballanabwee; Beal, or beul, *m.* Poss. _beιl, a mouth; Buιδe, yellow; The mouth of the yellow[2] ford[1] ! ... ... 47—250

> The final letter of aτa is scarce heard in speaking.

Beaιba, *Bearbha*, *f.* vulgò, the Barrow, 2lη beaιba, indecl. ... 142—158

Beιη-boιb, *Beinn-borb*, vulgò, Benburb; Beιη, *f.* Poss. beιηe, the summit of a hill or mountain; boιb, rough, fierce, ... 31—219—250

Beιη-£aδaιη, *Beinn-Eadair*, the hill of Howth; the hill of £aδaη,6—28—283

> "Beinn-Eaduinn, the hill of Howth in Ireland, nomen montis Hibernici." Dict. Scoto-Celt. voce Beinn.

Beιη-mόη,*Beinn-mhor*, vulgò, Benmore, ... 125

Beιηe, *Beire*, vulgò, Bear; see Beaηa, *O'B.* 79

Boιη, *Boinn*, vulgò, the Boyne; *f.* Poss. Boιηe, ... 32—34—35—36

> Some suppose it to be Buιδe amaιη, i.e. the Yellow River.

C.

Caιιeal-cηoc, *Caiseal-cnoc*, vulgò, Castleknock, the castle of hills, ... 171

Caιιaιʒ-aη-διοιcιδ, *Carraig-an-droichid*, vulgò, Carrigadrohid, the Rock of the Bridge; Διοιceaδ, *m.* a bridge, Poss. διοιcιδ,... 306

Caιιaιʒ-ℱeaιʒuιa, *Carraig-Fergusa*, vulgò, Carrickfergus, the Rock of Feargus, ... 27

Ceaη-maιa, *Ceann-mara*, vulgò, Kenmare, ... 298

> Ceaη, *m.* Poss. cιη. See the Welsh *pen*; and note a singular interchange between c in Irish and *b* or *p* in Welsh as in Mac, Mab (already noticed) ; ceaτaιη, pedr, Latin, *quatuor*; cuιʒ, *pump*, Latin, *quinque*, German, *funf*, ca, cu, cιa, *pa*, *pam*, *po*, *pwy*, *py*, Latin, *qua*, *quam*, *quo*, *qui*, English, *what*, *when*, *who*, *why*, &c. £luaιη, Latin, *planum*, English, *lawn*. Μuιη, *f.* the sea, Poss. maιa.

Cιaιιaιʒe, *Ciarraighe*, vulgò, Kerry, the name of a county, *O'B.* 18—299

Cιll-δaιa, *Cill-dara*, vulgò, Kildare, the name of a town and county, 129—142

> Cιll; this common prefix to the names of churches and burial-grounds seems, properly, to be the inflection of ceall, *f.* Poss.

cıll, though used as a nominative. The Highland Scotch have also cıll, Poss. cılle, and it is curious that this latter is generally prefixed by them to names of churches or burial-grounds, e. g. Cille-mhaillidh, Cille-bhride, Cille-mhaodhain, though before a vowel or fh *silent* it is cıll, as Cill-cobhain, Cill-fhin; Dict. Scoto-Celt. Daıṙ, f. an oak, Poss. ḋaṙaċ.

Claṅ-Rıocaıṅḃ (a búṅc) Clan-Riocaird, vulgò, Clanrickard, ... 6—72
    Claṅ f. a clan, tribe, children, descendants, Poss. cloıṅe, Subj. cloıṅ, Nom. plur. claṅa.
    Rıocaṅḃ a búṅc, Richard de Bourge, Burke, or de Burgo; the a is used in Irish for the Norman "de."

Claṙ, *Clar*, vulgò, Clare, a town and county. *O'B.* Dict. derives it from Thomas and Richard de Clare, but this is questioned. Claṙ, *m.* Poss. claıṙ, a flat, a board &c.; a word which, as well as its derivative claṙaċ, is much used in names of places. The people say Conḋae an Ċhlaıṙ, the county of Clare, i.e. of the plain, ... 214—290

Cléıṙe, *Cleire*, vulgò, Cape Clear; see *O'B.* Dict. 125
    Quære, from Cléıṙ f. the clergy, Poss. Cléıṙe.

Cloċ-Uaċtaṙ, *Cloch-Uachtar*, vulgò, Clough Oughter, ... 5
    Cloċ, f. a stone, Poss. cloıċe, Subj. ċloıċ, Nom. Plur. cloċa.
    Uaċtaṙ, upper, (So ıoċtaṙ, vulgò, Eighter, lower.)

Cluaıṅ-meala, *Cluain-meala*, vulgò, Clonmel, the plain of honey, 5—305
Cluaıṅ-taıṙḃ, *Cluain-tairbh*, vulgò, Clontarf, the plain of the bull, 31—178—225
    Cluaıṅ, f. a lawn, a plain; Poss. cluaṅa, Nom. Plur. cluaıṅte.
    Taṙḃ, m. a bull, Poss. taıṙḃ, Welsh *tarw*, Latin *taurus*.

Coṅaċt, *Connacht*, vulgò, Connaught, ... 3—66—72—226
    Coṅaċt, m. Poss. Coṅaċta.

Coıṙṙ-ṙıaḃ, *Coirr-sliabh*, vulgò, Curliew, ... 72
    Coṙṙ, m. a crane, also a turn, twist, or corner; it is a doubt in which sense the word is compounded. Slıaḃ, m. a mountain, Poss. ṙléıḃe, Nom. Plur. ṙléıḃte.

Cualaṅ, *Cualann*. Cṙıoċ cualaṅ, *O'B.* 173
Cúl-ḋaıṁ, *Cul-daimh*, vulgò, Culdaff, the back of the ox, ... 110
    Cúl, m. back, Poss. cúıl; Daṁ, m. ox, Poss. ḋaıṁ.

Cuṙṙaċ, *Currach*, vulgò, Curragh, ... 31—143
    Cuṙṙaċ, m. Poss. cuṙṙaıᵹ.

D.

Daıṅᵹeaṅ Uı Ċhúıṙe, *Daingean Ui Chuise*, vulgò, Dingle-y-cooch, ... 142
    Daıṅᵹeaṅ, m. a Fortress; Poss. ḋaıṅᵹıṅ, Fortress of the Son of Cúıṙ.

Dalcaıṙ, *Dalcais*, ... 178
    Dál, m. a division or region belonging to a tribe, there is also ḋaıl, f. Poss. ḋala, a share, separate tribe, meeting, plain, field, &c. Caṙ, Poss. Caıṙ, was Coṙmac Caṙ, (King of Leaċ Moᵹa, A.D. 20,) from whom descend the Uı Ḃṙıaıṅ.

Ⓕoᴆla, *Fodhla*, the word is sometimes written Ⓕoᴆla, Fodla; the effect of the ᴆ is to make the o long; the effect of ᴅl is ll 229
     Ⓕoᴆla, *f.* indecl. a name of Ireland from one of the three sisters Banba, Ⓕoᴆla and Éⳃe.

Ⓖ.

Ⓖaⳃlᴄe-móⳃ, *Gaillte-mor,* vulgò, Galtymore, ... 159—194
Ⓖaoⳃᴆeal, *Gaoidheal,* ⎫ vulgò, Gael, an Irishman, or Highland ⎫
Ⓖaoᴆal, *Gaodhal,*   ⎬   Scot, ...   ⎬ 7—43—97
Ⓖaoⳃᴅⳃⳃⱴ, *Gaoidhilig,* ⎱ vulgò, Gaelic, the language spoken in ⎬
Ⓖaoⳃleaⳉ, *Gaoileag,*   ⎭   these countries, ... ⎭
     It is remarkable that the Welsh call the language Gwyddeleg, as they say Cymraeg, Saesneg, &c. Gwyddel is an Irishman, or one in a sylvan state, said to be from Gwydd a wood, or woody, and hely to hunt, as it were a hunter in the woods.
Ⓖaⳃᴆa-Éóⳉaⳃⳃ, *Gardha Eoghain,* vulgò, Garryowen, the garden of Éóⳉaⳃ, 194
Ⓖleaⳃ, *Gleann,* vulgò, Glen, Glin or Glyn. Ⓖleaⳃ, *m.* Poss. ⳉleaⳃa, ... 142
Ⓖleaⳃ Ⓛolaⳃᴄ, *Gleann Colaich,* 194
Ⓖleaⳃ-ᴆa-loᴄa, *Gleann-da-locha,* vulgò, Glendalough, the Gleann of the two lakes, ... 153—173—80—99
Ⓖleaⳃ-ⳉaⳃb, *Gleann-garbh.* Ⓖaⳃb, rough; see the Welsh garw, ... 80

Ⓙ.

Ⓙⳃⳃⳃ-Éóⳉaⳃⳃ, *Innis Eoghain,* vulgò, Innishowen, ... 81
Ⓙⳃⳃⳃ-Ⓕaⳃl, *Innis-Fail,* 238
Ⓙubaⳃ, *Iubhar, m.* Poss. Ⓙubaⳃⳃ, the Yew-tree. Uⳃ Ⓙubaⳃ ᴄⳃⳃ ᴄⳃaⳉa, *An Iubhar chinn tragha,* vulgò, Newry, or the Newry, the yew-tree of the head of the Strand. 104
     This is as remarkable a corruption as is traceable in any language; see ceaⳃ, Beaⳃ-ᴄⳃaⳃⳉe, &c. 'ⳃ-aⳃ Ⓙubaⳃ, in Newry.

Ⓛ.

Ⓛaⳃⳉeaⳃ, *Laigheann,* vulgò, Lagenia and Leinster, ... 28—126
     Ⓛaⳃⳉeaⳃ, *m.* Poss. Ⓛaⳃⳉⳃⳃ.
Ⓛaoⳃ, *Laoi,* vulgò, the Lee, ... 126—247
Ⓛaoⳃⳉⳃⳃ, *Laoighis,* ⎫ vulgò, Leix, ... 66
Ⓛaoⳃⳃⳃeaᴄ, *Laoiseach, O'B.* ⎭
     O'B. says "now the Queen's County." There is a barony, parish, and Castle of "Lee" there, formerly of Ⓞ'Ⳃóⳃᴆa, whom *O'B.* names for the whole county.
     The modern names are translations; coⳃᴆae aⳃ ⳃⳃⳉ, the King's County; coⳃᴆae ⳃa baⳃⳃ-ⳃⳃoⳉⳃa, the Queen's County.
Ⓛeaᴄ, *Leath, m.* Poss. leaᴄa, a half, ... 28
     Hence Ⓛeaᴄ Ⓛuⳃⳃ, Conn's half; Ⓛeaᴄ Ⳃoⳉa, Mogh's half, in the two-fold division of Ireland. Ⓛeaᴄ Ⓛaᴄaⳃl, Cathail's half or portion, vulgò, Lecale.
    2 x

Lɪfe, *Life,* vulgò, the Liffey, ... 126—172—256
Loċ Léɪn, *Loch Lein,* vulgò, the lower Lake of Killarney, ... 277
Loċ n-Eaċaċ, *Loch n-Eathach,* vulgò, Lough Neagh, (loċ ꞃ-Ɠꞃeaċ,) ... 246
Loċ Súɪlɪ⸹, *Loch Suiligh,* vulgò, Lough Swilly, ... 118—246
Lonɜ-poꞃc, *Long-phort,* vulgò, Longford, a town and county, ... 159
　　　Lonɜ-poꞃc, *m.* Poss. Lonɜ-puɪꞃc. This is Lonɜ-poꞃc Uɪ
　　　Fheaꞃɜaɪll, the palace of the descendant of Fearghaill;
　　　from Lonɜ, *m.* a residence, and poꞃc, a fort.
Luɪmneaċ, *Luimneach,* vulgò, Limerick; the name of a city and county;
　　　in Norse, *Hlimric.* Luɪmneaċ, *f.* Poss. Luɪmꞃɪ⸹, 215—219—292—303
　　　Luɪmneaċ lɪoñ-ɜlaꞃ, of the azure² water¹; from lɪñ, *f.* Poss.
　　　lɪñe, a pool, water, (N.B. the *o* seems superfluous,) and ɜlaꞃ,
　　　green, azure.

ꞡ.

Maɜ-Nuaḋaɪc, *Magh-Nuadhait,* vulgò, Maynooth, ... 142
　　　Maɜ, *m.* Poss. Muɪɜe, a plain; the plain of Nuaḋac,
Maɜ Cꞃoṁa, *Magh Cromha,* vulgò, Macroom, or Macromp, the plain of 305
Maɜ-Raċ, *Magh-Rath,* vulgo, Moira; the plain of forts, ... 79
Maɪne, *Maine,*
　　　Uɪ Maɪne, vulgò, Hy Many; the descendants of Maine, ... 307
Malaɪñ, *Malainn,* vulgò, Malin, ... 28—307
Malla, *Malla,* (for Maɜ Ealla, *Magh Ealla,*) vulgò, Mallow, (Moyallow,) 136
　　　From Maɜ, a plain; Ulla, *O'B.;* Ealla, Ui Fiachrach, p. 52.
Moḋoꞃn, *Modhorn,* vulgò, Mourne, ... ⎫
　　　Slɪab Moḋuɪꞃn, *Sliabh Modhuirn,* vulgò, Mourne mountain, ... ⎬ 137
Mullaċ-maɪꞃcɪn, *Mullach-maistin,* vulgò, Mullaghmast, ... ⎪
　　　Mullaċ, *m.* Poss. mullaɪɜ, a top; Maɪꞃceaꞃ, *m.* Poss. Maɪꞃcɪn, ⎬ 65
Raċ mullaɪɜ Mhaɪꞃcɪn, the rath of Mullach Maistin, ... ⎭
Muṁa, *Mumha,* vulgò, Munster, ...3—126—194—241
　　　Nom. Muṁa, Poss. Muṁañ, Subjective, Muṁaɪn, Voc. a Mhuṁa.

O.

O'Faɪlɜe, *O'Failghe,* vulgò, Offaly, ... 66—86
Oɪleaċ, *Oileach,* vulgò, Ely, ... 110
　　　Oɪleaċ, *m.* Poss. Oɪlɪɜ; sometimes spelled with the initial a,
　　　as, Uɪleaċ, Uɪlɪɜ.
Oɪleán Mac Uoḋa, *Oilean Mac Aodha,* vulgò, Island Magee, see Uoḋ,
　　　Oɪleán, *m.* Poss. oɪleɪn. 27

P.

Poꞃc-móꞃ, *Port-mor,* vulgò, Portmore; Poꞃc, *m.* Poss. puɪꞃc, has many
　　　significations; a harbour or fort. The great harbour or fort, ... 47

R.

Roɪlɪɜ na Rɪoɜ, *Roilig na Riogh,* vulgò, Relignaree; the burial-place of
　　　the kings, ...
　　　Roɪlɪɜ, *f.* Poss. ꞃoɪlɜe, a burial-ground; it is also spelled ꞃeɪlɪɜ,
　　　see *O'B.* and *O'R.* Dict. The Highland-Scotch spell it,

even, as ᵱeᵩᴅᴸᴵc, and derive from ᵱeᵩᴅ, smooth; and ʟeᴀc,
a stone. "A famous burial-place near ᴄᵱuᴀᴄᴀᴎ, in ᴄoᵑᴀcᴄ,
where the kings were usually interred, before the establishment of the Christian religion in Ireland." *O'B.*
ᴿᵩᵹ, *m.* a king, Sing. indecl. Plur. Nom. ᵱᵩᵹᴄe, Poss. ᵱᵩoᵹ.

ᴿoᵱ, *Ros,* vulgò, Ross, *m.* Poss. ᵱuᵢᵱ, a promontory, peninsula, ... 305
ᴿoᵱ ᴄoᴍᴀᵩᴎ, *Ros Comain,* vulgò, Roscommon, a town and county; ᵱoᵱ, *m.*
Poss. ᵱoᵱᴀ, a wood. The wood of Coman, ...
ᴿuᴀċᴛᴀċ, *Ruachtach,* vulgò, Roughty, *m.* Poss. ᴿuᴀċᴛᴀᵩᵹ, ... 298

S.

ᴤᴀᵩᴍeᴀᵱ, *Saimear,* 118
ᴤᴀᵱᴀᵩᴎ, *Sasain, f.* England, ...
Nom. ᴤᴀᵱᴀᵩᴎ, Poss. ᴤᴀᵱᴀᵑ, Subjective ᴤᴀᵱᴀᵩᵑ, Voc. ᴀ ᴤʜᴀᵱᴀᵩᴎ.
ᴤᴀᵱᴀᴎᴀċ, *Sasanach,* Saxon, English, ... 14
ᴤᵢoᴎᴀᵩᴎ, *Sionainn,* vulgò, Shannon, *f.* Poss. ᴤᵢoᵑᴀ; ᴤeᴀᴎ-ᴀᵯᴀᵩᴎ, the
Old River, according to some. ... ...72—126—158—160—193
ᴤᵢuᵢᵱ, *Siuir,* vulgò, the Suir, ... 194
ᴤʟᴀᵩᴎe, *Slaine,* vulgò, Slane, ... 75
ᴤʟᵢᴀƀ ᴃʟᴀᴆᴍᴀ, *Sliabh Bladhma,* vulgò, Slieve Bloom. For ᴤʟᵢᴀƀ, see
ᴄoᵩᵱᵱ-ᵱᴸᵢᴀƀ; ᴃʟᴀᴆᴀᴍ, *m.* Poss. ᴃʟᴀᴆᴍᴀ, the Mountain of Bladham, 194
ᴤʟᵢᴀƀ ᴄuᵢʟᵩᴎ, *Sliabh Cuilinn,* ᴄuᵢʟeᵑ, *m.* Poss. cuᵢʟᵩᵑ, a holly; the mountain of holly, ...
ᴤʟᵢᴀƀ ᴅoᴍᴀᴎᵹoᵱᴄ, *Sliabh Domhanghort,* vernacularly Donairt, vulgò,
Slieve Donard, ... 97
ᴤʟᵢᴀƀ ᴎᴀ ᴍ-ƀᴀᴎ, *Sliabh na m-ban,* vulgò, Slievenamon; the mountain of
the (fair) women, ... 159—194
ᴤᵱᴀċ-ƀᴀᴎ, *Srath-bhan,* vulgò, Strabane; ᴤᵱᴀċ, a valley through which a
river runs; ƀᴀᴎ, white, ... 246

T.

ᴄᴀᵩʟʟᴄe, *Taillte,*, vulgò, Telltown, ... 105
Nom. ᴄᴀᵩʟʟᴄe, Poss. ᴄᴀᵩʟʟᴄeᴀᵑ, Subjective ᴄᴀᵩʟʟᴄᵩᵑ, Voc. ᴀ ᴄʜᴀᵩʟʟᴄe.
ᴄᴀᴎᴀᵩᵱᴄe, *Tanaiste,* vulgò, Tanist, ... 225
This is not the place to discuss the opinions as to the derivation,
whether from ᴄᴀᴎ, a region, or ᴄᴀᴎᴀᵩᵱᴄe, second, as some
intimate, or whether the latter be not the derivative.
ᴄeᴀᵯᴀᵩᵱ, *Teamhair,* vulgò, Tara, ... 105—160
Nom. ᴄeᴀᵯᴀᵩᵱ, Poss. ᴄeᴀᵯᵱᴀċ, Subjective ᴄeᴀᵯᴀᵩᵱ, Voc.
ᴀ ᴄʜeᴀᵯᴀᵩᵱ.
ᴄeᴀᴍᴩoʟʟ-ᴍóᵱ, *Teampoll mor,* vulgò, Templemore, ... 195
ᴄᵩᵱ-ᴄoᴎᴀᵩʟʟ, *Tir-Conaill,* vulgò, Tyrconnell; ᴄᵩᵱ, *f.* Poss. ᴄᵩᵱe, a country,
ᴄoᴎᴀʟʟ was ᴄoᴎᴀʟʟ ᴳuʟƀᴀᴎ, Son of Niall of the Nine Hostages, 119—126
ᴄᵩᵱ-ᴄóᵹᴀᵩᴎ, *Tir-Eoghain,* vulgò, Tyrone, the name of a county, ... 97
This ᴄóᵹᴀᴎ was also Son of Niall of the Nine Hostages.

Cobaṅoaṗaṅ,
Cịobṗao-Uṗaịṅ, the well of Uṗaṅ, *O'B.* ... { vulgò, Tipperary, the name
Cobaṗ a' oa ịuịṅ, the well of the two divisions; } of a town and county, 84—159
Cṗịoċa, *Triocha*, vulgò, Truagh or Triach, Cṗịoċa, *m.* a district,   28—151
    Cṗịoċa ċêao, Thirty hundred; a Cantred or Barony. *O'B.*
Cuao Ṁuṁa, *Tuadh Mumha*, vulgò, Thomond; Cuao, North; North
  Munster. See Ṁuṁa. 158
Culaċ óȝ ṗaċ, *Tulach og rath*, ... 245

U.

Ullao, *Ulladh*, vulgò, Ulidia or Ulster; Ullao, *m.* indecl. ... 26—226—228
  Uịṗo Ullao, the Heights of Ulladh, vulgò, the Ards, ... 245

EXPLANATION OF ABBREVIATIONS IN THE PRECEDING INDEXES.

O'B. refers to "J. O'Brien's Irish-English Dictionary."

O'R. refers to "Edward O'Reilly's Irish-English Dictionary."

Dict. Scoto-Celt. refers to the "Dictionarium Scoto-Celticum, a Dictionary of the Gaelic Language, compiled and published under the direction of the Highland Society of Scotland, 2 Voll. Edinburgh, 1828."

Nom. Poss. Subj. Voc.—indicate the four cases used in Irish;—Nom. stands equally for Nominative and Accusative. Poss., Possessive, is used instead of the Latin "Genitive," because the Irish case has not the derivative function of the Latin. Subj., Subjective, is used as a correlative to "preposition," because the single function of this Irish case is to follow a proper preposition. It is commonly divided into "Dative" and "Ablative;" but the Latin Dative is not used after a preposition, while the "Accusative" is. Nothing but complexity and confusion follows from the use of the words Dative, Accusative, and Ablative as applied to Irish cases. Voc. Vocative, speaks for itself. Those cases, which suffer no inflection or whose inflections are formed according to general rules, are not always noticed.

ADDENDA.

Index.

INDEX TO ORIGINAL MUSIC.

INDEX TO OLD IRISH MUSIC.

INDEX TO THE POEMS.*

* In this Index the preliminary article in all the names of the **Poems** is dropped. For instance, a person looking for " The Memory of the Dead," must refer to letter M, not letter T.

DUBLIN:

PRINTED BY T. COLDWELL,
50, CAPEL-STREET.